THE
POLITICS
OF
WARFARE

STEPHEN J. CIMBALA

THE POLITICS OF WARFARE

THE GREAT POWERS IN THE TWENTIETH CENTURY

The Pennsylvania State University Press
University Park, Pennsylvania

Library of Congress Cataloging-in-Publication Data

Cimbala, Stephen J.
    The politics of warfare : the great powers in the twentieth
century / Stephen J. Cimbala.
        p.   cm.
    Includes bibliographical references and index.
    ISBN 0-271-01597-7 (cloth : alk. paper)
    ISBN 0-271-01598-5 (paper : alk. paper)
    1. Military history, Modern—20th century.   2. Politics and war.
3. World politics—1989–   I. Title.
    U42.C55   1997
    355′.033′004—dc20   96-6450
                                                                    CIP

It is the policy of The Pennsylvania State University Press
to use acid-free paper for the first printing of all
clothbound books. Publications on uncoated stock satisfy the
minimum requirements of American National Standard for
Information Sciences–Permanence of Paper for Printed Library
Materials, ANSI Z39.48-1992.

Contents

Acknowledgments

A study of this scope would never have been started, much less finished, without the encouragement of many persons. Undoubtedly this acknowledgment will not do justice to all of them. I want to specifically thank the following for their contributions to my understanding of military strategy in general: Sam Sarkesian, John Allen (Jay) Williams, Paul Davis, David Tarr, Michael Pocalyko, and William J. Taylor, Jr. For my appreciation of nuclear deterrence theory, I am indebted to George Quester, Colin Gray, Patric Morgan, Richard Ned Lebow, Keith Payne, and Fred Ikle. I am especially grateful to Sam Sarkesian, James Motley, Richard Shultz, and Col. William Flavin, USA, for insights into special operations and low-intensity conflict. For Soviet and Russian military strategy, I have turned frequently to Jacob Kipp, Stephen Blank, David Glantz, Raymond Garthoff, Graham Turbiville, Timothy Sanz, and Timothy Thomas. Special gratitude is extended to Roy Godson and Richard Shultz, whose tutorials in intelligence and kind invitations to participate in intelligence conferences improved my awareness of the significance of that subject for overall national security policy. Finally, I owe Col. Joseph Collins, USA, the baton for encouraging me to undertake this seemingly impossible task and for putting me together with some of his outstanding colleagues at the U.S. Military Academy, West Point, who critiqued an early concept of it. And it was equally beneficial to have the opportunity to take part in the U.S. Air Force "2025" study commissioned by the Air Force Chief of Staff in 1995–96. All errors are my responsibility.

I would be remiss not to acknowledge the administrative support I have received during this study from the Delaware County Campus administrative staff, including Diane Wolf, Madlyn Hanes, and Edward Tomezsko. The university also graciously provided a semester of sabbatical so that I could complete the important finishing touches. I also appreciate the expert copyediting of Charles Purrenhage and the editorial guidance and production management of Cherene Holland and Peter Potter, Penn State Press. My wife deserves most of the credit for her management of my otherwise disordered life as well as her own busy work schedule. This book is dedicated to my mother, Helen Hartman Cimbala, whose exemplary performance as an educator offered an example.

INTRODUCTION

This is not a history of war in the twentieth century. There are many splendid studies covering that terrain.[1] My object is to draw the reader's attention to certain aspects of the relationship between war and politics in twentieth-century war. There are two reasons for bothering to do so at book length, although in a short book. First, the Western reader's understanding of how war and politics fit together is inescapably influenced by the Prussian military theorist Carl von Clausewitz: like Banquo's ghost, his apparition hovers over the table at all academic conferences on the subject. Second, a Clausewitz-derived understanding of the relationship between twentieth-century war and politics, left to itself, drives us into an intellectual cul-de-sac. The burden of this study is that Clausewitz got it right about the conventional, "ordinary" wars fought between uniformed forces clearly distinguished from noncombatants and duly accountable to, and only to, the government of a territorial state. As war drifted outside this normative model, it drifted away from Clausewitz.

Thus, an enormous amount of military history has been devoted to conventional warfare and to its political implications, but comparatively less to other forms of war, including intelligence wars, low-intensity conflicts, cyber wars, and nuclear-crisis management (which is the functional equivalent of war). The continuing relevancy of conventional warfare is not disputed here: it was apparent in the rapid, decisive victory over Iraq

1. In addition to other sources cited below, I recommend Donald Kagan, *On the Origins of War and the Preservation of Peace* (New York: Doubleday, 1995), chs. 2 and 4, and John Keegan, *The Second World War* (New York: Viking Press, 1989).

by the United States and the allies in 1991. What has happened in the twentieth century is that this form of war reached its zenith of destruction in World War II. The lethality of armed forces, even before nuclear weapons were first exploded in anger, was such that twentieth-century war had subsumed politics. War had become its own form of capital punishment, outside policy if not also outside politics.

Wars are political creatures. They are fought for political reasons, pushed forward with political passions, and terminated with political rationales for victory and surrender. To say that wars are political is not to say that the politics attendant to war are always handled well. It is the exceptional statesman who comprehends the military art. It is an even more exceptional leader who can relate this understanding of military art to the purposes of the state.[2] War, after all, predates the modern, territorial nation-state by millennia: nomadic tribes, preindustrial civilizations, knights-errant, and others took up arms before the Peace of Westphalia in 1648 confirmed the political supremacy of statehood over empire and church.

However, this supremacy of the state was established by being fought for, and it was by no means permanently settled. Various nationalities, political dissidents, and aspiring emperors contested the idea of state supremacy. The most successful of these was Napoléon Bonaparte, who turned a revolution against the ancien régime of France into a forced march against the other major armies and regimes of Europe. By the time Napoléon was done with and dispatched to St. Helena, the powers agreed that only dynastic legitimacy was a proper form of statehood. Revolutions against this concept, according the Congress of Vienna that followed the Napoleonic Wars, would not do. Austrian Chancellor Metternich's idea of a Congress system to deter or to repress revolutions against dynastic statehood lasted from 1815 until 1822: thereafter, the powers had to accept that more than one kind of state might coexist in Europe. Such coexistence has been uneasy, up to the present. The idea of state sovereignty is, even now, in the aftermath of Cold War and Soviet collapse, being sorely tested by political and social upheavals across the former Soviet republics, in Bosnia and in other ethnonationalist wars outside Europe.

But the period from 1648 until the end of the Second World War offered more consensus among the great powers on the question of state sovereignty than the period before or after. The twentieth-century experience

---

2. The point is effectively argued in Colin S. Gray, *Weapons Don't Make War: Policy, Strategy, and Military Technology* (Lawrence: University Press of Kansas, 1993), with comments especially pertinent to deterrence and arms control in lieu of war (161ff.).

of war, therefore, at least until the end of the Cold War in 1989–90, partakes of this period during which the monopoly of states over the legitimate resort to military force was judged to be more or less normative. What did we learn about the relationship between force and policy during this period?

Clausewitz on War

Some of the more important things that we learned were pulled together and explained by Carl von Clausewitz, in his work *Vom Kriege* [On War], first published in 1832.[3] No single work since has captured so much of the accepted relationship between sovereign states, their armies, and the requirements of war. Twentieth-century war includes not only conflicts between states but other kinds of conflicts. Clausewitz was better able to appreciate the first kind of war, statist war, than he was the second, wars between or among entities other than states.

Although this is not a book about Clausewitz, it starts with him because his understanding of statist war illuminates all other discussions of the relationship between war and policy. Clausewitz offers an ideal type or benchmark for heads of state and commanders to follow, recognizing that ideal war and real war are two very different things. Because they are different, actual wars risk undesirable outcomes for armed forces (defeat in battle) and for the state (disestablishment of the regime). However, states cannot always choose whether to avoid war: the legal anarchy of the international system places them in a situation of perpetual jeopardy. Therefore, the possibility of war remains a constant preoccupation for political leaders and for their militaries.

Clausewitz is best known for his insistence that war is only the instrument, and policy the controlling faculty, in a well-ordered state.[4] The distinction between "politics" and "policy" is very important in this context. Clausewitz used the term *Politik,* which is preferably translated as "policy." War should be subordinated to policy, but not necessarily to politics. Politics is a more inclusive category than policy, which refers to the authoritative decisions and actions taken by duly elected or appointed heads of state. Politics is the entire set of relationships having to do with the governance of communities.

3. Carl von Clausewitz, *On War,* ed. and trans. Michael Howard and Peter Paret; commentary Bernard Brodie (Princeton, N.J.: Princeton University Press, 1976).
4. Ibid., bk. 1, ch. 1, p. 87.

An important question is whether, in view of U.S. and other experience in twentieth-century war, Clausewitz's view now belongs to the dustbin of history. Of course, Clausewitz's highly regarded classic study, *On War,* emphasized the dangers of divorcing force from the control of policy. In order to do this, Clausewitz developed a philosophical construct that has bedeviled readers ever since: absolute war. Wars, especially those wars that aroused popular and national passions, tended naturally toward the expansion of violence. The inherent logic of war was to advance toward greater and greater levels of destruction. Absolute war was an ideal type in Clausewitz's mind: it was a philosophical thesis to be opposed in dialectical fashion by its theoretical opposite, actual war.[5]

For a number of reasons, according to Clausewitz, actual war did not tend to its absolute, utterly destructive limit. In book 8, chapter 6 of *On War,* he notes that "war does not advance relentlessly toward the absolute, as theory would demand. Being incomplete and self-contradictory, it cannot follow its own laws, but has to be treated as part of some other whole; the name of which is policy."[6] Policy converts the overwhelmingly destructive character of war into a mere instrument, according to Clausewitz. Accordingly, as policy becomes more ambitious, so shall war. Clausewitz argued with emphasis against the mistaken view, from his perspective, that once war had broken out, policy had failed and the purely military point of view should become dominant over the political:

> That the political view should wholly cease to count on the outbreak of war is hardly conceivable unless pure hatred made all wars a struggle for life and death. In fact, as we have said, they are nothing but expressions of policy itself. Subordinating the political point of view to the military would be absurd, for it is policy that creates war. Policy is the guiding intelligence and war only the instrument, not vice versa. No other possibility exists, then, than to subordinate the military point of view to the political.[7]

It is a measure of Clausewitz's influence that the inseparability of war and policy has become a professional academic and military truism. But Clausewitz meant for this relationship to take on specific form: the military art was to be subordinate to the policy guidance provided from state authorities *acting within their proper sphere of political competency.*[8] This

5. W. B. Gallie, *Philosophers of Peace and War: Kant, Clausewitz, Marx, Engels and Tolstoy* (Cambridge: Cambridge University Press, 1978), 37–65.

6. Clausewitz, *On War,* 606.

7. Ibid., 607.

8. For perspective on Clausewitz, see Peter Paret, *Clausewitz and the State* (New York:

is easier said than done. War, Clausewitz emphasized, had its own "grammar," but not its own logic. Once set in motion, the war machine was capable of movement toward its own self-generated imperatives, and away from the best interests of the state.

In Clausewitz's time, the first half of the nineteenth century, most of these state authorities were appointed, not elected. Nonetheless the supremacy of policy over the military instrument, in wars waged by accountable governments of state actors, is now assumed by theorists to apply to democracies and autocracies alike. Cold War theorists, U.S. and Soviet alike (albeit from different philosophical starting points), accepted Clausewitz's argument about the primacy of *state policy,* and they cited the influential Prussian repeatedly to support the argument. The living impact of the dead Prussian philosopher on modern ideas about war and politics remains strong, acting as the point of departure for all others.[9]

However, twentieth-century warfare has done much to contravene Clausewitz's nineteenth-century view of the relationship between politics and war. First, the world wars were major coalition wars of unprecedented scope and destructiveness. They remade or undid empires, created new polities where once only the politically dispossessed had existed, and set performance standards for war machines that made militaries even more difficult to control than hitherto. Second, the de-Europeanization of global politics after World War II—in particular, the rising importance of national and other nongovernment actors after the Cold War—renders old notions of military obedience and professionalism subject to dispute. Third, the collapse of any meaningful distinction between "internal" or "domestic" politics and "foreign" policy, tied to the erosion of the concept of state sovereignty in modern times, means that immigration, environmental degradation, and other issues previously fenced off from security studies are now very much a part of the field.[10]

Oxford University Press, 1976), and Michael I. Handel, ed., *Clausewitz and Modern Strategy* (London: Frank Cass, 1986). Also informative are H. Rothfels, "Clausewitz," ch. 5 in Edward Mead Earle, ed., *Makers of Modern Strategy: Military Thought from Machiavelli to Hitler* (Princeton, N.J.: Princeton University Press, 1943), 93–116, and Peter Paret, "Clausewitz," ch. 7 in Paret, ed., *Makers of Modern Strategy: From Machiavelli to the Nuclear Age* (Princeton, N.J.: Princeton University Press, 1986), 186–216. A critical assessment of Clausewitz's thinking on modern war appears in B. H. Liddell Hart, *Strategy,* 2d rev. ed. (New York: Frederick A. Praeger, 1967), 352–56.

9. Critical assessment of Clausewitz's influence on twentieth-century war appears in John Keegan, *A History of Warfare* (New York: Alfred A. Knopf, 1993), 13–24 and 372–92.

10. Paul Kennedy, *Preparing for the Twenty-first Century* (New York: Random House, 1993), esp. pt. 1, argues for this with considerable cogency.

Force and Policy after the Cold War:
What Kind of War?

The end of the Cold War means that the threat of global war or major coalition war which hung over Eurasia and North America for forty-five years has receded into glacial quietude. It has been replaced by the more plausible threat of numerous smaller wars, of various sizes, including major regional wars (as in the Persian Gulf, 1991), low-intensity conflicts (as in Grenada, 1983), terrorist threats (as in sources too numerous to mention in this paragraph), and other conventional or unconventional perturbations of the status quo.

In addition, states outside economically developed Eurasia, including Third World regional antagonists such as Iran, North Korea, India, and Pakistan, have acquired or seek to acquire weapons of mass destruction and/or long-range delivery systems, including ballistic missiles. The sophisticated weaponization of Third World regional adversaries also poses at least indirect threats, potential and actual, to U.S. and allied NATO armed forces. One has only to imagine Saddam Hussein in 1991, had his nuclear weapons program matured in time for the Gulf War of that year, to foresee the potentially destabilizing consequences of advanced technology weapons in the hands of rogue state, or nonstate, actors.

If statist wars fought by professional armies under the control of accountable governments become the exception rather than than norm, as some experts foresee, then "war" as Clausewitz knew it will be swallowed by a larger set of forces.[11] Social and cultural *stasis,* or general turbulence, to use the preferred term of Aristotle for upheavals in ancient Greece, would then overwhelm state-directed wars with conflicts among ethnic and religious groups, private warlords, military dissidents, and others not frocked by a territorial state ruling authoritatively over a given territory. History provides some basis for anticipating an outcome of turbulence triumphant over statism. Reasons of state and the exertion of control over the military by states are historical exceptions, not the rule. Prior to the heyday of armed forces monopolized by territorial states, the killing grounds were fields of dreams for mercenary armies and others seeking private gain and having little or no concept of the public good.

To the extent that wars slip out of the hands of accountable heads of state or parliaments, Clausewitz's arguments imply greater opportunity

---

11. For this argument, see Martin Van Creveld, *The Transformation of War* (New York: Free Press, 1991), esp. chs. 1 and 2. Keegan, *A History of Warfare,* argues that even the statist wars of the twentieth century failed to correspond to Clausewitz's model.

for the corrosion of strategy by improper politicization. The term "politicization" is to be distinguished from "policy guidance," which Clausewitz judged to be the appropriate and necessary context for strategymaking. By politicization, I mean three things. First, politicization is at work when political leaders *interfere,* or attempt to interfere, in the details of military operations, planning, and tactics which are customarily left to professionals.[12] Second, politicization of war results from *obscurity or indeterminacy of political aim* on the part of one or more military combatants. Indeterminacy or obscurity of aim may result from a variety of causes: disagreements among allies, misperception of the threat, poor understanding of one's own or one's adversaries' intentions, and other sources.[13] Third, politicization implies that the public is at least *generally aware* of the war and its costs, though not necessarily well informed about strategy, and that this public awareness has *anticipated domestic political costs* for leaders. My use of the term "politicization" (not Clausewitz's term, but influenced by his writing) leads to the advancement of some hypotheses of my own about the dimensions of military politicization, summarized in Table 1.

The three attributes of politicized wars, as defined here, are not presented as a scientific formula. Nor, by themselves, do they describe the difference between good wars and bad wars. They are political hypotheses deserving of scrutiny on the basis of historical evidence. In addition, the characteristics listed are not functionally equivalent. The first, interference, involves a subjective judgment, but if the judgment in a particular case is a valid one, it may provide a necessary *and* sufficient case for

Table 1. Dimensions of War Politicization

Attributes of Politicization	Politicized Wars	Unpoliticized Wars
Leader interference with operations	High	Low
Ambiguity of aims	High	Low
Public involvement and expected costs	High	Low

12. Gray, *Weapons Don't Make War,* 167–69, explains well the point that although military technology and weapons are not autonomous from policy and strategy, it is nonetheless the case that war has its own "grammar," or subordinate logic, per Clausewitz's assumption.

13. Writing about World War I decisions by the great powers that led to ultimate disaster, Williamson Murray and Mark Grimsley note that "when one views matters as they appeared through the lens of government and public opinion, and above all in the uncertain light of what was actually known at the time, it becomes harder to sort out reasonable from foolish courses of action." Murray and Grimsley, "On Strategy," ch. 1 in Williamson Murray, Macgregor Knox, and Alvin Bernstein, eds., *The Making of Strategy: Rulers, States and War* (Cambridge: Cambridge University Press, 1994), 4.

a politicized war. The second and third attributes, singly or paired, do not necessarily *cause* dysfunctional relationships between strategy and politics, but the conditions are often *associated with* an incorrect relationship by Clausewitz's standards.

"Military politicization," as I am using the term, is thus a form of political-military corruption. Why should this form of corruption be of concern to political leaders, to military strategists, and to the general public? The chapters that follow give some of the answers in detail. But I want to anticipate some of those answers here and now. Military politicization is marked off from political control of the military: the latter is a cornerstone of any legitimate political order. Military politicization is to political control of the military as junk bonds are to investing, or as purchased term papers are to education. It marks a debasement of the currency by which soldiers are given their proper marching orders and by which politicians accept responsibility for setting those orders.

In the history of twentieth-century warfare, both the largest interstate wars and the smallest intrastate civil wars have been highly politicized or politically corrupted conflicts. In between are the wars that continued to adhere to the Clausewitzian paradigm: wars of medium intensity between several major powers or their proxies, fought for limited objectives and with limited means. Nuclear war stands as an oxymoron for the Cold War years. Any U.S.-Soviet nuclear "exchange" threatened to escalate into total societal destruction. Whether use of smaller numbers of nuclear weapons in the post–Cold War era falls outside the proper scope of "war" is controversial.[14]

If the thesis argued here is correct, it bodes ill for expectations about world peace. Although the threat of large-scale, intercontinental war is absent in the aftermath of Soviet collapse and Russian beginnings of democratization, the predominance of intrastate, primordial wars of civil violence in the late twentieth century warns us against complacency. If my arguments are correct, these politically corrupted civil wars will be the most bitterly fought and difficult to terminate by traditional truces, cease-fires, and other means of war termination. The very arrangement of the chapters in this book emphasizes the secular drift of war away from statist, or relatively depoliticized, wars and toward nonstatist, or highly politicized, conflicts based on ethnonationalist, religious, or other basic communitarian values. War has become coterminous with the struggle to define basic values of civilized life, by the most uncivilized means.

---

14. For pertinent arguments with regard to nuclear use by nonstate actors, see Louis René Beres, "On International Law and Nuclear Terrorism," *Georgia Journal of International and Comparative Law,* no. 1 (1994): 1–36.

This study divides itself into two compartments. In the first, we review findings about the relationship between policy and war in major twentieth-century conflicts of the old world order prior to the collapse of the Soviet Union and the end of the Cold War. The second part considers the Gulf War, intelligence, special operations, and low-intensity conflict as aspects of the new world order. A separate chapter on nuclear weapons and strategy focuses mostly on the Cold War years, but it also addresses problems of proliferation which are most pertinent to the post–Cold War order. An assumption underlying both parts of this study is that war or other armed conflict is a social interaction based on opposed political interests. Wars have been considered and evaluated in other ways: as epidemics, psychological misperceptions, miscalculated escalations, and so forth. We do not deny the existence of military or political dysfunctions of these types. For our purposes, though, such models serve less well than the simpler, and theoretically more useful, assumption of intendedly rational resort to force on the part of state or nonstate actors.

Each of the chapters that follow looks at one aspect of the force and policy relationship as that relationship has been played out in twentieth-century conflict. We shall use historical and contemporary information to investigate which wars and other conflicts are more politicized and which are less politicized. We are equally interested in why conflicts are politicized, and in what ways. The twentieth century includes samples of virtually all the kinds of conflict that heads of state and military planners might ever have to fight. Does the integrity of the force–policy connection hold despite this variety, or does the complexity of twentieth-century conflict leave the connection in doubt? The concluding chapter provides an overall assessment, including some cautionary notes about the future of U.S. armed forces and military policy.

1

WORLD WAR I
and the
END of EMPIRE

World War I was neither an accidental nor an inadvertent war. Nevertheless, it strained the relationship between force and policy to the breaking point. This is not to suggest that the leaders who embarked upon this unprecedented misadventure in mass destruction knew, prior to the outbreak of war, exactly what they were getting into. Their prewar expectations were very wide of the mark. On account of this, historians have argued ever since the end of World War I about its causes. Beyond dispute is the rising tide of nationalism which heads of state and warlords exploited for military purposes. At the turn of the century, this nationalism was manifest in rising levels of support for autocratic and for democratic governments among the powers. The results of World War I were very different: nationalism helped to destroy the Austro-Hungarian and Ottoman empires, and national self-determination was used as a principle by which the European postwar peace settlement was organized.

A useful classification of the causes of war is to distinguish three types of causes in terms of their proximity in time to the war's beginning. This suggests that causes of war can be divided as follows: (1) *deep* causes, those most remote from the immediate decisions for war; (2) *precipitating* causes, those most immediate to the war's outbreak; and (3) *intermediate* causes, somewhere between the remote and precipitating causes. Joseph S. Nye, Jr., using this classification, summarizes some of the causes for World War I (see Table 2).

Table 2. Various Causes of World War I

Deep Causes	Intermediate Causes	Immediate Causes

Changes in the structure of the balance of power
  a. Rise of German strength
  b. Tightening of bi-polar alliance systems (Triple Alliance and Triple Entente)
	German policy (vague and vacillating on the part of Wilhelm II; alternately belligerent and conciliatory)	Assassination of Archduke Franz Ferdinand at Sarajevo by Serbian terrorist

Rise of nationalism	Rise in complacency about peace (absence of great-power war for previous forty years; successful crisis management between 1908 and 1912)	Misperceptions on the part of leaders about each other's goals and commitments (e.g., perception by Germany's leaders until too late that England would remain neutral in any continental war)
Declining empires of Austria, Turkey	Personal idiosyncrasies of leaders (kaiser's mercurial temperament; tsar's dependence on incompetent advisers)	Leaders' ideas about the dependency of war outcomes on prompt offensives; leaders' inability to improvise around prewar plans fixed to jumping the gun on potential opponents
Advances in technology related to large-scale military operations (railroads making possible movement of large numbers of troops; industrialization)	Military plans for war which depended on prompt offensives and made crisis management more difficult (e.g., Germany's Schlieffen Plan for a swift, decisive victory against France before turning against Russia)	

SOURCE: Adapted from Joseph S. Nye, Jr., *Understanding International Conflicts: An Introduction to Theory and History* (New York: Harper Collins, 1993), 59–65.

Society, Technology, and War

Twentieth-century warfare grew from social and technical forces which exceeded the ability of political and military leaders with nineteenth-century outlooks to contain those forces. The social forces included the social and political repercussions of industrialism and the culmination of the age of empire. Among the technical forces were the flowering of invention during the nineteenth century and the implications of invention for military art.[1] The weapons of war became more lethal and more widely available to the mass armies that were being created by political leaders. The increased lethality of weaponry was accompanied by a growth of nationalism, manifest at outset of the nineteenth century in the march of Napoléon's *grande armée* across the breadth of western and central Europe. Nationalism was further manifest in midcentury with the beginning of movements that would culminate in the unification of Germany and Italy. When the armies of the French were put paid to by the Prussians in 1870, German nationalism had its revenge against the ghost of Napoléon.

Nationalism provided the psychological support for mass armies, and industrialism equipped those armies with greater numbers of precision-firing weapons. The U.S. Civil War and the Franco-Prussian War offered contrasting cases of a prolonged war of attrition, in the first instance, and of a rapid campaign of annihilation in the second. In both wars, however, it was evident that the relationship between infantry attack and defense had changed to the detriment of the attacker. Rifled weapons and the invention of the minié ball allowed for precision aiming at greater distances. Cavalry charges and linear formations going against bunkered defenders would almost always have to endure an unfavorable ratio of friendly to enemy dead and wounded. Infantry firepower dominated Civil War battlefields, relegating artillery to primarily a defensive role (because artillerymen could not be got close enough to enemy infantry to deliver their most effective offensive fire).[2]

The U.S. Civil War not only showed the improved capabilities of defenders to stand off frontal attackers. It also demonstrated, for the first time on a multitheater scale, a new relationship between the strategic

---

1. Martin Van Creveld, *Technology and War: From 2000 B.C. to the Present* (New York: Free Press, 1989), esp. 217–34.

2. Charles C. Fennell, Jr., "The Civil War: The First Modern War," ch. 4 in John M. Carroll and Colin F. Baxter, eds., *The American Military Tradition: From Colonial Times to the Present*, 61–95, esp. 67.

rear and the tactical front.[3] Railroads and telegraph lines were now part of the central nervous system that connected the industrial sinews of military power with the sharp ends of bullet and bayonet. Railroad transport and telegraphic communications were exploited by both sides in the Civil War, although ultimately to greater Union advantage. The Union was forced to invade the South and subdue its resistance; to "win" in a political sense, the Confederacy had only not to lose decisively. The requirement for more ambitious military and political aims forced onto the North a strategy of attrition against Confederate soldiers and civilians alike. Sherman's march through Georgia marked the virtual disappearance of any distinction between noncombatants and combatants: the will of a resisting people was as much a military objective for Grant's forces as were the uniformed effectives volunteered or forced under arms.

Some European interpretations of the U.S. Civil War experience wrongly assumed that American tactical and operational conditions were unique to the North American continent. But other Europeans had already taken notice of the technologies of transport and communication and their uses for troop deployment and for command and control. Railways made possible the prompt deployment of previously mobilized and trained forces on a hitherto unprecedented scale. The side that first succeeded in deploying large and combat-ready forces near the front might conceivably win the war in its initial period, catching the opponent off balance and undermobilized for defense. Moreover, although the distances over which any war in North America might have to be fought would be vast, the distances that railroads would have to cover in Europe would be comparatively short.

Contrasting Visions

At the turn of the nineteenth century, therefore, the war planners of the powers of Europe were offered contrasting visions of the implications of military-related technology. Developments in weapons, armaments, and tactics favored defenders; the rapid mobilization and concentration made possible by railways and telegraph lines favored the attacker. Or, to express the same point in a somewhat different and more military-technical way, the strategic technologies favored offensive doctrines and war plans, but the technologies pertinent to field weapons seemed to favor the de-

3. Theodore Ropp, *War in the Modern World* (Durham, N.C.: Duke University Press, 1959), 157ff.

fender.[4] Then, too, the professionalization of armed forces during the nineteenth century included the development of general staffs along the lines of the Prussian/German model. With the development of general staffs came the advance preparation of intricate and detailed war plans, tying together assumptions about available transport and communications technology with the preferred military doctrines of each planning staff.

These judgments about the implications of strategic and tactical technologies, however, are more apparent to historians after the fact than they were to those contemporary European and American war planners. In Europe, the alliance flexibility of the nineteenth century had given way to rigidity, with the Triple Alliance of Germany, Austria-Hungary, and Italy coalescing to counterbalance the alignment of France, Russia, and ultimately, when war in 1914 could no longer have been avoided, Britain. As the powers moved toward military confrontation, their strategic proclivities not to be caught second in mobilizing for war contributed to the sense of foreboding among general staffs that war was imminent. Germany's strategy in the years immediately preceding the outbreak of World War I reflected this defensive-offensiveness of mobilization plans dictated to the last jot and tittle of trains departed and telegrams sent.[5]

It would be an exaggeration, and something of an evasion of political responsibility, to charge the German General Staff and the other powers' mobilization planners with the main responsibility for the deterioration of the July 1914 crisis into war at the beginning of August. The powers had been positioning themselves for war for decades, were overconfident that wars might be won decisively in their initial period, and preferred not to draw too many pessimistic conclusions (about a possibly prolonged war) from the evolution of infantry weapons and tactics.[6] Nor did the European powers learn much from the turn of the century Boer War, or from the Russo-Japanese War of 1904–5 in which the resistance of large armies to rapid campaigns of annihilation was all too apparent. The Polish economist Ivan Blioch, who foresaw that mass warfare and mobilized industrial economies favored a longer war rather than a shorter one, was dimissed as a crank.

4. Paul M. Kennedy, ed., *The War Plans of the Great Powers, 1880–1914* (London: Allen & Unwin, 1979).

5. L.C.F. Turner, "The Significance of the Schlieffen Plan," ch. 9 in Kennedy, ed., *The War Plans of the Great Powers, 1880–1914,* 199–221. See also Sidney Bradshaw Fay, *The Origins of the World War,* 2d rev. ed. (New York: Free Press, 1966), vol. 2, chs. 10 and 11.

6. Geoffrey Blainey, *The Causes of War* (New York: Free Press, 1973), 35–56. Blainey's arguments find support in John J. Mearsheimer, *Conventional Deterrence* (Ithaca, N.Y.: Cornell University Press, 1983), 23–66.

It proved to be something of a shock to British sensibilities at the very outset of World War I, therefore, when Lord Kitchener, the hero of Khartoum, announced on being appointed war minister in 1914 that Britain was in for a long and costly war. This opinion could not be dismissed as that of a crank, and both Blioch and Kitchener were in the event proved to be prescient concerning the horror to come. Britain's nineteenth-century strategy emphasized the avoidance of any continental commitment that would entail sending a mass expeditionary force across the English channel to rescue French from Germans, Germans from French, or either of those from the Russians. Even as the German forward strategy of risk-fleet shipbuilding challenged British hegemony in the waters surrounding northern Europe, British planners held to the previous century's order of strategic and political priorities: first the homeland, then the empire, and only third the protection of Europe against aspiring hegemons.

Of course, once aspiring hegemonic European land powers threatened Britain's imperial domain or sea lifeline, as did Napoléon's Continental System, then the dispatch of a British fighting force to the European continent was judged both necessary and appropriate. On the other hand, in the minds of British nineteenth-century strategists, sufficient forethought and planning should have allowed Britain to play its best hand against Imperial Germany or others aspiring to dominate continental Europe. Its best hand was an offshore sea-denial and blockade strategy which would strangle the German economy until its people demanded that its leaders sue for peace. Meanwhile, France and its land armies would hold the line against the westward thrusts of the kaiser's armed forces. As the British reorganized their national security planning in the first decade of the twentieth century, and as they tied their military fortunes more closely to those of their French allies, it became clear that a sizable commitment of British ground forces to continental Europe would be an unavoidable necessity.[7]

Germany's Schlieffen Plan for a quick and decisive victory against France fell short on the Marne. It followed, according to military lexicon, that a counteroffensive should be mustered to push the Germans back onto their own territory, followed by an agreeable peace settlement which left the balance of power (prewar) more or less intact. The counteroffensive could not be prepared with sufficient effectiveness to push the boche out of Belgium and France, however, and a stalemate on the western front continued until the armistice of November 1918.

---

7. J. McDermott, "The Revolution in British Military Thinking from the Boer War to the Moroccan Crisis," ch. 4 in Kennedy, ed., *The War Plans of the Great Powers, 1880–1914*, 99–117.

One reason that no counteroffensive was in readiness to push back the invading Germans was that French prewar doctrine, like the German, emphasized taking the offensive at the outset of war. The two plans for a prompt offensive bypassed one another: had the French successfully consummated their Plan 17, they would have yielded French territory to invading Germans that much faster. Fortunately for France, Germany's timetable for advance through Belgium and France was more appropriate for the motorized and mechanized armies of World War II. The armies of Helmuth von Moltke (the younger) had to march on foot or advance on horseback, thus overextending the supply lines on the critical right wing of the attack which was to sweep toward the English channel and then envelop Paris from the west.[8]

Strategic miscalculation was not confined to the western front in World War I. The Russians and French could agree that Germany's military power constituted a major threat to both. Russia, however, had other concerns, including a disagreeable Austria-Hungary on its southwestern flank, committed to side with Germany in the event of war against Russia. Further, Russia had to consider the possibility that a Balkan crisis could propel the tsar's armies into battle on behalf of Serbia against Austria-Hungary, leaving open the back door for German invaders to take much or all of Russian Poland (as they eventually did after a series of battles in 1915). Russia's German and Austrian fronts committed Russia to consider whether a one-front or a two-front emphasis in defensive planning would pay the most dividends.

Russia's alliance with France meant that, should Germany direct the bulk of its attack westward against the French, then Russia would have time to concentrate the majority of its forces against Austria. If, on the other hand, Germany was likely to direct its main initial forces against Russia, then Russian prewar deployments should emphasize the German and not the Austrian front. The Russian General Staff, unable to resolve this dilemma prior to war, settled for a compromise two-plan formula: Plan A would be activated if Germany was expected to make its main attack against France, Plan G if Russia was about to absorb the stronger of Germany's opening moves.[9] This compromise was further complicated by French insistence that Russia must mobilize and thrust promptly into

8. Holger H. Herwig, "The Dynamics of Necessity: German Military Policy during the First World War," ch. 3 in Allan R. Millett and Williamson Murray, eds., *Military Effectiveness,* (London: Unwin Hyman, 1988), 1:80–115.

9. Norman Stone, *The Eastern Front* (New York: Charles Scribner's Sons, 1975), and Jack Snyder, *The Ideology of the Offensive: Military Decision Making and the Disasters of 1914* (Ithaca, N.Y.: Cornell University Press, 1984), chs. 6 and 7. See also Iurii Danilov, *La Russie dans la Guerre mondiale* (1914–1917) (Paris: Payot, 1927).

East Prussia (by the fifteenth day of mobilization) in order to tie down some of Germany's divisions for defense in the east, instead of attack in the west. Russian mobilization according to Plan A, following the Instructions of 1912, called for the deployment of the First and Second armies on the German front and the Third, Fourth, and Fifth armies on the Austro-Hungarian front (19 first-line infantry divisions against the Germans, 29 first-line infantry divisions against the Austrians). The times required for units to complete their concentration according to this plan were actually as listed in Table 3, in contradiction to the Russian war minister's commitment to the French for prompt attacks after fifteen days of mobilization.

Russia ended by planning for a two-front war in which neither front was allocated enough forces to ensure victory.[10] Austria proved to be less formidable for the tsar's armies than Germany. Rot within the Russian armed forces high command, problems of supply (especially munitions and rifles), and political discontent with tsarist conduct of the war ultimately forced the monarchy to abdicate.[11] The provisional government was un-

Table 3. Time Required for Concentration of Russian Armies against Germany and Austria-Hungary, August 1914

	Days Needed for 50% Concentration	Days Needed for 75% Concentration	Days Needed for 100% Concentration
First Army	15	20	36
Second Army	10	15	40
Third Army	15	22	40
Fourth Army	20	30	41
Fifth Army	20	27	38
Sixth Army[a]	20	27	36
Seventh Army[b]	10	15	20

SOURCE: Adapted from Nicholas N. Golovine, Lt. Gen., Imperial Russian Army, *The Russian Campaign of 1914: The Beginning of the War and Operations in East Prussia* (Ft. Leavenworth, Kans.: Command and General Staff School Press, 1933), 71.

[a]An "independent army securing the flanks," tasked to guarantee the safety of the capital (St. Petersburg, later named Petrograd) and the guard the Baltic coast.

[b]An "independent army securing the flanks," tasked to cover the Romanian flank and to guard the Black Sea coast.

10. Nicholas N. Golovine, Lt. Gen., Imperial Russian Army, *The Russian Campaign of 1914: The Beginning of the War and Operations in East Prussia* (Ft. Leavenworth, Kans.: Command and General Staff School Press, 1933), esp. 70–71.

11. Alan K. Wildman, *The End of the Russian Imperial Army* (Princeton, N.J.: Princeton University Press, 1980). See also David R. Jones, "Imperial Russia's Forces at War," ch. 8 in Millett and Murray, eds., *Military Effectiveness*, 1:249–328, and William C. Fuller, Jr., *Strategy and Power in Russia, 1600–1914* (New York: Free Press, 1992), 432–51.

able to do better, and the Bolshevik revolution of November 1917 was made possible in part by Lenin's pledge to seek immediate peace with Russia's enemies. At great cost, this pledge was fulfilled at Brest-Litovsk in 1918, and Russia quit the war.

The French offensive strategy and Russia's two-front dilemma had contributed to the obsession with winning wars in their initial period. As strategy bogged down in the mud of Flanders, expedient solutions commended themselves to British, French, and German planners. The most daring was the Gallipoli campaign (approved by Kitchener, but blamed by most Britons on the influence of then First Lord of the Admiralty Winston S. Churchill) to force the Dardanelles, knock Turkey out of the war, and storm through the Balkans to subdue Austria and then Germany. The plan, if brought to fruition, would also have opened a lifeline of supply through the Black Sea to Imperial Russia. Gallipoli, although tantalizingly near to success, ultimately failed owing to the risk aversion of commanders on the spot and insufficient appreciation of the need for joint land and maritime operations.

With the failure of Gallipoli in 1916, the British and French turned to the western front strategy of bleeding the Germans. Repeated offensives across no-man's-land would waste German manpower to such an extent that Germany would rather seek a negotiated peace than continue fighting. Unfortunately for British and French planners, there was not sufficient political wisdom in Germany, nor in London or Paris, to seek any peace so long as either side could replace unprecedented casualty lists with fresh recruits or draftees.[12] Germany's imperial government had in any event fallen into de facto control of the military oligarchs Paul von Hindenburg and Erich von Ludendorff. The latter, emboldened by Russia's defection from the allied cause in 1918, ordered a series of final offensives intended to break the back of the allied defense in France. When these failed and counteroffensives threatened to destroy what remained of the Imperial German Army, Ludendorff implored his nominal civilian superiors to sue for peace.

The United States had not planned to send an expeditionary force to Europe prior to World War I. President Woodrow Wilson preferred to maintain an isolationist stance with regard to outbreaks of war in Europe, and he discouraged advance military-staff planning for American involvement in such a war. Events, primarily Germany's unrestricted submarine-warfare campaign against allied shipping, changed his position. In 1917

---

12. Interesting analysis of why the war was prolonged appears in Charles S. Maier, "Wargames: 1914–1919," in Robert I. Rotberg and Theodore K. Rabb, eds., *The Origin and Prevention of Major Wars* (Cambridge: Cambridge University Press, 1989), 249–80, esp. 264–71.

the United States thus found itself at war without a force suitable for the task and with only the potential for wartime mobilization. This lack of experience was soon put right with the designation of General John J. ("Black Jack") Pershing as United States commander-in-chief of the U.S. Army expeditionary force. Pershing insisted upon maintaining U.S. forces under a separate national command, and he succeeded in preparing his charges for their involvement in the decisive battles of 1918 that finally defeated German military strategy.

An Improbable War

The First World War was the result of an improbable crisis and it had an improbable outcome, ending in a military stalemate on the western front and in the collapse of Russia on the eastern front. The Russian, Austro-Hungarian, and Ottoman empires were destroyed. This remade the map of Eurasia, though not necessarily in a direction more conducive to subsequent peace. It is sometimes argued by historians that there is nothing like the experience of a costly and protracted war to pave the way for a period of prolonged peace in international relations. World War I shows that there is no necessary connection between the costliness of a war and the durability of the peace that follows it.

Russia, Turkey, and Austria were removed as major players on the international chessboard, yet Germany remained temporarily defeated and forced to acquiesce in Weimar democracy and harsh peace terms. The balance of power that had supported European political order prior to the outbreak of World War I was thus at least temporarily destabilized. This power vacuum could only have been filled in one of two ways. The United States, having come to the temporary rescue of the Old World, could stay and maintain a permanent military commitment to oppose aspiring hegemons in Europe. Or the League of Nations could work as intended: the majority of states basically satisfied with the international status quo would keep in check the revolutionary aspirations of revisionist states unhappy with the prevailing order.

Events conspired so that neither of these two options proved successful. The United States wanted no enduring transatlantic security commitment, and its refusal to join the League of Nations further attested to American suspicion of internationalism. The League of Nations was fated to be as successful as the least common denominator of agreement among its most powerful members. When these gatekeepers proved in the 1930s that they were unequal to the task of international peacekeeping and security, the aggressive designs of Germany, Italy, and Japan encountered no serious international opposition.

As the diplomatic settlement of World War I was mistaken for an enduring peace, so too were the military-strategic lessons mislearned. World War I had seemed to result from an excessive amount of alliance-making: hardening of the diplomatic arteries when flexibility might have avoided war. This was true to an extent but also misleading in the larger compass of events leading up to war. Alliances were the symptoms of distrust, not the causes of fighting. World War I was caused by a peculiar combination of military optimism and strategic pessimism. The optimism was that major coalition wars, even those involving most of the major powers of continental Europe, could be won decisively in their initial period. The pessimism was that no modern economy could stand a prolonged war. Since the British economy was thought to be the most capable of enduring prolonged war among the Eurasian continental and maritime powers, this pessimism as felt in London was to some extent about the expected fate of Germans and Russians, not the English.

The miltary-strategic lesson of World War I—that the stalemated trench warfare in the west proved the technological superiority of the defense over the offense—was a contingent lesson since subjected to a great deal of historical overstatement. The German plan for the invasion of Belgium and France certainly did pull up short on the Marne, but that had as much to do with inherent difficulties of the plan itself as it had to do with the superiority of the defensive form of war. The near success of the Schlieffen Plan in the autumn of 1914 might just as easily be pointed to as evidence of the superiority of a new form of offensive warfare. Mobile artillery, modern rifled weapons, massive flanking maneuvers, and mobilized reserves were all used effectively by the German attackers—who nearly succeeded on one throw of the die.

Moreover, in the east, where battles between the Germans and Russians could take advantage of more room for maneuver, the confinement of trench warfare was not nearly so pronounced as it was in the western theater of operations. British World War I operations in the Middle East, particularly those under the command of Archibald Percival Wavell, also used to great advantage various forms of surprise and operational maneuver.[13] The protracted nature of World War I was caused primarily by the number of states and the geographic expanse of the fighting, not by the particular tactics used in fighting over no-man's-land. This is not to say that those tactics were ones to which postwar British or French generals

13. Capt. B. H. Liddell-Hart, *The Real War, 1914–1918* (Boston: Little, Brown, 1930, 1964), 439–48.

could point with pride: problems of command and control, including poor tactical judgments based on misinformation, have been well documented for the western front.

World War I, its particular origins and preferred tactics aside, demonstrated that major coalition wars could not easily be brought under the control of politicians to any useful end. Once under way, such wars had a momentum of their own, especially when the age of mass industrial society allowed political leaders to propagandize their enemies as the devil incarnate before an audience of unprecedented size and diversity. This practice has continued to the present day, with unfortunate results insofar as sober public appreciation of the real travails of warfighting and policymaking is concerned. World War I was the first global coalition war in which home-front propaganda became a part of military strategy. If the entire populace could not be enlisted under arms, it could participate vicariously in the excoriation of the "Huns" and "Kaiser Bill."

The flexibility of alignment on which a balance of power depends did not return to the international system after World War I. For one thing, a propagandized public had become used to ideological appeals, and these now resonated throughout postwar Europe and in North America. The former Russian allies became dangerous "Reds" and could not be acknowledged by the United States as a legitimate member of the international community until the 1930s. Germany, on the other hand, was readmitted to the international community so long as Berlin maintained the institutional façade of democracy, which it was able to do well into the 1930s. The assumption that good democracies were inherently peaceful and bad autocracies inherently warlike had supported Woodrow Wilson's wartime and postwar diplomacy. It continued to be a talisman of the U.S. understanding of international politics, and the assumption that democracy is an inherently peaceful form of government rides herd over political science debates even today.

The notion that democracies are inherently more peaceful than autocracies was arrived at by World War I and postwar politicians by statistical sleight of hand. The autocratic Germans were blamed for starting World War I, but the equally autocratic Russians and Austro-Hungarians were less often charged. Presumably the Germans' real sin was the effective fighting power of their armies compared to that of their autocratic neighbors. One should worry, then, only about those autocrats who are militarily competent, such as Frederick the Great and Napoléon, as potential disturbers of the peace. On the other hand, the assumption that democracies are inherently peaceful cannot be grounded in experience immediately preceding World War I, during it, or immediately afterward.

Peace is not the result of a deterministic unwillingness to fight, but of a judicious weighing by a state of the balance between fighting when necessary and negotiating when possible. A democracy that is unwilling to fight when its vital interests are threatened is not "peace seeking" in any serious sense of that term: it is simply mistaken. As the interwar years of the 1920s and 1930s were to show, if by "peaceful" we mean acquiescent in the demands of aggressors, then the leading democracies of Europe were certainly peaceful. They also invited into the peace of Europe the disturbance of Hitler's unslaked thirst for German expansion and genocide.

Although the pre-1914 European democracies cannot be accused of mistaken pacifism in the preceding sense, they were certainly uncertain about how to balance the deterrent effect of war-preparedness with the equally significant capacity for negotiated peace settlement short of war.[14] Their attempts to balance force with diplomacy failed spectacularly. Of course, one school of thought, the so-called Fischer school of German revisionist writers, maintains that Germany's desire for world power was the major cause for war: other factors were contributory and relatively insignificant.[15] While Germany's part cannot be excused, most historians would be loath to attribute to Kaiser Wilhelm the same single-minded ruthless sense of imperial purpose as was later manifested by Hitler. Imperial Germany desired to be first among equals in the European balance of power, not to topple the entire balancing mechanism.

Continuing Controversy

Who Caused the First World War?

The victors of World War I imposed on Germany a peace treaty which included an acknowledgment of German guilt for starting the war. The causes of World War I are deep and complex, but even some noted German scholars have argued that Germany bears most of the responsibility. Germany is certainly one of the three most popular villains nominated by historians and political scientists, not to mention contemporary politi-

14. Multipolar power systems create opposed incentives for alliance formation: "chain ganging" and "buck passing." See Thomas J. Christensen and Jack Snyder, "Chain Gangs and Passed Bucks: Predicting Alliance Patterns in Multipolarity," *International Organization* (Spring 1990): 137–68. Related to this is the question of whether states will "bandwagon" with rising hegemons or will balance against them: see Stephen M. Walt, *The Origins of Alliances* (Ithaca, N.Y.: Cornell University Press, 1987), esp. ch. 2.

15. See Fritz Fischer, *War of Illusions: German Policies from 1911 to 1914,* trans. Marian Jackson (New York: W. W. Norton, 1975), esp. 389–92 on the Schlieffen Plan.

cians and generals. The other two combatants receiving numerous nominations for the dubious honor of principal cause for World War I are Austria-Hungary and Russia.

The case for Germany is based on several points. First, the ambitious foreign policy undertaken by that country at the turn of the century caused its European neighbors to doubt its commitment to continental stability. Germany asserted itself outside Europe in imperial domains formerly thought to be the preserve of Britain or France, as in Morocco. Second, Germany sought to modernize its navy so that it was either equal in size and capability to the British or, if not equal, sufficiently capable for deterrence. Admiral Alfred von Tirpitz's idea was that even a German navy that could not take on Britain single-handedly could serve as a "risk fleet" capable of imposing unacceptable losses. Third, Germany's alliance with Austria was yet another source of concern among its political rivals, and it contributed directly to the July crisis of 1914 and to the outbreak of war immediately thereafter. Fourth, Germany had an apparently aggressive military doctrine and strategic war plan, based on the rapid and decisive defeat of its opponents by speedier mobilization and deployment.

Russia's candidacy, like that of Germany, involves several factors. First, Russian foreign policy was overcommitted to the defense of Serbia against Austria. After previous crises, including the Bosnian crisis of 1908, the Russian leadership felt it had to support Serbia against future Austrian pressure or lose an unacceptable amount of prestige. Second, Russia allied itself to France, making a war between Germany and Russia inevitable if Germany attacked France. Third, Russia could not mobilize and deploy forces to the frontier as rapidly as Germany could. Therefore, Russian mobilization might have to start sooner than German mobilization, raising tensions contributory to war. Fourth, Russia's government was the worst possible for crisis management. The tsar was the center of decision on war policy, and he was predominantly influenced by whichever adviser had most recently briefed him.

Austria-Hungary can also be seen as the principal culprit for the outbreak of war. First, Austria set the July 1914 crisis in motion with its ultimatum to Serbia, a list of demands imposed on Belgrade following the assassination of the Archduke Ferdinand and his wife in Bosnia. The demands on Serbia by Austria were calculatedly excessive: Austria was looking for a pretext for war, not an escape hatch. Second, Austria fired the first shots in anger. It did so in cold blood, deliberately allowing a lapse of time between the ultimatum and the bombardment of Belgrade in order to lull public opinion and the governments of the other powers. Third, Austria obtained from Germany in June a blank check for whatever measures it might subsequently take to punish Serbia. Although Germany can be faulted for its incompetence in providing such an empty-headed commitment, Austria obtained the blank check without full candor about its long-term intentions.

Some argue that the system was the villain, not the individual state participants. Two alliances, the Entente and the Central Powers (Triple Alliance), were poised for an outbreak of war by the end of the first decade of the twentieth century. It needed only a spark to set off the conflagration of war throughout Europe. That spark was nearly provided in 1912 by an earlier Balkan crisis, but the danger abated when Russia and France, less cohesive than in 1914, backed away from war. Nevertheless, Russian War Minister Vladimir Sukhomlinov had on his own accord authorized a partial mobilization of the forces located near the Austrian front. This was discovered inadvertently by others in the Russian leadership and pulled back with sharp remonstrances from the Russian foreign minister, Sergei Sazonov.

Imperialism is also in the docket, according to some historians, as the primary cause for World War I. For imperialism dictated that the powers perceived a security dilemma: if they were not expanding, then they were losing ground. This zero-sum (one side's loss is another's gain) perception of the balance of power in pre–World War I Europe was inaccurate. Neither the autocratic nor the democratic prewar regimes of Europe needed imperial expansion beyond that already achieved before the twentieth century in order to maintain their status in the military pecking order. Imperial acquisitions outside Europe may have brought trade and other economic benefits, but outer empires also had to be garrisoned with troops and protected with fleets. The costs of imperialism in the industrial age were certainly equal to, if not greater than, the costs of improving a state's own national armed forces and economic strength by judicious investment.

Few nominate Britain for the role of primary cause of the fighting in the First World War. But it can be argued that Britain contributed to the outbreak of war by what she did *not* do, rather than by what she did. Britain was late in warning Germany that British support for France was all but guaranteed if Germany should attack France. Too late in the day was the kaiser finally persuaded that Britain could not remain nonbelligerent if Germany fought France. Had the British Foreign Office made it clearer that a victory of Germany over France was completely unacceptable and that the British commitment of a continental army to support Paris was firm, it is possible that some small chance existed that Germany would have pulled back from Austria. The kaiser had already urged Austria to settle on terms with Serbia, and although he vacillated, the frantic diplomatic communications with his cousin Tsar Nicholas II indicated that the kaiser was wishy-washy, not bent irretrievably on war.

The most obvious strategic planning deficiency of the powers was their expectation that war would be short. Their economies and military production systems were not geared for a long war. In one sense, their economic planners underestimated their production capabilities. Once the possibility of protracted war was faced up to, most of the combatants outproduced their prewar expectations. Even the oft-criticized Russians, whose forces fought with notorious shell and rifle shortages, had by 1916 substantially improved their factory production of weapons and ammunition (and had made arrangements to purchase more from abroad).

Had the powers anticipated a longer and more costly war, it is not obvious that they would have desisted. Only a crystal ball which clearly forecast the demise of their regimes (as occurred in Russia, Austria, and Germany) might have deflected them off the collision course of their diplomacies. Using as their model the Franco-Prussian War of 1870 and not the more protracted U.S. Civil War or Russo-Japanese War, the great powers of Europe mobilized for victory in a short conflict, only to find that there was no victory to be had at an acceptable social and political cost. Thus, one cause of the war lay in the policymaking process used in chancelleries, militaries, and foreign offices of the powers: the result was a willingness, in almost every case, to substitute estimation based on the desirable for intelligence based on the necessary.

2

INTERWAR and WORLD WAR II POLICY and STRATEGY

The First World War, judged by the Clausewitzian standards which had informed much prewar military planning and training, horribly disconnected war from prudent state policy. Germany and Russia lost their empires. Britain and France, though nominal victors, were terribly weakened. The United States, despite its late entry into the war in 1917, had emerged with more prestige intact than any other participant. Technology seemed to favor military stalemate, not the exploitation of military power for victory in battle at an acceptable cost. During the interwar period of the 1920s and the 1930s, the powers tried to put back into place the stable and predictable relationship between war and policy which was thought to obtain in the previous century. As we know, they failed.

World War I ended with expectations about strategy and policy that were incongruent with the actual unfolding of war and politics in the 1920s and 1930s. Leaders concluded in the aftermath of World War I that replacement of autocracies with democracies would contribute to peace. They assumed that Germany could be reintegrated into a peaceful and democratic family of nations. They assumed that the Soviet Union could be excused from participating in a European security system. They assumed that the League of Nations would successfully internationalize the responsibility for world peace and security. Although each of these assumptions had some theoretically compelling reasoning behind it, the world refused the follow a course conducive to those arguments.

The world of the 1920s was for many political leaders in Europe and North America a time of make-believe. The U.S. return to "normalcy" in the 1920s meant noninvolvement in European security issues. Europeans pinned their hopes on postwar economic recovery and on a variety of diplomatic expedients to ward off war. In addition to the League of Nations, these expedients included disarmament agreements and conferences, reciprocal security guarantees (as at Locarno), and a proliferation of new democracies in east-central Europe. The need of the powers of Europe to rebuild their economies after World War I and the near-term memories of the costs of that conflict dictated that military adventurism remain dormant for a decade or so.

Nevertheless, the Peace of Versailles was a "worst case" of leniency combined with harshness: sufficient to enrage the defeated Germans but insufficient to keep down their economic and military potential for military mischief. A defeated nation is vulnerable to appeals on nationalistic, ethnic, and other ideological grounds, and it is further susceptible to scapegoating. All of these appeals were used by the Nazi leadership to great effect during the 1930s. Once the bottom had fallen out of Germany's economy, democracy seemed to coincide with incompetency. Germans turned to a führer whose rearmament and public works campaigns put people to work and seemed to guarantee a more secure future. Once convinced of their dependency on Hitler for economic solvency, the German masses were all the more vulnerable to his racist and xenophobic appeals. (See Table 4.)

Belligerent Nonbelligerence

If the Peace of Versailles failed to support the postwar balance of power in Europe, it also failed to damp the noxious fumes of triumphant pacificism among Europe's postwar elites. This statement should be qualified: there was little pacificism in Moscow, where the political leadership felt encircled by capitalism, or in the German General Staff, which was biding its time for better days ahead. However, in the Western democracies as a whole there was a belligerent nonbelligerence. World War I had been a "war to end all wars," and it was against accepted canon to argue otherwise. The assumption was that if only leaders wished hard enough to purge war as a viable political option, its purgation would come to pass.

The apotheosis of this belligerent nonbelligerence was the Kellogg-Briand Pact, which closed the 1920s on a foreign policy note about as realistic as the Harding and Coolidge domestic economic policies. By the terms of the Kellogg-Briand Pact (1928), signatories renounced war as an option for foreign policy. How the renunciation of war under all condi-

Table 4. Chronology of Events between the World Wars

Date	Events
1919	Opening of peace conference at Versailles
	Adoption of Weimar Constitution for Germany
1920	Creation of League of Nations
1921–22	Washington Conference on naval arms limitation
1922	Permanent Court of International Justice established
	Treaty of Rapallo normalizes Soviet–German relations
	Mussolini takes power in Italy
1923	France and Belgium occupy the Ruhr
1926	Germany admitted to League of Nations
1928	Kellogg-Briand Pact outlawing war signed
1931	Japanese invasion of Manchuria
1933	Hitler named chancellor of Germany
	Germany withdraws from League of Nations
1934	Soviet Union joins League of Nations
1935	Germany renounces disarmament clauses of Versailles
	Italy invades Ethiopia
	Franco-Russian alliance formed
1936	Germany reoccupies the Rhineland, renounces the Locarno security-guaranty pacts of 1925
1936–39	Spanish Civil War
1937	Japan wages full-scale war against China
1938	Germany annexes Austria
	Munich agreement cedes Sudeten Czechoslovakia to Germany
1939	Germany occupies all of Czechoslovakia
	Britain and France pledge to defend Poland
	Germany invades Poland, September 1, beginning World War II
1940	After "phony war" respite, Hitler attacks and defeats France
1941	Hitler invades Soviet Union
	Japan attacks United States at Pearl Harbor
	Hitler declares war against the United States

SOURCE: Adapted from Joseph S. Nye, Jr., *Understanding International Conflicts* (New York: Harper Collins, 1993), 96–97.

tions was presumed to contribute to peace was not made clear. Wars, after all, have political causes, and among those causes are the unwillingness of states to coalesce against aspiring hegemons as well as the aspirations of the aggressors themselves. The League of Nations, a first and last experiment in the application of universal collective security, was founded on the assumption that disturbers of the peace would meet with immediate resistance from an outraged and unified international community. This assumption, like the Kellogg-Briand assumption of war renunciation, failed to jibe with events.

The 1930s saw a global economic recession coincide with the arrival of new regimes in Germany, Japan, and Italy whose mass appeal was based on chauvinism and militarism. The stress placed upon the international status quo was considerable. There are many well-known markers by which historians of this decade have plotted the demise of European and global security. Italy's invasion of Ethiopia was met with a slap on the wrist by the League's leading states. Japan's invasion of Manchuria was unmet by counterforce, as was Japan's later sweep across the rest of China, placing in imminent jeopardy the British, French, and Dutch holdings in South Asia. Hitler's occupation of the Rhineland could easily have been bluffed out or snuffed out by resolute diplomacy or military action, but the French claimed they did not have a plan for limited war. In 1934, the Japanese government, fearing internal political crisis and under navy pressure to modernize the fleet, announced its intention to abrogate the Washington arms-limitation agreements designed to maintain a balance of maritime power in the Pacific.[1]

Neither the temerity of the major status quo powers nor the collective machinery of international organization was sufficient to persuade the revisionist Germans, Japanese, and Italians that there was any willingness to fight to uphold the balance of power. Even deterrent measures were suspect and controversial. On account of the Soviet Union's ideologically suspect status, its forces were not enlisted in any deterrent alliance prior to war. One might justifiably argue that Russia's aid had been enlisted prior to World War I, with the result that the Entente was more tightly bound to rapid mobilization plans and prompt offensives. But the problem of war avoidance in the 1930s was different from the problem during the July 1914 crisis. In 1914, no power really wanted war to the extent that it was willing to pay *any* price, including the possible collapse of its regime, to gain the spoils of war.

Hitler and Imperial Japan were willing to pay almost any price, though not all at once. Hitler prepared to lay out his design in stages. What he could bluff the Allies into giving up without a fight he would not have to seize by force. The German General Staff was more afraid of war than Hitler was between 1936, when he marched into the Rhineland and tore up the Versailles treaty, and the time of the Munich agreement over Czechoslovakia (September 1938).[2] Some leading German officers had conspired to overthrow Hitler if the British and French decided to fight over Czechoslovakia, but diplomatic concessions at Munich gave Hitler

---

1. Emily O. Goldman, *Sunken Treaties: Naval Arms Control between the Wars* (University Park: Pennsylvania State University Press, 1994), 223.
2. John Keegan, *The Second World War* (New York: Viking Press, 1989), 36.

all the impetus he needed in 1939 to subdue doubting generals and invest the remainder of Czechoslovakia over allied protest.

At this point, Hitler had run out of victories by bluff (although he did not yet realize the point). Having conceded so much previously, the Neville Chamberlain government decided to draw the line at Poland. In the spring of 1939, Britain made public a security guarantee to Poland which was a diplomatic surprise to Hitler and a military anomaly to others. A Polish security guarantee would be enforceable not by Britain but by Russia, but Whitehall was reluctant to involve Russia in its diplomatic demarches. Britain was allied to France, but geography placed both on the western side of Germany. Without Russian connivance against Germany, pledges to come to the defense of Poland were empty.

Unfortunately for British-French policy and strategy, both Hitler and Stalin deduced the fact of Polish vulnerability as well as the irrelevance of British pledges to Warsaw. If only the two dictators could agree not to fight one another, they could dismember Poland more or less at will. Such an agreement was accomplished by Foreign Ministers Joachim von Ribbentrop and V. M. Molotov in August 1939, setting the stage for Hitler's attack on Poland, which began the Second World War on September 1, 1939. There is some evidence that Hitler did not expect Britain and France to redeem their pledge to Poland, anticipating that they would concede at the last minute as they had at Munich. If Hitler so supposed, he reckoned badly.

Hitler's Misestimate

Hitler failed to reckon with the British public sense of indignity at having been double-crossed over Munich and with the British government's sense of propriety over keeping agreements that have been publicly proclaimed. The British government had deliberately burned its diplomatic bridges over Poland: they could only go forward into world war, not backward into still another concession to Hitler. The French were no more able to save Poland than the British. But they, too, recognized that the invasion of Poland amounted to a point of no return.

However united the British Parliament and public were, once the Chamberlain government saw clearly into Hitler's designs, the French Third Republic was torn by an ineffective multiparty system and hobbled by professional military arteriosclerosis. Having retroactively seen the error of their ways against the absurdly optimistic plans of 1914, the French

General Staff now reverted to optimistically defensive plans for containing any German offensive by means of the Maginot line.[3] The French prewar strategy was to allow the Germans to bleed themselves in futile offensives against the defensive bulwarks, and then to assume a counteroffensive into Germany. The strategy depended upon Hitler offering some variant of Germany's World War I strategy: a main thrust sweeping through Belgium with diversionary thrusts elsewhere.

Hitler originally adopted such a strategy on the basis of the recommendations of his General Staff. But he was never comfortable with it, and as soon as he learned of the more audacious Manstein Plan for a main attack through the seemingly impenetrable Ardennes he was all for it. The plan fitted his personality and his gambling instincts. Fortunately for Hitler and not for the French, the plan's audacity was compensated for by brilliant field leadership, primarily that of panzer group commander Heinz Guderian. Guderian raced through French defenses faster than even Manstein's breathless timetable had called for, causing Wehrmacht logistics to strain and Hitler to worry about his overextended panzers being outflanked and encircled.

He need not have worried. For the French government, recognizing that once the Ardennes was pierced its game plan for defense of the Third Republic had failed, preferred to surrender instead of fighting on. The British evacuated from Dunkirk and left the Vichy regime behind, in the control of Hitler's Reich. This defeat and humiliation was unacceptable to Churchill, who resolved to fight on with or without France (though the American arsenal of democracy had somehow to be got into the war). Meanwhile, Hitler's overconfidence caused him, immediately following the demise of France, to demobilize thirty-five divisions in the expectation that Britain would now have to sue for peace.

Hitler's strategic position in June 1940 was not as enviable as it appeared at first glance. He had pushed the British off the Continent and subdued France and Poland. Russia, however, remained at his back, and Stalin was the least trustworthy of allies. It had been Hitler's obsession for a long time to acquire lebensraum at the expense of Slavic peoples between Poland and the Caspian Sea. He also wanted to secure Germany's control over the granaries of Ukraine and the Ploesti oil fields of Romania. In addition, communist ideology was repugnant to his National Socialist soul. In 1940 there was no doubt in Hitler's mind that eventually Russia had to fall, but that would be easier to bring about if British resis-

3. Ronald Chalmers Hood III, "Bitter Victory: French Military Effectiveness during the Second World War," ch. 6 in Alan R. Millett and Williamson Murray, eds., *Military Effectiveness* (London: Unwin Hyman, 1988), 3:221–55.

tance were nullified first. America Hitler dismissed as a military nonentity.

But Britain would neither be conciliated nor deterred from continuation of what appeared even to its friends to be a desperate and potentially bootless struggle. This prospectus changed significantly after Hitler's air force was unable, during the Battle of Britain in 1940, to induce London's capitulation. Hitler was actually willing to offer very favorable terms for war termination, but who could trust him? Churchill was the least likely, and how long could the British Empire endure with Hitler in command of everything from Narvik to Astrakhan? Hitler decided that England counted on rescue by the Soviet Union. By knocking Moscow out of the war, Germany could find the back door to England's capitulation.[4]

Germany against Russia

It happened in 1940 that the Soviet Union was more vulnerable than it should have been. Stalin's purges of the military and virtually everything else between 1936 and 1939 resulted in a collective Soviet military leadership unable to prepare for the kind of war Hitler was about to launch on June 22, 1941.[5] The Soviets' costly war with Finland in 1940–41 and their own war games under Stalin's watchful eye convinced the Soviet leader that he needed to placate Hitler and buy as much time for rebuilding as possible.[6] Ironically, the westward push of the Soviet frontier in 1940 made it more vulnerable to the rapid thrust of Germany's attacking legions in 1941. The older border would have been more easily defended.

Hitler's intelligence about Soviet military and economic power was lacking. Stalin's purges convinced Germany's military leaders that there was a feeble brain at the head of the Soviet armed forces in 1941. This judgment was correct, but Stalin was able to find capable generals to replace those who had failed in the initial weeks and months of humiliating retreat across western Byelorussia and Ukraine. A younger generation of Red commanders matured during the Second World War and, by the time of the climactic battles of Stalingrad in 1942–43 and Kursk in 1943,

4. Jürgen E. Forster, "The Dynamics of *Volkegemeinschaft:* The Effectiveness of the German Military Establishment in the Second World War," ch. 5 in Millett and Murray, eds., *Military Effectiveness,* 3:195–96.

5. John Erickson, "Threat Identification and Strategic Appraisal by the Soviet Union," ch. 13 in Ernest R. May, ed., *Knowing One's Enemies: Intelligence Assessment before the Two World Wars* (Princeton, N.J.: Princeton University Press, 1986), 375–423, esp. 390.

6. Keegan, *The Second World War,* 47.

Soviet capability for offensive mobile warfare over great distances was at least equivalent to that of the Germans.[7]

Historians still debate whether Hitler overshot his bolt by invading Russia in Operation Barbarossa, begun in June 1941 but halted within sight of the gates of Moscow in December of that year. Had Hitler's invading forces concentrating on the Moscow axis pushed for the taking of that sector more decisively, it is conceivable that Stalin and his entourage would have had to decamp to Yekaterinburg for at least a year or two.[8] The conquest of the Soviet Union in its entirely was another matter. Hitler's armored spearhead was only the tip of his lance: most of Germany's ground forces marched or rode on horseback well behind the rapidly moving panzers. Logistics ran out on Hitler as fast as Russian resistance ground him down, and the Russian winter, though taxing to both sides, found Germany's planners more unprepared than Russia's for climatic conditions.

Another uncertainty for Hitler and for Stalin was what Japan would do. A nominal ally of the Third Reich, Japan had its own scores to settle with Moscow. In all likelihood, a Japanese attack on Russia's rear, coincident with Hitler's Barbarossa, would have sealed Stalin's fate. Stalin was obsessive about power but not evidently unwilling to face military facts. Faced with a Japanese invasion of the Soviet Far East and a simultaneous German attack from the west, Stalin probably would have cut a deal with one side in order to direct all of his surviving power against the other. Japan could have been conciliated easier than Hitler, and in the event, such a decision was unnecessary. Japan sought to expand its empire in other directions, making the war a truly global conflict and provoking America's entry.

Undoubtedly it was Winston Churchill's greatest day when he learned of Pearl Harbor, for Hitler fortuitously jumped in to declare war against America.[9] In Churchill's mind, this represented Britain's salvation. How-

7. Col. David M. Glantz, *The Great Patriotic War and the Maturation of Soviet Operational Art: 1941–1945* (Draft) (Fort Leavenworth, Kans.: Soviet Army Studies Office, 1987), is an excellent overview with illustrations. See also G. Isserson, "Razvitiye teorii sovetskogo operativnogo iskusstva v 30-ye gody" [The Development of Theory of Soviet Operational Art in the 1930s], *Voenna-istoricheskii zhurnal,* no. 1 (January 1965): 36–46, trans. and repr. in Harold S. Orenstein, ed., *Selected Readings in the History of Soviet Operational Art* (Fort Leavenworth, Kans.: Soviet Army Studies Office, May 1980), 29–46.

8. Hitler's Army High Command (OKH) certainly held to a view favoring a headlong drive toward Moscow. See Keegan, *The Second World War,* 192–93. See also Col. Albert Seaton, *The Battle for Moscow* (New York: Jove Books, 1983), 27ff.

9. Historical perspective on Hitler's decision is provided by Hans L. Trefousse, "Germany and Pearl Harbor," in Robert A. Divine, ed., *Causes and Consequences of World War II* (Chicago: Quadrangle Books, 1969), 123–42.

ever long the war might continue, the American economic superpower would now become a military giant to help smash Hitler. Churchill was right beyond his wildest dreams. The United States put 12 million troops under arms and turned American factories into the greatest makers of planes, tanks, and munitions in world history. The United States so out-produced the Axis powers that even the most inept strategy would still have led to an inevitable result. Pearl Harbor ensured that the U.S. leadership would be as determined to pursue the matter to unconditional surrender, or the disestablishment of the entire German regime, as was Churchill. Neither Hitler nor Germany would rise again in his lifetime.

America and Global War

The United States was no better prepared for war in Asia than it was for war in Europe until the deterioration of relations with Japan, culminating in the Japanese attack on Pearl Harbor, brought an aroused America into the world war. Imperial Japan ran riot over the South Pacific until U.S. success at the Battle of Midway in 1942 began to turn the tide. Years of tough fighting in some of the world's most remote and forbidding outposts (Guadalcanal, Tarawa) lay ahead of American sailors and marines. The United States having also entered the war for Europe, it was judged by President Franklin Roosevelt that the defeat of Germany had priority over war against Japan. Accordingly, U.S. forces in the Pacific were off-stage compared to the public and news media attention lavished on those in Europe until V-E Day. It took massive Soviet pressure from the east and U.S. and allied pressure from the west between June 6, 1944 (the Normandy invasion), and the fall of Berlin in 1945. With the subsequent defeat of Japan after the August bombings of Hiroshima and Nagasaki, the Eurasian balance of power had reduced itself from a many-sided balance of five or six powers to a two-sided, or bipolar, balance.

One might ask, in view of the outcome of the Second World War, whether the Allies' objective of unconditional surrender was necessary on strategic grounds or expedient for rallying their national publics.[10] Evidence suggests that unconditional surrender might have prolonged the war against Japan, although peace feelers prior to August 1945 were confounded by Russian concern about Allied abandonment and by Japanese fears that the emperor would be slain or exiled after national defeat.

10. John L. Chase, "Unconditional Surrender Reconsidered," in Divine, ed., *Causes and Consequences of World War II*, 183–202, takes a favorable view of the decision for unconditional surrender.

Hitler's offers of peace to Britain in 1940 suggest to some that a negotiated agreement could have left the Allies with the British Empire and North America while Hitler gorged on continental west-central Europe and European Russia.

Hitler's deservedly poor reputation for bargain keeping and Churchill's justified ardor for putting the Nazi dictator onto the ash heap of history are two strong arguments why "conditional" surrender or peace on terms with Nazis remaining in power seemed farfetched to statesmen at the time. It still does. Hitler was willing to compromise with Britain in 1940 in order to obtain European hegemony at low cost. By 1944 he had paid enormous costs and was less willing to settle for partial victory. In addition, the attempt on his life by members of his own military high command in 1944 caused Hitler to distrust even more fervently the judgments of his generals and to doubt fully their loyalty to his person and cause. If the plot against Hitler provides evidence for some that war termination short of unconditional surrender was a near miss, Hitler's vindictive purging of the military command afterward shows a tyrannical force no longer open to political compromise.

Hanson W. Baldwin, former military correspondent for the *New York Times,* has indicted President Roosevelt and his advisers for allegedly defective policy and strategy decisions, including open-ended definitions of war aims.[11] According to Baldwin, unconditional surrender was a policy of "political bankruptcy" that delayed the military objective of victory over the Axis armed forces and revealed the lack of any clear U.S. and Allied program for peace. Baldwin summons Clausewitz to his side of the argument:

> We fought to win, period. We did not remember that wars are merely an extension of politics by other means; that wars have objectives; that wars without objectives represent particularly senseless slaughters; that unless a nation is to engage in an unlimited holocaust those objectives must be attainable by the available strength and are limited by the victor's capacity to enforce them and by the willingness of the vanquished state to accept them; and that the general objective of war is a more stable peace.[12]

The United States arose from its slumber in 1941 to become a global military power by 1943 and the preeminent one by the end of the Second World War. When Russians and Americans met at the Elbe a bipolar

---

11. See Hanson W. Baldwin, "Our Worst Blunders in the War: Europe and the Russians," in Divine, ed., *Causes and Consequences of World War II,* 163–82.

12. Ibid., 164.

world had arrived. This world would have less flexibility of alignment than a multipolar rivalry among five or six great powers. It would have to depend on something other than the counterpoint of balancing and band-wagoning by leading states. Shifting alliances would be replaced after World War II by relationships of domination and subordination. This great power dealignment was accompanied by the advent of nuclear weapons, creating a need for strategic rethinking of the first order. Unconditional surrender of the Axis powers had not yielded unconditional victory: seen from 1945, the postwar world looked as dangerous as the prewar one.

Continuing Controversy

Was "Unconditional Surrender" a Mistake?

The United States, Britain, and the Soviet Union agreed during a wartime conference at Casablanca, Morocco, that the terms for the cessation of hostilities with Germany, Italy, and Japan would be nothing less than unconditional surrender. In the ABC-1 meetings between U.S. and British military planners, held beginning in January 1941, it was agreed in principle that the first priority was defeat of the European Axis powers, especially Germany.[13] Unconditional surrender meant that the Allies would not deal with the governments in Berlin, Rome, and Tokyo as legitimate state actors. These governments were judged to have committed illegal aggression against the international order. They had to be unseated and replaced by legitimate regimes in order to restore peace.

This decision of the Allies was controversial in its own time and subsequently. Some have claimed that either Germany or Japan would have sued for peace without having their armed forces totally defeated in battle. The case of Japan has stirred special interest among historians and other students of war termination in 1945. The U.S. decision to drop the atomic bomb on Japan made the character of Allied war termination with Hirohito's empire a matter of academic and popular debate from 1945 to the present. Skeptics have doubted that the atomic bomb was really necessary to end the war with Japan, and Cold War "revisionist" historians have suspected that the bombings of Hiroshima and Nagasaki were designed to intimidate Stalin as much as they were intended to subdue Japan.

13. Russell F. Weigley, *The American Way of War: A History of United States Military Strategy and Policy* (New York: Macmillan, 1973), 316.

The U.S. strategic bombing survey conducted in Japan after the war concluded that, in all probability, Japan would have surrendered by November 1945 without the use of atomic bombing and without an invasion of the Japanese home islands which the Allies had thought necessary prior to Hiroshima and Nagasaki. The issue of expected losses in any invasion of Japan is an important aspect of Harry Truman's decision to authorize the use of atomic weapons. Military estimates provided to Secretary of War Henry Stimson suggested that up to 1 million *U.S.* casualties (killed and wounded) would result from any invasion of the Japanese homeland.

Paul Fussell, a noted writer and cultural historian of both the world wars, tells poignantly of his feelings as a G.I. in 1945 awaiting imminent transfer to the Far Eastern theater of operations.[14] His unit was expected to take part in the invasion of Japan: few of his buddies assumed that they would return to the United States when it was over. There were good reasons for their fears. U.S. casualties in amphibious island-clearing operations in the Pacific from 1942 through 1945 had been daunting. At Iwo Jima, more than 24,000 marines had died to take an island from die-hard Japanese resisters who were dug into coral and rock redoubts. A Japanese population which was determined to fight to the last man, woman, and child for its homeland would suffer deaths and injuries even more numerous than those inflicted on the attackers.

There is a strong likelihood that the faction within the Japanese cabinet favoring continued resistance in August 1945 would have prevailed in their policy debates and prolonged the war for some time. The personal intervention of Emperor Hirohito, after the bombing of Nagasaki, decided the issue in favor of surrender. The willingness of the Allies to allow the Japanese emperor to remain on his throne as a symbol of national unity expedited the arrangement of surrender terms, although some hothead politicians in Washington and many of their constituents would have preferred to see Hirohito executed. Reconstruction of the Japanese constitution under postwar proconsul General Douglas MacArthur fitted the terms of unconditional surrender imposed on the Japanese.

With or without the atomic bomb, then, it appeared improbable to the Allies that anything less than total military defeat would cause Japan to quit fighting. What about Germany? Some historians and other writers have cited Hitler's desire for peace with Britain in 1940 after it became clear to the German dictator that a cross-channel invasion of the British Isles was not feasible. After the defeat of France in May-June 1940, Hitler

---

14. Paul Fussell, *"Thank God for the Atom Bomb" and Other Essays* (New York: Summit Books, 1988), 13–37.

proposed through direct and indirect means that he would be satisfied to divide up the spoils with an England that retained its independence and most of its global empire. Hitler wanted "only" a free hand in continental Eurasia: even in the spring of 1940, Hitler's always latent designs on Russian territory were never far below the surface of his actual war plans.

Undoubtedly, appeasers of Germany within the British upper classes existed not only before World War II had broken out but afterward. With the fall of France in 1940, there were those influentials in London political and literary circles who maintained that Hitler's forces were irresistible: better to make a good peace while it could be had. However, the pro-appeasement group was never able to rally a sufficient number of cabinet ministers or leading opposition parliamentarians. Of utmost significance, Churchill, once having assumed the position of prime minister within a coalition government, ruled out absolutely any negotiated peace with Hitler. His celebrated remark that if Hitler invaded hell, Churchill would at least remark favorably about the devil in the House of Commons, testifies to the determinism of Churchill's convictions on this point.

Two other claims are put forward by those who argue that a negotiated peace short of unconditional surrender might have been possible in Europe. The first is that Rudolf Hess's unexpected and clandestine arrival in Britain during the war was in fact a peace feeler, though not an officially acknowledged one, from the Nazi regime. Alternatively, the Hess visit has been interpreted to suggest that a group of anti-Nazis were planning to seize power and would welcome British cooperation in a negotiated peace once Hitler had been disestablished. Actually U.S. and Allied leaders received more than one diplomatic and intelligence feeler from sources within Germany, suggesting conspiracies against the Third Reich and the possibility of peaceful settlement with a post-Hitler government. Postwar studies have revealed that Rear Admiral Wilhelm Franz Canaris, a high-ranking German military intelligence officer, provided a great deal of highly sensitive information about German plans to Allied sources. The difficulty with these various informal peace feelers from German dissidents, anti-Nazi and otherwise, was the dubious reliability of the sources as capable of overthrowing Hitler in the first place. The Allies judged, probably correctly, that Hitler's rule was secure. (One assassination plot against the führer nearly succeeded in 1944 as the Allies were landing at Normandy, but Hitler escaped death and then purged many officers, including suspected plotters).

The second claim concerning the possibility of a negotiated peace short of unconditional surrender is the idea that Stalin might have settled for a deal with Germany. The argument here is that the early stages of the war went very badly for the Soviet Union, and in 1941 and 1942 its fortunes remained quite uncertain. Only after the decisive turning point at Stalingrad in the winter of 1942–43 did the momentum swing against German forces fighting in Russia. In addition, Stalin was reportedly stunned to the point of psychological paralysis in the first few weeks of Germany's invasion, which began on June 22, 1941. Although Stalin subsequently regained his composure and reorganized his military and political administration for war, the story of his temporary breakdown lends some credibility to claims that in 1941 or 1942 a sincere peace initiative from Germany would have met with a favorable reception in the Kremlin.

It is possible that Stalin sent some very indirect and discreet peace feelers to Hitler in 1941 or 1942. The Soviet dictator was extremely secretive about diplomatic and military decisions. Such initiatives, if indeed they were undertaken at Stalin's behest, would have been done covertly and deniably: the Soviet Union was undergoing a struggle for its imperiled existence. Having rallied the Soviet people with all the nationalistic and antifascist appeals that his propagandists could muster, Stalin would have been at some pains to persuade them that Germany could be trusted to observe the terms of any negotiated peace. Hitler had, after all, double-crossed Stalin by launching the German attack in the first place, while the two states were supposedly linked by a nonaggression pact made in 1939.

It is doubtful, even if Stalin had cared to make carefully concealed approaches to a negotiated peace with Germany, that Hitler would have accepted the offer. While his forces were apparently getting the upper hand against Soviet forces, Hitler had no immediate interest in negotiating. Once the military tide had reversed, it became a point of pride for Hitler to show that the inferior peoples to the east of Germany could not inflict defeat on the master race. Hitler's National Socialist ideology regarded the Slavic peoples as subhumans who were destined to be enslaved by the culturally superior Germanic-Nordic peoples. Some skeptics argue, however, that Hitler's ideological bombast contained a great deal of camouflage, and that hard geopolitical facts had more to do with Hitler's decision priorities than his adversaries acknowledged. A geopolitically minded Hitler, in this view, might have agreed to settle for the Ukrainian granaries and Romanian oil fields under German control, allowing the remainder of Russia west of the Urals to exist under a Soviet equivalent of the German-controlled Vichy regime in wartime France.

A final point about unconditional surrender is that it served to sustain the Allied coalition of the United States, Britain, and Russia. Stalin, from the moment of Hitler's invasion of the Soviet Union, was suspicious that his American and British allies would sell him out by negotiating a separate peace with Hitler. A deal of this sort would throw the entire weight of Germany and its probable co-belligerent Japan against the Soviet Union.

Stalin's "worst case" scenario would have arrived at his Kremlin doorstep. Soviet fears of this scenario were marked by some paranoia but, given the prior history of relations between communist and capitalist powers, were not altogether unrealistic. Stalin's suspicions were sufficiently acute that he reacted with great alarm to news that U.S. and British intelligence sources were receiving in 1943 feelers from German forces in Italy expressing a desire for local surrender and war termination.

3

THE COLD WAR

Most Americans, including President Roosevelt, expected during World War II that the unlimited force used in that conflict would force postwar politicians to agree to put aside the sword on behalf of policy. The United Nations organization embodied not only the hopes for future concord among the victors of the war, but also the frustrations of those states at the events of the preceding twenty years or so. The taming of force on behalf of policy was accomplished during the next forty years by the politics of fear, or mutual deterrence, and only to the extent that a global war or continental European war was avoided. The Cold War relationship between the Americans and the Soviets, neither true peace nor true war but very deadly at the margin, brought the atmosphere of uncertainty and the fear of battle into the time period of nuclear-crisis management. Crises were now ersatz wars, for no real war fought with nuclear weapons could possibly serve as a rational policy instrument. Absolute war and real war were joined by nuclear embrace: it was now the task of policymakers to prevent war from happening.

Historians are still fighting the Cold War, after its abandonment as a topical focus by politicians. During the 1960s and 1970s there were intense U.S. scholarly debates, between "orthodox" and "revisionist" schools of thought, about the origins of the Cold War. Orthodox thinkers contended that the Soviet military challenge had been serious and vital and that, by and large, U.S. Cold War containment policy was a realistic and successful response to that challenge. Revisionist thinkers argued, to the contrary, that the United States overreacted to Soviet postwar insecurity and defense-mindedness, which were a result of Russian-Soviet historical experience and communist ideology. By the 1980s a "postrevisionist" school had seemed to take something useful from each of these two schools and to have calmed down the arguments.[1] However, no truce lasts forever, and the 1990s have witnessed a new surge of debates over the proper distribution of responsibility between Moscow and Washington for the Cold War.[2]

Ideology and economics commonly receive more attention from historians in these Cold War debates than does military strategy. Yet the armed forces of the United States and the Soviet Union and their preferred military strategies are an important part of the story of Cold War politics. The Cold War remained cold instead of erupting into a U.S.-Soviet shooting war for many reasons, among them Soviet postwar exhaustion and U.S. willingness to accept a status quo in Europe based on wartime and immediate postwar agreements. But nuclear weapons and their influence on military strategy figured into this equation of cold versus hot war, too: the weapons, and strategies supported by those weapons, had stabilizing and destabilizing effects on policy. On one hand, the effects of nuclear weapons were so hideously disproportionate to the political objectives that the disconnection between war and policy restrained planning for deliberate aggression. On the other hand, both sides flirted with crisis brinkmanship and other variants of coercive diplomacy made possible by nuclear weapons, creating a shared danger from which escape was not always easy.

A Durable Peace?

If the peace settlement of World War I served only as an interlude between major coalition wars, the end of World War II was marked by ar-

1. The enormous literature here is not easily summarized. For political science students, I recommend the following: John Lewis Gaddis, *The United States and the Origins of the Cold War, 1941–1947* (New York: Columbia University Press, 1972), on the early years of the Cold War; Walter LaFeber, *America, Russia and the Cold War, 1945–1975,* 3d ed. (New York: John Wiley & Sons, 1976), an excellent overview of Cold War political history; Richard K. Betts, *Soldiers, Statesmen, and Cold War Crises* (Cambridge, Mass.: Harvard University Press, 1977), a superb study of decisionmaking and civil–military relations in the Cold War; H. W. Brands, *The Devil We Knew: Americans and the Cold War* (New York: Oxford University Press, 1993), a refreshingly novel and well-written study carrying forward to the present; and John Lewis Gaddis, *The United States and the End of the Cold War: Implications, Reconsiderations, Provocations* (New York: Oxford University Press, 1992), which summarizes some of Gaddis's more important thinking on Cold War history and shows an uncommon appreciation of the relationship between policy and strategy.

2. See Karen J. Winkler, "Scholars Refight the Cold War," *Chronicle of Higher Education,* March 2, 1994, for a discussion of recent controversies.

rangements that appeared much more durable. Germany and Japan were eliminated as major powers, much of Europe lay in ruins, and the Americans and Soviets moved toward bipolar competition for diplomatic influence and military suasion. The situation between the two "superpowers," as the United States and the Soviet Union were subsequently known, was one of deadlock. The Soviet Union was not about to yield up its sphere of influence in Eastern Europe, and the United States and its allies were reluctant to make any additional concessions to Stalin beyond those already flowing from wartime and immediate postwar agreements.

Among historians there are at least three schools of Western thought about the origins of the Cold War. One holds that the Truman reversal of Roosevelt's benign policy toward Stalinist Russia was responsible for the breakdown of wartime amity into postwar suspicion. A second school, to the contrary, maintains that Stalin's diplomatic pressure backed by Soviet military power placed into jeopardy vital American interests and called forth allied resistance. Still a third school acknowledges that there is truth both in the "blame Russia" and the "blame the West" approach: hostility is never one-sided. Russian historians are only now weighing in, and many of their archives remain to be declassified in post–Cold War *glasnost.*

Regardless of schools of thought, the United States has been commended for responding to *perceived* peacetime foreign policy challenges after 1945 with uncharacteristic foresight and commitment. Previously uninterested in peacetime military alliances, the United States signed onto NATO in 1949 and encouraged its forces to be placed under the command of a U.S. general. The Truman Doctrine declared, perhaps with excessive zeal, that any free (noncommunist) people under attack by aggression or revolution could expect American help. The Marshall Plan provided funds to rebuild a Europe devastated by war. The cumulative effect of these and other initiatives in the Truman administration was to establish secure conditions for the growth of capitalist democracy despite the shadow of Soviet military power.

Stalin had his own economy to rebuild after 1945. His threat to the West was not so much one of military invasion of Western Europe as it was one of diplomatic coercion and intimidation backed by the Red Army. There was also the potential danger that communists might win parliamentary elections in Italy, France, or other Western countries, then invite in the Red Army under the terms of a "treaty of peace and friendship." We now know that the Soviet tide had already reached its high point with the fall of Czechoslovakia into Moscow's orbit in 1948. From then on, Stalin and his successors struggled to hold together their empire, in Eastern Europe and elsewhere.

The United States and the Soviets were held in check not just because most of Eurasia had already been parceled out; they were also check-mated by the reality of nuclear weapons. After a few years of American monopoly (until 1949), atomic (and later hydrogen) weapons gave to both Moscow and Washington the means for unprecedented destruction. At first this appeared to make their militaries more formidable than any in history. The Americans and the Soviets soon discovered that there was more to the relationship between nuclear weapons and political power than how much destruction those weapons could cause. Because both sides had nuclear weapons and because each side could eventually de-ploy many of them in survivable basing modes, the weapons of one side could not be used to disarm those of the other. Nuclear weapons became disconnected from classical military concepts of surprise, the offensive, and victory in battle.

Nuclear Weapons and Cold War

On account of nuclear weapons and their terrible destructiveness, civilian scientists and policy advisers were brought into the U.S. government and became influential in the development of American military strategy. These U.S. civilian strategists had no counterpart in Soviet military-plan-ning circles; therefore, the Soviets continued to think of war in the tradi-tional way as a series of combats, the purpose of which was to prevail on the battlefield. The battle space was now understood to be global, of course, but the objective of military attacks in the early Cold War think-ing of the Soviets—including nuclear attacks—was to disarm the oppo-nent and to destroy those warmaking capacities of the economy that might threaten world communism.

U.S. nuclear strategic thinking of the early Cold War years was unset-tled. The Truman administration did not think very much about the use of nuclear weapons: bombs were relatively few, and delivery systems con-sisted only of long- or medium-range bombers. Under President Dwight Eisenhower, the size of the U.S. nuclear arsenal expanded dramatically as more bombs became available in more varieties. The United States in the 1950s was also moved toward a more nuclear-dependent military strategy by the desire of the president to reduce government spending, including defense spending. Nuclear weapons offered "more bang for the buck" than conventional weapons.

The arrival of ballistic missiles as the weapons of choice for interconti-nental delivery of nuclear warheads made the possibility of nuclear sur-prise attack on a strategic scale a realistic one. The U.S. bomber force was theoretically vulnerable to long-range ballistic missile strikes, against which no known defense was viable. After the alarms created by the Soviet launch of *Sputnik* in 1957, the U.S. public and congressional critics of Eisenhower's defense policy questioned whether America was in danger of losing the nuclear arms race to the Soviet Union. U.S. strategic thinkers argued for the significance of the distinction between a first- and a second-strike capability: a nuclear force had to be survivable in order to act as a credible deterrent. Once survivable, such a force should be able to deter prospective opponents from launching any deliberate first strike.

For U.S. and allied NATO military strategy, however, the problem was not only the possibility of a nuclear first strike. That problem was simple compared to the more complicated role that tactical nuclear "first use" played in NATO defense. The assumption by NATO was that forward-deployed nuclear forces of limited range would deter any Soviet attack by acting as "tripwires" or detonators, escalating to the use of more destructive nuclear exchanges and ultimately to strikes against the American and Soviet homelands. This great chain of escalation theory was not automatic, and it was thought to be all the better that the Soviets could not know in advance whether NATO would, or would not, choose to activate this doomsday machine by increments. NATO sought further to turn vice into virtue by contending, not without some tongue in cheek, that the independent national deterrent of France and the NATO-coordinated British nuclear deterrent complicated Soviet decisionmaking.

The very idea of independent nuclear-decision centers vexed U.S. Secretary of Defense Robert McNamara more than almost anything else. Thus the United States attempted by means of the MLF (Multilateral Force) proposal to provide for mixed European and American crews on naval vessels, with more than one finger required to pull the nuclear trigger. This proposal died in the Johnson administration after it had died in Europe, but the United States continued to regard French nuclear forces as loose cannons and as inconsistent with the tight alliance command and control needed for the Kennedy-Johnson "flexible response" doctrine. In 1967 the French withdrew from the NATO integrated military command structure and expelled NATO installations from their territory. Undoubtedly this complicated the entire equation of NATO conventional defense, apart from its implications for nuclear deterrent strategies.

The idea of an "alliance" nuclear strategy was something of a misnomer. Nuclear weapons were ultimately so destructive that they argued against divisibility of risk or the extension of protection by nuclear states to nonnuclear allies. The United States attempted to provide "extended" nuclear deterrence of this sort by means of its theater and strategic nuclear weapons. This amounted to guaranteeing Europe's security by promising to blow it up in self-defense, perhaps sparing North America from similar destruction and perhaps not. Europeans, on the other hand, were not interested in being decoupled from American nuclear protection: the alternative was to provide for their own deterrence and defense at a greater cost than before.

Nuclear strategy itself, even apart from the complications of alliance management, was something of a misnomer. Nuclear weapons lent themselves to brinkmanship and other experiments in applied psychology. In this regard, the theory of brinkmanship, or the use of nuclear weapons for coercive politics, was more convincing than its practical applications. Prior to the Cuban missile crisis of 1962, some U.S. and Soviet sources talked with great hubris about the coercive utility of nuclear weapons in international bargaining situations. After the missile crisis was concluded, there was less of this. In the aftermath of the "missiles of October," Soviet and U.S. leaders decided that brinkmanship with nuclear weapons was a process less controllable than theorists had supposed. Being less controllable, it was more liable to escalation and to undesired outcomes for both sides.

Professional military dissatisfaction with U.S. nuclear strategy in both the earlier and the later phase of the Cold War was based on either of two concerns. Some military experts deplored the intellectual impact of nuclear weapons on American strategy. Other experts contended that traditional strategy could still be applied to the nuclear age if the United States were willing to invest in deploying antinuclear defenses (ballistic missile defense) as well as offensive nuclear weapons. The first dissatisfied group of military traditionalists fought against what they saw as the corrosive impact of nuclearism on the relationship between America's political aims and its military means. The second group acknowledged that nuclear strategy might be a thing in itself, but they argued that as presented by U.S. administrations from John F. Kennedy through Jimmy Carter it was misconceived.

The first critique of nuclearism was that overreliance on nuclear weapons diminished the willingness of presidents and congresses to create those conventional forces which were much more likely to be used in battle. If, for the sake of argument, a war really began between NATO and the Warsaw Pact in Central Europe, nuclear weapons might cancel one another out. The outcome would then be determined by the side which had superiority in conventional forces. U.S. Army planners throughout the 1950s excoriated the Eisenhower-Dulles overreliance on massive nuclear retaliation. Indeed, Army Chief of Staff Maxwell D. Taylor retired from active duty to write *The Uncertain Trumpet,* a critique of Eisenhower's "New Look" strategy and of the implications of its reduction in U.S. land power.

It was also charged by military professionals that nuclear strategy brought to prominence persons who imported ideas from psychology and economics and dressed them up as insights about war. The writings of Thomas Schelling, Bernard Brodie, Henry Kissinger, and other influential civilian nuclear strategists made great academic splashes, but many military readers were appalled. Especially controversial were two notions that Schelling did much to make prominent in strategic debates: the need for gradual escalation and the manipulation of risk by means of ambiguous threats. Military Clausewitzians, who felt that to attack the enemy's main force and destroy it was the essence of war, lamented the influence of civilian strategists on the policymaking process. In Vietnam, the civilians would be charged specifically with contributing to Lyndon Johnson's commitment to a strategy of gradual escalation that ultimately doomed the U.S. military effort.

A second critique of U.S. nuclear strategic thinking was offered by dissenting nuclear strategists, including Donald Brennan, Colin Gray, and Keith Payne. This group of adherents to nuclear heterodoxy claimed that U.S. nuclear strategy could be made less logically absurd and less inconsistent with traditional principles of strategy if defense were combined with offense. Never in the history of warfare had one-sided thinking paid dividends: a well-rounded military force had capabilities for both offensive and defensive missions. These nuclear apostates further contended that the U.S. lack of commitment to strategic defenses was not a result of technical difficulties. Rather, according to these dissenters from U.S. nuclear orthodoxy, the lack of interest in strategic defenses stemmed from the U.S. commitment to an arms control orthodoxy which had a noxious spillover for military strategy.

The arms control orientation which bothered the nuclear dissenters was the concept of assured destruction, or "mutual assured destruction" (MAD) in the terminology invented by its critics and later adopted with pride by its advocates. The argument was that the United States and the Soviet Union would remain in a position of nuclear stalemate so long as neither side had a first-strike capability (primarily against the retaliatory forces of the other) and both sides had a survivable second-strike capability. The second-strike capability could be aimed at a variety of targets, but the bottom line was that it had to be able to destroy the first-striker as a modern society. Assured destruction did not guarantee prevention of a nuclear "Pearl Harbor," but it did seek to guarantee that the first-striker would have no consolation in anything comparable to "victory" as victory had been understood prior to the invention of nuclear weapons.

Dissenters pointed out that assured destruction left U.S. presidents with an "all or nothing" choice in the event that deterrence failed, but actual U.S. targeting doctrine was more subtle than that. A variety of Soviet military, economic and command targets were programmed into the U.S. Single Integrated Operational Plan (SIOP) for nuclear retaliation. However, the creation of additional retaliatory options did not do much to change the bottom line on the relationship between nuclear destruction and political purpose. Flexible targeting slowed the rate at which unacceptable damage would be accomplished by first- or second-strikers, but no one doubted that unacceptable and historically unprecedented damage to American or Soviet society would take place very soon after war began.

In order to move the bottom line on the relationship between nuclear weapons and political purpose, the U.S. nuclear dissidents felt that the deployment of American ballistic missile defenses would, together with the modernization of offensive weapons, restore traditional strategic flexibility despite the destructiveness of nuclear weapons. Nuclear retaliation based only on offensive weaponry offered no protection to the American people in case of deterrence failure. Defenses could protect societal values and provide a shield to go with the U.S. sword. The credibility of limited nuclear options, or waging ultimate war on the installment plan, would be enhanced (some felt) by deploying defenses, even if those defenses were less than perfect.

Soviet military thinkers agreed to some extent with the U.S. critics of assured destruction. They distrusted *American* strategic defenses as possible nullifiers of a Soviet retaliatory strike. But the Soviet military establishment sought to develop and to deploy its own ballistic missile defenses. Eventually they did so, in the form of the Galosh system surrounding Moscow. By the early 1970s, though, this primitive system had been overtaken by U.S. technology then being developed and tested. The United States, in the sum of all Moscow's fears, might deploy defenses superior to those of the Soviet Union and combine those U.S. defenses with offensive weapons to create an American theoretical first-strike capability. Faced with this possibility, the Soviets agreed in the ABM Treaty of 1972, as part of the Strategic Arms Limitation Talks agreements (SALT I), to limit ballistic missile defense deployments to two sites in each country (later amended to one site each, with the U.S. site dismantled in 1975).

Moscow's signature on SALT I was not an endorsement of the logic of mutual assured destruction as an operational military strategy. Rather, Moscow's participation in SALT represented the more modest convergence of U.S. and Soviet views concerning the possible basis of an arms control consensus. Arms control went forward on a track almost entirely separated from serious military-strategic planning from the early 1970s until the later 1980s. It fit with the U.S. and Soviet desire to dampen their global Cold War conflicts in the 1970s, in particular with the U.S. desire to obtain Soviet help in concluding the war in Vietnam on terms acceptable to both the Nixon administration and the U.S. Congress. Arms control was more significant as an ambience which pervaded U.S.-Soviet détente in the 1970s (and entente in the last half of the 1980s) than it was for any influence it had on the U.S.-Soviet military balance.

Conflict outside Europe

Nuclear stalemate between the superpowers for most of the Cold War permitted the stirring of troubled waters outside Europe by means of proxy war. From the 1950s through the 1980s, the Americans and Soviets took sides in civil and revolutionary wars throughout the Third World in order to advance their respective ideological appeals and deny supposedly vital resources to the other side. There was something tragically ironic about this competition between the superpowers for Third World influence. The newly independent states of Asia, Africa, and the Middle East were only too happy to use Washington against Moscow and vice versa. Many of these states were run by unrepresentative elites who had contempt for the U.S. and the Soviet way of life, and who distrusted both Washington and Moscow as interlopers into regions where American and Soviet influence did not really belong.

The most significant political force in the Third World during the Cold War was neither communism nor Americanism, but nationalism. For example, only the continuing force of nationalism could drive Vietnamese to persevere against Japanese, French, and American opponents in succession. Mistaking the Vietnamese revolution for an expansion of the Sino-Soviet bloc, itself torn apart by the later 1950s, the Johnson administration turned the limited-risk commitment of the Kennedy and Eisenhower years into a full-scale war. But Johnson stopped short of asking for a legal declaration of war, was unwilling to mobilize the reserves, and alternated signals of escalation with those of de-escalation in such a way that traditional military strategists and peace advocates alike remained dissatisfied. The war in Vietnam was lost when the U.S. public and the government mind tired of it, despite the performance of U.S. armed forces under fire which was exemplary against North Vietnamese regular units.

For the United States, it was especially ironic that the greatest Cold War setback to its global power would be dealt not by communist advance but by the aftermath of the October War of 1973. The supposedly moderate Arab states such as Saudi Arabia led the charge to impose an oil embargo against the United States and others who supported Israel in that conflict. The U.S. paralysis in the face of this economic imperialism was in part a result of the Vietnam syndrome. Another factor, though, was the lack of viable military-strategic planning for an eventuality of just this sort. Since the Truman Doctrine of 1947 and the U.S.-imposed defeat of Britain and France in the Suez crisis of 1956, U.S. political leaders and military planners should have been on alert that the U.S. and allied oil jugular in the Persian Gulf was vulnerable. As American and especially allied European and Japanese dependency rose in the 1960s, neither an economic strategy for Western self-reliance nor a military strategy for Western rescue was on the shelf when OPEC struck.

U.S. policy in the Middle East and Persian Gulf had been based on Israel, Iran, and Saudi Arabia. The latter two states were regarded for several decades as the twin pillars of anticommunist stability astride the Persian Gulf. Tehran and Riyadh were not so much anticommunist as they were anti-Israel and very suspicious of Western economic and moral values. The government of the shah of Iran was deposed early in 1979 by a coalition which included Shiite religious leaders seeking a return to social tradition, disgruntled middle classes wanting to move away from tradition even faster, and an uncertain military and security apparatus that was divided within itself and was not as able as experts supposed to suppress revolutionary outbreak. The fall of the shah left U.S. policy dependent on a single pillar and ushered in the theocratic regime of Ayatollah Ruholla Mussaui Khomeini, removing Iran as a reliable U.S. and Western ally in the Gulf region.

The breakthrough made possible by Richard Nixon's opening to China in 1972 and the options made available by the newly triangularized relationship among Beijing, Moscow, and Washington were only partially exploited to U.S. advantage on account of the Nixon, Ford, and Carter preoccupation with fiascoes in the Middle East and Southwest Asia. The events from 1973 to 1979 revealed that Cold War fixation on Soviet foreign and defense policy had left the United States and its NATO allies with insufficient expertise and doubtful intelligence about areas outside Europe but nonetheless critical to U.S. security. The superpower relationship vis-à-vis grand strategy (i.e., between policy and military strategy) had been allowed to deteriorate into a merry minuet with Moscow over nuclear deterrence and arms control. Seeing the United States becalmed, Moscow was all the more encouraged to adopt a forward strategy, culminating with its march into Afghanistan in 1979.

The invasion of Afghanistan was the Soviets' last military hurrah of the Cold War. Already creaking from years of bureaucratic sclerosis, the Soviet economy of the 1980s crashed beneath of the floor of its overly subsidized military and heavy-industrial sectors. Mikhail Gorbachev's arrival as party chairman in 1985 and his talent for popularizing political slogans (*glasnost, perestroika*) suggested to some that a younger generation of Soviet leaders could cast off the chrysalis of the old order while retaining the essence of a new communism. But it was too late for that. Gorbachev fell between the failures of the past and the unmet expectations of the future. When he fell, the old political order, including the politico-military system of the communist regime and the Red Army, fell with him. The United States had seemingly won the Cold War by default.

Despite the claims of a victorious United States, both sides actually lost. A great deal of unnecessary military spending and a plethora of politically unaccountable covert actions were among the U.S. costs inflicted by the forty or so years of the Cold War. U.S. military spending peaked (in constant 1995 dollars) at $390.5 billion in 1985 and began falling immediately thereafter (even Ronald Reagan could only coax so much defense largess from the U.S. Congress), continuing a downward trajectory for the next decade (see Table 5).

The Soviet costs included the postponement of economic and political cleanup from Stalinism and the ossification of an already outdated imperial design. The most significant and surprising thing about the liberation of Eastern Europe from 1989 to 1991 was that it occurred without triggering even a serious crisis, let alone a war, between East and West. Such an outcome would have been inconceivable just a decade earlier. The re-

Table 5. U.S. Department of Defense Budget Authority, FY 1985–1995

	Current Dollars	Constant Dollars	Percent Real Growth
1985	286.8	390.5	
1986	281.4	373.2	−4.4
1987	279.5	359.2	−3.8
1988	283.8	351.7	−2.1
1989	290.8	346.7	−1.4
1990	290.9	336.7	−2.9
1991	276.0	304.2	−9.6
1992	272.2	294.0	−3.4
1993	267.3	279.5	−5.0
1994	249.0	254.4	−9.0
1995	252.2	252.2	−0.9

SOURCE: Les Aspin, Secretary of Defense, *Annual Report to the President and the Congress* (Washington, D.C.: GPO, January 1994), 255.

NOTE: Cumulative change for FY 1985–95 in constant dollars = −35.4 percent. Data for FY 1990–93 do not include costs of Desert Shield/Desert Storm.

lighting of the lamps of freedom in East-Central Europe was made possible by Soviet nonresistance, and Soviet nonresistance was the product not of generosity of spirit, but of Soviet retrenchment forced by imperial incompetency. Few would have suspected that the Soviets would end as the Ottomans of the later twentieth century: imploding by their own devices instead of exploding after outside pillage and invasion.

Continuing Controversy

The Cuban Missile Crisis: Diplomatic Triumph or Near Disaster?

The Cold War between the United States and the Soviet Union proceeded for about forty years with variable levels of intensity. Periods of confrontation alternated with periods of détente, or relaxation of tensions. The most severe period of U.S.-Soviet tension occurred between 1958 and 1962. Several crises in Berlin and other disagreements between the Cold War superpowers set the stage for the most dramatic and dangerous confrontation of the nuclear age in October 1962. President John F. Kennedy appeared on national television on October 22 to announce that the Soviet Union had secretly deployed medium-range ballistic missiles in Cuba despite previous U.S. warnings not to do so. Kennedy announced that the United States would enforce a "quarantine," or blockade, of further military shipments to Cuba and demanded that the Soviet leadership withdraw immediately the offensive missiles already deployed there.

Although a bookshelf of material now exists on the Cuban missile crisis, two issues remain at issue. The first controversy among scholars and policymakers has to do with Nikita Khrushchev's reasons for taking such a risky decision. The second controversy is about whether President Kennedy and his advisers in the Executive Committee of the National Security Council, or ExComm, chose the best course of action in deciding in favor of a blockade accompanied by demands for removal of the Soviet missiles from Cuba.

Khrushchev's reasons for his decision to deploy medium- and intermediate-range missiles in Cuba (the latter were scheduled for deployment but never actually reached the island) were undoubtedly complicated and less than totally clear in his own mind. His memoirs give two reasons for the decision: (1) to equalize the balance of strategic nuclear power between the United States and the Soviet Union and (2) to defend Cuba against any attempt by the United States to repeat the failed Bay of Pigs invasion of 1961 (this time, with forces sufficient to guarantee success).

According to Khrushchev, the second motive was the more important for him.

U.S. scholars and policymakers have acknowledged that Khrushchev and Castro might reasonably have expected another U.S.-sponsored invasion of Cuba. During conferences held many years later among U.S., Soviet, and Cuban policymakers and academics, former U.S. Secretary of Defense Robert S. McNamara (in charge of President Kennedy's Department of Defense during the 1962 crisis) denied that the United States had any actual *plans* for another Cuban invasion. But he admitted that, putting himself in the shoes of Soviet and Cuban planners, he might have attributed such an intent to the United States. Thus Khrushchev's claim that the missile deployments were necessary for Cuban defense (meaning deterrence of another U.S. invasion attempt) was an incorrect but understandable estimate of probable intentions in Washington.

On the other hand, if Khrushchev's primary motive was to deter attack against Cuba, his surreptitious deployment of the missiles seemed to contradict the objective of deterrence. There is some evidence that Khrushchev planned to make the deployment of medium- and intermediate-range ballistic missiles (MRBMs and IRBMs) public during a November 1962 visit to the United Nations. He would then expect to exploit the completed and previously undetected deployments for political capital, within the NATO alliance and within the world communist camp. Khrushchev apparently sought a diplomatic coup of this sort in order to gain leverage against the United States and its allies with respect to Berlin and to keep at bay Chinese hawks who contended that the Soviet leadership had gone soft or "revisionist" on the issue of East-West confrontation.

The second reason given by Khrushchev for his missile deployments to Cuba was that they were intended to equalize the strategic nuclear balance of power. U.S. academics, intelligence analysts, and policymakers have been more willing to accept this explanation than the "Cuban defense" argument. Even some Russian academics contend that this must have been Khrushchev's primary motive for the missile deployments. The strategic problem for Khrushchev in the early 1960s was that his use of nuclear diplomacy to intimidate the West, from the launch of *Sputnik* in 1957 through the autumn of 1962, ran far ahead of his actual military capabilities. Khrushchev must have suspected as much after his air defenses shot down the U.S. U-2 spy plane in 1960 and recovered alive the pilot, Francis Gary Powers. Khrushchev knew that previous U-2 flights which had not been shot down would have revealed a great deal about the actual, as opposed to the putative, deployments of Soviet land-based intercontinental missiles, or ICBMs.

Khrushchev's suspicions of a U.S. awareness of the gap between Soviet policy and Soviet forces were confirmed publicly by the Kennedy administration in October 1961. Almost a year before the Cuban missile crisis, Deputy Defense Secretary Roswell Gilpatric gave a speech in which he announced that the United States had achieved nuclear superiority, or the closest thing to it, over the Soviet Union. According to Gilpatric's presentation before an open forum of U.S. news media, previously cleared by the White House, the United States as of October 1961 had a stronger second-strike capability against the Soviet Union than the Soviet Union had a first-strike capability against the United States. This meant that, even after absorbing a "worst case" Soviet first strike, the United States could retaliate and do more damage to Soviet forces and society than the Soviets had done striking at U.S. targets out of the blue.

Gilpatric's speech must have sent shock waves through the Soviet defense establishment. The U.S. policy pronouncement conveyed signals beyond the fact, already apparent to Soviet military leaders, that the United States had more nuclear weapons than they. It was now clear that the United States had established the exact locations of land-based intercontinental missiles located on Soviet territory. From the standpoint of conservative Soviet defense specialists, the United States had the potential, if not the policy, for a disarming first strike against the entire Soviet missile force. Even short of war, that potential could be exploited to coerce Moscow to do Washington's diplomatic bidding.

Missiles in Cuba might have appeared to Khrushchev and to the Soviet military establishment as a short-term corrective for the U.S. lead in land-based missiles. By completing the first wave of medium- and intermediate-range ballistic missile deployments to Cuba in early November, the Soviet nuclear strike capability against U.S. cities or military targets, especially Strategic Air Command bomber bases, would be improved significantly. This, at least, was the estimate provided to the ExComm by expert U.S. intelligence analysts. For one thing, the U.S. air-defense radar warning system was oriented northward, toward the most likely direction for a massive Soviet missile and bomber attack on North America. Nothing equivalent existed facing south: missiles launched from Cuba against U.S. air bases in 1962 would have faced an improvised radar warning network which was untested even under simulated crisis conditions.

There may have been other reasons for Khrushchev's decision in addition to the ones he later acknowledged. First, he may have sought to win a diplomatic coup against President Kennedy by announcing the presence of Soviet missiles deployed in Cuba. Then Khrushchev could have offered to trade those missiles for U.S. Jupiter IRBMs deployed in Turkey that were capable of rapid strikes into Soviet territory. The idea of trading

Jupiters in Turkey for Soviet MRBMs in Cuba was raised explicitly by the Soviets during the Cuban missile crisis bargaining. The crisis was finally settled with an understanding that the United States would agree tacitly to remove the Jupiters from Turkey provided this was not made an explicit bargaining condition for withdrawal of the Soviet missiles from Cuba.

Khrushchev may also have been motivated by the desire to restore his image as a decisive leader within the Presidium (the highest circle of Soviet party leaders, later called the Politburo) and among fellow communist governments. His domestic policies had proved to be controversial and even, in cases such as agriculture, disastrous. His military reforms emphasized buildup of the newly created Strategic Rocket Forces, and his military strategy emphasized the nuclear character of any European or world war. From this the Soviet premier deduced that he could make large reductions in the Red Army ground forces, but such cuts were not pleasing to most senior military leaders. Ultimately Khrushchev was forced to retrench both on his domestic reform and his military-restructuring policies, but only after a great deal of political blood had been spilled. His desperate gamble in Cuba reinforced his reputation among his colleagues for risky adventurism and contributed to his fall from power in 1964.

The other controversy over the Cuban missile crisis is about whether President Kennedy chose wisely in favoring the blockade instead of either of two other options. The first option would have been a more decisive military move against the missile sites, perhaps accompanied by an invasion of Cuba and the removal of the Castro regime. The second option would have been to initiate diplomatic negotiations with the Soviet Union over removal of the Cuban missiles, leaving the threat or use of force for later if negotiations proved to be unproductive.

Those who favored a more decisive military option to destroy the Soviet missiles in Cuba felt that the blockade was insufficient to remove the danger posed by the missile deployments. A blockade could prevent other missiles from being shipped to Cuba, but it could not remove those missiles which had already arrived and which were being erected. The blockade critics became especially vocal on October 27, 1962, the day before the crisis ended in Khrushchev's announced willingness to remove the missiles in return for Kennedy's public pledge not to invade Cuba. October 27 was a day of frustration for U.S. officials. The Soviets, having earlier sent a conciliatory telegram offering terms for settling the crisis that were ultimately adopted, sent a harsher message the next day and upped the ante. They now demanded not only a U.S. pledge not to invade Cuba, but also a quid pro quo removal of the Jupiter missiles in Turkey.

Several incidents on October 27 added to the crisis tension. A U.S. U-2 aircraft accidentally strayed over Soviet airspace near the Chukotski Peninsula. As Soviet fighter aircraft were scrambled from Wrangel Island to intercept the intruder, U.S. fighter interceptors were sent from Alaska in an effort to rescue the American pilot. The U.S. aircraft were armed with nuclear weapons (air-to-air missiles). The U-2 eventually found its way back into American airspace before converging Soviet and U.S. fighters made contact. Khrushchev, apprised of the intrusion, later chided Kennedy: "The question is, Mr. President: How should we regard this? What is this, a provocation? One of your planes violates our frontier during this anxious time we are both experiencing, when everything has been put into combat readiness. Is it not a fact that an intruding American plane could be easily taken for a nuclear bomber, which might push us to a fateful step?"[3] Tension was also exacerbated on October 27 when U.S. officials learned of the shootdown of a U.S. U-2, conducting reconnaissance over Cuba, by a Soviet SA-2 surface-to-air missile (SAM). Since U.S. officials believed (correctly) that the Soviet SAMs were entirely under Soviet and not Cuban control, it seemed possible that the action had been taken deliberately by Khrushchev to escalate the crisis. U.S. officials also wondered whether hard-liners in the Soviet leadership had ordered the U-2 shootdown without Khrushchev's knowledge. A former aide to Cuban Premier Fidel Castro claimed that Castro had mistakenly or deliberately fired the missile during an inspection tour of Soviet facilities.

It turned out that the U-2 had been shot down on the orders of Soviet air-defense commanders in Cuba who believed mistakenly that their standing orders included this possibility. Moscow had not intended that air-defense missiles be fired at U.S. aircraft unless a U.S. *invasion* of Cuba was already in progress. Field commanders interpreted this guidance broadly, to include U.S. reconnaissance aircraft that were overflying sensitive military sites and violating Cuban airspace. Soviet Defense Minister Marshal Rodion Malinovsky immediately reprimanded the commanders and emphasized Moscow's view of standing orders: U.S. aircraft were not to be fired on "prematurely."[4] The correction was timely, for U.S. leaders had originally decided that the shootdown of U.S. aircraft by any Soviet SAM would be a necessary and sufficient cause for retaliatory air strikes against the offending missile-defense site. Fortunately, President Kennedy opted against implementing this previously taken decision after he

---

3. Quoted in Scott D. Sagan, *Moving Targets: Nuclear Strategy and National Security* (Princeton, N.J.: Princeton University Press, 1989), 148.

4. Raymond L. Garthoff, *Reflections on the Cuban Missile Crisis,* rev. ed. (Washington, D.C.: Brookings Institution, 1989), 84–85.

learned of the U-2 shootdown, even as the Air Force leadership was preparing to send retaliatory strike orders through channels.

The U-2 shootdown over Cuba and the U-2 "stray" into Soviet airspace on October 27 contributed to an atmosphere in Washington in which the more hawkish members of the ExComm urged President Kennedy toward an air strike or invasion. Even after the crisis had been resolved peacefully, some U.S. military leaders argued that Kennedy had missed an opportunity to embarrass Moscow and dislodge Castro. On the other hand, we now know that the Soviet Union had more nuclear weapons in Cuba and a larger number of combat troops on the ground than U.S. intelligence surmised at the time. An invasion of Cuba would have been costly to U.S. forces even if we assume that no Soviet tactical nuclear surface-to-surface missiles would have been launched in response. (Tactical nuclear warheads were deployed as standard operating procedure with Soviet motor rifle divisions for Luna short-range missiles.)

If hawks saw the resolution of the Cuban missile crisis as an opportunity missed, doves saw it as an unnecessarily provocative flaunting of U.S. strategic nuclear and conventional military power. From this perspective, once the missiles had been discovered, Washington had Khrushchev over a barrel. The United States had an approximate superiority of seventeen to one over the Soviets in strategic nuclear warheads and an overwhelming superiority in its ability to dominate any non-nuclear conflict in the Caribbean theater of operations. Since the United States could rest assured that its military preeminence was incontestable, doves felt that Kennedy's opening move could have been more diplomatic and less military, or more carrot and less stick.

Some participants in the ExComm deliberations did argue for a first diplomatic overture to Moscow, with U.S. force remaining in the background as a tacit but meaningful threat. The argument against a strictly diplomatic approach by a majority of Kennedy's advisers was that it would not be taken seriously enough by Khrushchev. President Kennedy, having been through some tough negotiating sessions with Khrushchev, felt instinctively that a diplomatic approach, by itself, was insufficient and might mislead Khrushchev into a conclusion of American weakness.

Participants in the U.S. decisionmaking process offered two sets of diplomatic moves short of military action. One approach would send a secret U.S. emissary or messenger to Khrushchev indicating U.S. awareness of the missiles and offering Khrushchev some interval of time to withdraw the missiles before the United States would take public, and more escalatory, steps. Another diplomatic variation would have had the United States approach the U.N. secretary-general and ask for intervention by the United Nations as an impartial third party to resolve the situation short of military confrontation. These approaches shared a similar weakness: Khrushchev, aware of the U.S. discovery of his missiles, could stall for time while his forces in Cuba rushed feverishly to make them launch-ready. Once the missiles were launch-ready, Khrushchev would be in a much tougher bargaining position, and the time for preventing missile shipments by blockade or other means would have passed.

Kennedy chose the blockade after having been persuaded by the majority of his advisers that it was a first turning of the screw on Khrushchev, one that allowed the Soviet leader time to reconsider his previous decisions. The blockade allowed Kennedy to maintain control of events and to signal resolve without forcing Khrushchev into a diplomatic and military cul-de-sac. Eventually the blockade was accompanied by an ultimatum delivered to Moscow's U.S. ambassador, Anatoly Dobrynin, by Robert Kennedy. Although there is some disagreement among sources, it seems evident that this message, conveyed either on Robert Kennedy's own initiative or with President Kennedy's prior approval on October 27, helped Khrushchev to see that the U.S. decisionmaking process was moving toward escalation and that time for an agreement based on the terms of the president's first letter (October 26) was running out.

Kennedy admirers have since referred to the Cuban missile crisis as that U.S. president's finest hour. He had stood down the Soviets in the most important confrontation of the Cold War and had obtained his basic objective: removal of the unacceptable Soviet missiles from Cuba. Kennedy's own reaction was more sober and thoughtful. He regarded the Cuban missile crisis as a narrow and fortuitous escape from mutual disaster. He resolved not to test nuclear brinkmanship again and to place renewed emphasis on U.S.-Soviet nuclear arms control. Kennedy's assessment of the crisis was that he and the Soviet leadership had both had less control over the flow of events than was optimal for successful crisis management.

4

THE GULF CRISIS and WAR, 1990–1991

For some, the end of the Cold War held promise for a reuniting of force with international policy on behalf of peace. The disruption of that connection by two world wars and the Cold War seemed to end with the demise of Soviet communism and the advent of a "new world order" proclaimed by President George Bush. U.N. Security Council authorization for military action to expel Iraq from Kuwait, accomplished by the U.S. and allied members of the anti-Iraq coalition, caused optimism to rise about the future application of military power by peace-loving states against regional aggressors. The Gulf War of 1991, seen in proper historical and political context, fell short of accomplishing this reunification of policy and strategy, either from the American perspective taken alone or from the more complex coalition perspective.

On August 2, 1990, Iraqi forces invaded Kuwait. U.S. and allied intelligence had observed the buildup of Iraqi forces along the Kuwaiti border and reported this information to political leaders. The Bush administration was reassured during the last weeks of July 1990 by Saudi Arabian, Egyptian, and other Arab leaders that Iraqi President Saddam Hussein was only using force for diplomatic suasion. According to this predominant interpretation of Saddam's intentions, the Iraqi ruler sought to coerce the Kuwaiti emirs into supporting higher oil prices but not to get into a shooting war in the Persian Gulf.

The assumption that Saddam wanted to avoid war rested on twin pillars. First, the United States had sided with Iraq during the Iran-Iraq War from 1980 to 1988, when both sides agreed to a stalemate. Iraq, a relatively secular and modernized republic among countries with predominantly Muslim adherents, was thought useful in maintaining a Mideast balance of power against Iran. Iran's Islamic republic regarded the United States as a satanic force, and relations with Washington had been bad since the overthrow of the shah and the seizure of American hostages during the Carter administration.

Second, the United States judged that it had considerable influence on Saddam's behavior on account of the many dealings that Western companies had in Iraq, including agreements to provide military communications, command, and control systems for the Iraqi armed forces and political leadership. As Iraq's nondeclared ally during the Iran-Iraq war, the United States had made available to Baghdad intelligence derived from satellite reconnaissance and other highly technical and expensive sources. This support for Iraq was not as under the table as were the ill-fated negotiations with Iran to swap arms for hostages. However, the United States had to be somewhat discreet given its (misguided) desire to arrange a political opening to Iranian "moderates" and on account of Saddam's many overt ties to Soviet military support. In terms of military hardware, particularly in armored forces and air-defense systems, Iraq was very much a Soviet client.

U.S. leaders acknowledged that Saddam's dictatorial treatment of his own people left a great deal to be desired from a human rights standpoint. But he was a secular Arab leader with whom we could do business, without the distraction of ideological anti-Western fanaticism. It was therefore supposed that his remonstrations against Kuwait toward the end of July 1990 were professions of hubris rather than a call to arms. The United States may have given unintentional encouragement to Iraq by sending a number of misconceived diplomatic signals in 1990, including State Department and congressional expressions of support or indifference with respect to any grievances Iraq might have against other Arabs.

A Deterrence Failure?

For these reasons, it cannot be said that the Iraqi invasion of Kuwait on August 2 was a failure of deterrence, for it is not clear how hard the Bush administration had worked to signal Baghdad that it would disapprove of an attack on Kuwait. Much depends on what we assume of Saddam Hussein's intentions immediately prior to the attack. His original objective may have been simply to occupy part of Kuwait, especially certain oil fields claimed by both countries and two offshore islands. Once the invasion got rolling, the rapid decomposition of Kuwaiti resistance created an inertia in favor of continued fighting until Kuwait had been totally subdued. Whether the complete conquest of Kuwait was originally intended or not, that was not the major concern of the Bush administration.

The Bush administration was worried about Saudi Arabia, which held so much of the world's readily available oil supply that its capture by hostile forces would be a serious policy reversal for Washington and for its European and Japanese allies. Kuwait was mostly a symbol, Saudi Arabia the "big enchilada." Nor were the Kuwaitis much beloved in the Muslim and Arab worlds. The government of Kuwait was a hereditary monarchy, and the bulk of the country's wealth was controlled by members of the al-Sabah family. Menial work was done by Palestinian, Pakistani, and other guest workers. Nonetheless, Kuwait was important, especially for George Bush, a former oil wildcatter whose Zapata Oil Company had sunk the first offshore oil drilling for the government of Kuwait.

When Iraqi forces, having completed the conquest of Kuwait, were reported to be massing on the border with Saudi Arabia, U.S. officials responded with alacrity to the apparent threat to vital U.S. interests. According to a study later by Les Aspin, then chairman of the House Armed Services Committee, the United States had three major interests at stake in reversing the Iraqi attack on Kuwait: oil, aggression, and nuclear weapons. The threat to Saudi control over their oil supplies, and thus to the oil jugular which supplied the United States and its European and Japanese allies, was the most imminently perceived danger. Aggression was a more abstract, but nonetheless salient, issue for the Bush administration. This issue had to do with the Bush administration's perception of an emerging new world order following the end of the Cold War. More will be said on this point below.

Aspin's and Bush's third issue was the potential that Iraq had for developing nuclear weapons if its military aspirations to regional hegemony were unchecked. Iraq had signed the Nuclear Nonproliferation Treaty (NPT), and regular International Atomic Energy Agency (IAEA) inspections had been conducted of its nuclear production facilities. Unknown to the inspectors and concealed by the Iraqis were other facilities devoted to the development of crude nuclear devices for eventual delivery by aircraft or short-range missiles. After Iraq's defeat in the Gulf War of 1991, U.N. inspectors uncovered a cornucopia of efforts using various technologies to develop nuclear weapons. Although the Bush administration can be accused of overselling the *immediate* threat of Iraqi nuclear capability, evidence revealed by U.N. inspections leaves no doubt that the *eventual* danger to other states in the region was considerable.

The U.S. Response

Once Iraq had completed its conquest of Kuwait, the Bush administration had to decide how to respond. It was not immediately obvious that responses on the scale of Desert Shield and Desert Storm would be undertaken. President Bush declared almost immediately that the invasion could not be allowed to stand. Secretary of Defense Dick Cheney and Chairman of the Joint Chiefs of Staff Colin Powell were tasked by the president to come up with viable military options to expel Iraq from Kuwait if necessary. Ironically, the day of Iraq's invasion, August 2, was the same date on which President Bush had delivered a major speech in Aspen, Colorado, about new directions in U.S. security policy. On account of the Iraqi attack, the significance of the president's Aspen speech was drowned out in the foreground noise of crisis in Southwest Asia.

Bush's Aspen speech outlined a defense posture for the post–Cold War world based on the absence of the global threat formerly posed by the Soviet Union. The Bush strategy would center on the need to deal with regional contingencies outside Europe, perhaps more than one at a time. This strategy, largely the work of Powell, Cheney, and Assistant Secretary of Defense Paul Wolfowitz, sought to repackage U.S. global forces and to reorganize defense tasks around four principal mission categories: strategic deterrence, forward presence, rapid response, and reconstitution. The geographic distribution of active duty forces would change to return more of the U.S. base force to the continental United States. Adjusted deployments overseas were expected, for example, to reduce U.S. troops deployed in Europe to about 150,000 or fewer by 1997. If a global threat rematerialized, the existing base force would have to be supplemented by reconstitution or by the creation of new units.

Saddam struck as the U.S. Department of Defense was putting the icing on the cake of its rethinking for the new world order. He caught the United States with forces still in place for doing battle against the bearish Soviet Union and the Warsaw Pact in Europe. This immense U.S. and allied NATO combat machine for "AirLand battle" was on the shelf to be applied as a template against Iraq. It would prove to be Saddam's undoing once Desert Shield, the defensive buildup of U.S. and allied troops in the Gulf theater of operations, was supplanted by Desert Storm, the air-ground offensive to restore the government of Kuwait. Iraq's attack timing provided the U.S. Air Force and Army with an opportunity to test AirLand battle doctrine against a far weaker opponent than the formerly hostile Soviets and on a series of geographic and terrain features even more advantageous to the anti-Iraqi coalition.

President Bush proceeded from the outside—in order to build domestic support for waging offensive war against Iraq, should Saddam refuse to acquiesce in U.N. resolutions for an Iraqi withdrawal. Bush lined up support from NATO allies, from a majority of Arab states, and (most symbolic of the new world order into which the administration thought it was heading) from the Soviet Union under Gorbachev. The refusal of the Soviet Union to support its former military client in Baghdad left Saddam diplomatically isolated and cleared the principal obstacle that might have inhibited Bush from launching an offensive military campaign. Gorbachev did maneuver, in late December 1990 and early in the following month, to try to arrange an Iraqi agreement for phased withdrawal which would satisfy both the United Nations and Bush. But Saddam Hussein doubted that the United States would actually go to war and so neglected to take advantage of Soviet mediation.

We have no diary of Saddam Hussein's strategic thinking on the eve of war. I judge that his strategy, intuitive or well considered, included the following elements. First, attempt to deter the Americans from war by loading up defensive entrenchments in the Kuwaiti theater of operations and threatening the coalition with protracted, high-casualty ground combat. Second, should deterrence fail, inflict high casualties on attacking forces in order to discourage the U.S. and allied home fronts. Third (once the war was under way), launch missile attacks against Israel in order to bring Israel into the war and divide the coalition, which included a majority of Arab powers. In short, his strategy would be based, in rank order, on deterrence, attrition, and horizontal escalation. If neither of these stratagems worked, a fourth option was to seek war termination before Saddam's armed forces were entirely destroyed and while Saddam remained in control of the state. Only the last of these was accomplished.

Coalition War Planning

The coalition war plan involved two phases: (1) an air war, which inflicted most of the damage on Iraqi military forces and other targets, and (2) a ground war, which clinched the victory and brought the Iraqi government to an agreed war termination. The air war was a spectacularly one-sided show. U.S. and allied air power struck early and decisively at Iraqi air defenses and command-and-control systems. Within not even one week of battle, Iraq's air force was a nullity. Iraq's modern fighter aircraft were either pinned down in their shelters for fear of destruction, destroyed on the ground or in the air, or flown out of harm's way to Iran.

Iraq did end the war with several hundred planes still under its control, but these exerted no influence on the air war during Desert Storm.

The initial period of the air war provided the first wartime demonstration of reconnaissance–strike complexes, used with devastating effect against Iraqi air defenses and command-and-control systems. Reconnaissance–strike complexes combined the effects of (1) precision-guided munitions for more accurate target destruction and less collateral damage, (2) improved observation of enemy movements in the air and on the ground, using observation platforms such as AWACS (Airborne Warning and Control System) planes, and (3) communications and control systems designed to provide real-time feedback to commanders about the results of strike plans.

Phase 1 of the offensive air campaign was designed as a six day program to incapacitate Iraqi leadership and destroy some of Iraq's principal military capabilities. Developed by Colonel John A. Warden III, deputy director for warfighting of the U.S. Air Staff, and an Air Staff division known as Checkmate, the plan emphasized attacks on Iraqi "centers of gravity."[1] These centers of gravity were assessed as the most important target sets for the purpose of disrupting the Iraqi leadership's control over its armed forces and for destroying those elements which would influence the Iraqi military against continued fighting. According to operations orders for Desert Storm, the six theater military objectives and the three centers of gravity for the Phase 1 air war were as follows:

Theater Military Objectives
(for entire war)
- Attack Iraqi political/military leadership and command and control
- Gain and maintain air superiority
- Sever Iraqi supply lines
- Destroy chemical, biological, and nuclear capability
  (including delivery systems, such as Scud mobile missiles)
- Destroy Republican Guard forces
- Liberate Kuwait City

Centers of Gravity
(Phase 1 campaign, air war)
- Iraqi National Command Authority
- Iraq's nuclear, chemical, and biological capabilities
- Republican Guard Forces Command
  (Republican Guard forces were the most modern and capable armored

1. *Gulf War Air Power Survey*, 6 vols. (Washington, D.C.: GPO, 1993), "Abbreviated Summary," pp. 13–14. Hereafter, *GWAPS* Abbreviated Summary.

forces, held in reserve for climactic phases of the land battle and judged by U.S. and allied intelligence to be the most loyal among Saddam Hussein's forces.)

Air-war planners determined that the "strategic core" of the air campaign would consist of eight of twelve target categories: (1) command, control, and communications; (2) leadership facilities; (3) nuclear, chemical, and biological warfare capabilities and weapon programs; (4) military-support facilities (e.g., logistics, ammunition storage); (5) ballistic missile launchers and their supporting infrastructure; (6) electric power; (7) oil refineries; and (8) bridges and railway facilities. The target list for these categories as of January 15, 1991, numbered 295; by February 26, the number had risen to 535. The growth in the number of targets within these eight categories was produced by intelligence obtained once the war was under way.[2]

Approximately 30 percent of the precision-guided bombs that were used in Desert Storm were employed against these eight core strategic-target categories, or about double the percentage of total strikes that those eight target classes received.[3] Only about 14.8 percent of the total air strikes in Desert Storm were directed against these "core targets." Table 6 summarizes the total numbers of strikes from all air-delivered weapons by target category.

In order to accomplish these missions, the first priority of coalition war planners was to establish command of the air, and this was done by the rapid destruction of Iraqi strategic air-defense systems and airfields. The attacks against leadership and command-and-control targets included television and radio transmitters, telephone and telegraph facilities, military command posts, relay stations, buildings of the Ministry of Defense and Baath Party headquarters, and facilities where Saddam Hussein might be located.[4] It was not an explicit objective of the air campaign to remove Saddam Hussein from power, although planners would have welcomed his fortuitous presence beneath appropriately timed ordnance. The U.N. resolutions authorizing the use of force to expel Iraq from Kuwait did not address the removal of Iraq's leadership. That would have stimulated an unnecessary and counterproductive controversy within the twenty-nine-nation hodgepodge that fought the Gulf War. So removal of the regime and displacement of Saddam was left to the possibility, adumbrated by Bush in his public pronouncements the

2. Thomas A. Keaney and Eliot A. Cohen, *Gulf War Air Power Survey: Summary Report* (Washington, D.C.: GPO, 1993), 64.
3. Ibid., 65.
4. *GWAPS* Abbreviated Summary, pp. 14–16.

TABLE 6. Gulf War Coalition Air Strikes

Target Categories	Number of Strikes
Iraqi ground forces	23,430
Airfields	2,990
Scuds	1,460
SAMs	1,370
Lines of communication	1,170
Military industry	970
Nuclear/biological/chemical	970
Integrated air defense	630
Telecommunications/C3	580
Oil	540
Naval targets	370
Electric power	345
Leadership	260

SOURCE: Adapted from Thomas A. Keaney and Eliot A. Cohen, *Gulf War Air Power Survey: Summary Report* (Washington, D.C.: GPO, 1993), 65, fig. 12.

NOTE: Totals have been rounded to the nearest multiple of ten and include strikes still uncategorized but mostly assigned to ground forces. C3 = command, control, and communications.

preceding autumn, that a defeated and demoralized Iraqi armed forces command would overthrow him.

Decapitation and Other Missions

U.S. policy with regard to replacement of the Iraqi leadership was a matter of public controversy during and after the Gulf crisis and war. In September 1990, then Air Force Chief of Staff Michael Dugan was quoted in press sources on the topic of targeting Saddam Hussein. Dugan, apparently in off-the-record interviews, suggested that the United States might deliberately target Saddam personally as well as his immediate professional entourage, family, and mistress. Secretary of Defense Dick Cheney judged that these comments, not cleared with higher authorities and potentially controversial from a Bush policy standpoint, were unacceptable. Dugan was asked to resign. The dispute about removal of Saddam Hussein from power continued into the postwar period. Saddam's postwar defiance of U.N. inspectors and his attempts to reimpose subjugation on domestic political opponents angered Americans who wondered why his removal was not included in the original list of political objectives.[5]

Saddam had carefully seeded the high command with his own loyalists, thus precluding a coup as the means of his removal. Coalition intelligence was never able to determine with sufficient fidelity the exact location of Saddam Hussein among the many fixed and mobile command posts to which the Iraqi leader had access. The physical destruction of the Iraqi command-and-control system was immense and impressive, but insufficient to disconnect totally the head of the serpent from its tail. In Phase 3 of the air campaign, on the other hand, attacks on Iraqi surface forces yielded both physical and psychological benefits for the coalition.

The greater part of coalition air war was flown either directly against Iraqi ground forces in the Kuwaiti Theater of Operations (KTO) or against the supply lines sustaining those forces.[6] According to the *Gulf War Air Power Survey* commissioned by the U.S. Air Force, the air war against Iraqi ground forces was one of attrition or gradual destruction, unlike the roundhouse or knockout punches delivered against Iraqi air and air-defense systems.[7] Air interdiction was intended not only to cut the flow of supplies to the KTO, but also to prevent movement of forces within the theater and to prevent Iraqi forces from leaving the theater intact. Lines of supply and communication between Baghdad and the KTO crossed a number of rivers; therefore, coalition air attacks sought to destroy as many bridges as possible. Iraqi ingenuity in designing around these attacks was considerable: alternatives used included temporary bridges, amphibious ferrying vehicles, and earthen causeways. Since the Iraqi army was deployed in the KTO with most of its supplies and equipment already on hand, coalition attacks on supply lines during the air war did not preclude the transshipment of the necessary amount of replenishments. Later, however, it became clear that Iraqi supply lines could not have kept pace with an extended ground war: Iraqi front forces could not have been sustained in ammunition and in petroleum, oil, and lubricants (POL) during protracted land battle.[8]

Coalition air attacks also destroyed a great deal of Iraqi ground-force equipment and killed many troops. There was considerable variation in the rate of unit armor attrition: an armored division in the middle of the theater might suffer attrition at a rate of 10 percent, but a comparable division close to the front lines could have attrition figures close to 100

5. *Gulf War Air Power Survey.* Vol. 2: *Operations and Effects and Effectiveness* (Washington, D.C.: GPO, 1993), 77.

6. *GWAPS* Abbreviated Summary, pp. 14–29.

7. Ibid.

8. Ibid., pp. 14–32.

percent. By the end of the air and ground wars, the Iraqi army had paid the price of 76 percent attrition in tanks, 55 percent in armored personnel carriers or infantry fighting vehicles (APC/IFV), and 90 percent in artillery.[9]

Sensitive to the issue of "body count" estimates that became so notorious during the Vietnam War, U.S. Central Command (under General Norman Schwarzkopf) declined to give estimates of Iraqi personnel losses either during or after the war. Postwar Department of Defense studies also preferred not to tackle the issue. The *Gulf War Air Power Survey* includes the following estimates. About 336,000 Iraqi military personnel were in the theater at the start of the air war. Desertions were 25–30 percent. Somewhat less than 10 percent of the force were casualties to air attacks. The remaining strength of the Iraqi army in the KTO by February 24 (the start of the ground war) was approximately 200,000 to 222,000.[10]

There is some evidence that the psychological effects of air bombardment on Iraqi front-line troops were both considerable and more significant than the number of casualties inflicted. Captured Iraqis said they had expected an air campaign of several days to a week. After weeks of bombardment, ground transportation fell apart, training ceased, supply stocks were destroyed, and units ran out of food, water, fuel, and spare parts. Pinned down in forward positions by Saddam's strategy and forced to endure this apparently ceaseless air attack, many Iraqi grunts developed a "sense of futility and inevitability" about an unfavorable outcome.[11] Many Iraqi soldiers decided during the air war that they had no more interest in fighting. Some of these troops deserted their units while others remained in place; the deserters were not there when the ground war began, and those who were left surrendered immediately without offering resistance.

As desertion and a sense of hopelessness caused Iraqi front-line resistance to crumble, Iraq's overall strategy went down with the disillusionment of its forward forces in the KTO. That strategy had planned for crack units in the Iraqi operational and strategic reserve to move against coalition armored spearheads when the main axes of the coalition attack became clear. As it turned out, the speed and direction of the main attack successfully deceived Iraqi planners, but even if it had not "the utter collapse of the Iraqi front lines made any planned movements by the re-

9. The Central Command estimates for equipment attrition were inflated, but the target base against which these estimates were made was also inflated. Therefore, the *percentage* figures for attrition given by the command are consistent with later assessments. Ibid., pp. 14–34.

10. Ibid., pp. 14–35.

11. Ibid.

serves irrelevant."[12] Lack of determined Iraqi resistance once the ground war began made the issue of close air support for ground operations a less important issue than in many other wars. Close air support was useful but not vital to the success of the coalition ground-force attacks.[13]

The Air War: Decisive or Indecisive?

From all of this one might conclude that the air war against Iraq was an unparalleled success story in the history of warfare. And some commentators were not slow to boost the decisive role of air power in modern combat, based on Gulf experience. Experts cautioned, however, that air power could be oversold in the present as it had been in the past.[14] There were several areas in which the accomplishments of air attacks fell well short of political and military objectives. These included attacks against Scud mobile, land-based missiles and against suspected Iraqi nuclear weapon sites.

The Iraqi nuclear program was "massive," for all practical purposes "fiscally unconstrained," and "closer to fielding a nuclear weapon and less vulnerable to destruction by precision bombing" than coalition air planners or U.S. intelligence experts realized prior to Desert Storm.[15] As of January 16, 1991, the coalition target list included two nuclear-related aiming points. U.N. inspectors later discovered more than twenty sites related to the Iraqi nuclear weapons program, of which sixteen were referred to as "main facilities."[16] The redundancy, advanced status on the eve of war, and elusiveness of the Iraqi nuclear program, together with wartime concealment efforts, caused the United Nations to conclude that the air campaign had merely "inconvenienced" Iraqi plans to construct atomic weapons.[17]

Another category of disappointment for the air war was the effort to destroy Scud missiles that might be launched against Israel or Saudi Arabia. The danger was perceived to be great that Iraq might launch ballistic missiles with chemical warheads into Israel, causing Israeli retaliation despite the protests of the United States and its coalition allies. During the war, mobile Scud launchers proved to be difficult to detect and to

12. Ibid.
13. Ibid., pp. 14–36.
14. Eliot A. Cohen, "The Mystique of U.S. Air Power," *Foreign Affairs* (January/February 1994): 109–24.
15. *GWAPS* Abbreviated Summary, pp. 14–26.
16. Ibid.
17. Ibid., pp. 14–27.

destroy. Coalition air crews reported the destruction of about eighty mobile launchers, and another dozen or so were claimed by special operations forces. The attacks did destroy something in the general vicinity of the Scud launch areas, but after-action reports now suggest that most of these objects were decoys.

Although some 1,500 strikes were made against targets associated with Iraqi ballistic missiles, included in this total are fixed launch sites and Scud-related production and support facilities. Only about 15 percent of the total, or 215 strikes, were targeted specifically against mobile launchers.[18] U.S. air planners had initially hoped that attacks on fixed Scud sites in the opening hours of the air war would virtually eliminate Iraq's ability to launch ballistic missiles against Israel or against regional members of the coalition. Unfortunately, the fixed Scud launchers in western Iraq on January 16 and 17 served as decoys that directed coalition attention away from the mobile Scuds, the latter already having been deployed to wartime hiding sites from which the attacks on Israel would be launched.[19]

The short duration of the ground war (about four days) suggested to some that this phase of the conflict was inconsequential. Air power alone had come close to inflicting strategic military defeat on Iraq. In this regard, all was not as it seemed. It was still necessary for the U.S. and allied ground forces to close with their Iraqi counterparts by means of a wide envelopment through western Iraq. This envelopment, or "left hook," cut off Saddam's retreating armored forces and subjected them to murderous carnage from tactical air power and coalition armor. By the time of the cease-fire it was clear that the capability of Iraq to sustain regional, large-scale offensives had been crippled decisively. The terms of the settlement imposed by the United Nations, though permitting the existing government to remain in Baghdad, nonetheless established limitations on Iraqi activities (e.g., "no fly" zones in northern and southern Iraq, thus protecting Kurds and Shiites respectively) and also imposed a postwar regime of inspections for nuclear weapons and other weapons of mass destruction.

Assessment

Because the Gulf War was the last war of the Cold War era or the first of the post–Cold War, depending on one's perspective, it received a great deal of scrutiny in official and other sources. I have cited extensively in

18. Keaney and Cohen, *Summary Report*, 84.
19. Ibid., 86.

the preceding pages the *Gulf War Air Power Survey* on account of the significance of the air war for the outcome of fighting between January 17 and February 28, 1991. The following discussion emphasizes the relationship between war policy and the instruments and techniques of warfare. Did the U.S. and allied coalition planners accomplish their political objectives, and were those political objectives the right ones?

President Bush, recognizing the unusual nature of the wartime coalition he had put together, did not deviate from his original and limited objective of expelling Iraq from Kuwait. Bush strategy thus consisted of the pursuit of limited aims, but with unlimited means relative to those aims. In Korea and in Vietnam, the United States had taken a somewhat different approach. It had limited both its political objectives and, relative to those political objectives, its means of fighting. The result was to make the two Asian wars more protracted and less popular on the home front. In both wars, the politically imposed constraints on tactics and operations relative to the set political objectives also filled field commanders with resentment over micromanagement (especially in Vietnam) and over the self-denial of an attainable military victory (especially in Korea).

Bush resisted the temptation to decimate additional Iraqi forces and to use a more extended ground and air war to dislodge Saddam Hussein from power. The Iraqi dictator was not expected by U.S. officials to survive for very long after the humiliation inflicted on him by Desert Storm. This expectation was proved false, as we now know. President Bush had to stand for reelection in 1992, and the ironic outcome of the two countries' domestic politics was that Saddam outlasted Bush as head of state. Some of Bush's critics during the war expressed regret that the coalition did not pursue Saddam to his grave and establish postwar U.N. control over all of Iraq. Instead, the United States stuck to its original U.N. objective and stopped fighting with many of Saddam's forces still intact and with his political power secure.

On the other hand, by sticking with his original policy aim, Bush had kept together the strange collection of political bedfellows who joined in the military operations to liberate Kuwait. Continuation of war against Iraq to the point of taking over its government would have been widely resented by political factions within the Arab and Muslim worlds. This is so even though Saddam's effort to represent his military campaign under the ideological smokescreen of Pan-Arabism was rejected by Egyptians, Saudis, Syrians, and other coalition partners. Expelling Iraq from Kuwait did not smack of Western imperialism in the way that taking over the government of Iraq with a U.S.-dominated military coalition would have.

On balance, it seemed that Bush's decision about policy objective was the right one. He had not made the mistake Truman made in Korea: allowing favorable military developments to influence a change in war policy. Subsequent to General Douglas MacArthur's dramatic landing at Inchon and the routing of North Korea's armies south of the 38th parallel, Truman had acquiesced when MacArthur asked to continue north in order to unify all of Korea under U.N. auspices. This meant sweeping of the regime in Pyongyang into the dustbin of history. China read this as a clear military threat to its own safety, and the Soviet Union could not but regard Kim Il Sung's demise as a rollback of the supposedly irresistible historical tide of communism.

The appropriateness of coalition military means for the desired policy objectives was testified to by the one-sided nature of the conflict, by its rapid termination, and by the comparatively small loss of life (relative to prewar projections) among coalition fighters. Within the context of a specific and limited political objective, the United States and its allies had used unrelenting military means. Continuation of the air bombardment until useful targets had virtually run out demoralized Iraqi defenders and disconnected the national command-and-control system from its forward detachments. Blinded by coalition attacks on its warning, communications, and air-defense systems, Iraq lost control of the air within a few days of combat.

With regard to the relationship between war policy and military means as conducted by Baghdad, some surprises were in store for the United States and its allies. Saddam's system of political control over his armed forces, security services, and other aspects of the state was more resistant to cracking under the strain of military defeat than prewar intelligence estimators suspected. On the other hand, the performance of the Iraqi armed forces in an environment of high-technology, combined-arms combat was much worse than U.S. and allied planners had suspected. Prewar assessments credited the Iraqi army for being one of the world's largest land forces, for possessing much modern equipment for ground and tactical-air forces, and for its seemingly battle-hardened qualities resulting from an eight-year war with Iran.

It may be that Iraq's success against the much larger but poorly trained and equipped Iranian armies between 1980 and 1988 led it to misperceive the kind of war for which its forces were headed in 1990. Saddam's deployments in the KTO suggested that he anticipated a war of attrition in which coalition forces would charge into fortified positions, expending their assets in futile offensives comparable to those launched repeatedly on the western front in the First World War. The refusal of the United States and its allies to fight this kind of war, together with the early domination of the skies by coalition aircraft, showed the importance of technology, properly employed, for the conduct of warfare. Technology favored the attacker, not the defender, in the theater of operations within which Saddam's harried defenders sought to hold off coalition attacks.

Saddam's grossest miscalculations were not military but political (in the sense of diplomatic). His poor prewar diplomacy alienated potential allies and allowed Bush to mobilize a coalition that included a majority of Middle Eastern Arab powers. Isolated diplomatically, Saddam was thus unprotected militarily from U.S. vengeance. The defection of his former Soviet ally should have been a clue to Saddam Hussein that a political solution prior to 1991 was in his interest. Instead, he clung stubbornly to an indefensible and isolated diplomatic position from which he was easily pushed by Bush into a military corner. Bush used Saddam's inept diplomacy to his advantage in still another way. President Bush was able to obtain U.N. authorization for the use of force; having accomplished that, he used the Security Council's approval for war to position his domestic political doubters.

U.S. policy was served in the narrow sense that Bush's war aim was accomplished at an acceptable cost. The larger issue—the fate of postwar Iraq—was undecided even as Bush left office in 1993. Iraq remained under U.N. inspection and supervision with respect to its potential for weapons of mass destruction, and Kurds in northern Iraq remained under the protection of U.S. and allied air power. The evolution of postwar Iraqi politics was uncertain so long as Saddam retained his tenuous grip on power. The clearest regional winners (apart from Kuwait) seemed to be Iran, now weighing much heavier in the Gulf as a military and political player, and Saudi Arabia, which had more firmly tied itself to U.S. military protection without having to endure a more permanent and embarrassing U.S. military presence.

Continuing Controversy

The News Media and the Gulf War

Prior to the outbreak of fighting between Iraqi and coalition forces on January 16, 1991, President Bush had repeatedly announced that this war would "not be another Vietnam." By this he meant several things. Sufficient force would be used to destroy the opponent's fighting power decisively and in the shortest possible time. He also meant something else. The U.S. news media would not be permitted to sabotage the war effort, from the adminstration's perspective, to the extent that U.S. reporters and anchors had turned American public opinion against the war in Vietnam.

The Bush strategy for dealing with the news media was as important as the strategy for defeating Saddam Hussein, and it consisted of at least three parts. First, reporters' knowledge of battlefield conditions and access to operational information was to be severely restricted. Second, carefully controlled briefings emphasizing the U.S. government point of view were to be staged repeatedly in the coalition headquarters at Riyadh, Saudi Arabia, and in Washington. Third, Saddam Hussein was to be personified as evil incarnate, and his regime would be presented as the "Republic of Fear." This strategy worked, from the perspective of the Pentagon, even beyond its wildest dreams.

The first component—restriction of the independent access of reporters in the field to U.S. and allied troops and plans—could be justified as a legitimate national security need. Bush administration planners argued with some justice that the existence of "real time" international networks such as CNN made it essential to exercise extreme care that operational security was not compromised inadvertently by news reports. In addition, it was easier in the Kuwaiti-Saudi theater of operations than it had been in Vietnam to impose restrictions on news media travel and access to troops. There were clearer boundaries between friendly and enemy turf, and unauthorized travel outside the coalition defense perimeter was extremely hazardous for journalists.

The second element of the Bush news media strategy was the carefully controlled use of military briefings as devices for persuasion. Briefings for reporters emphasized the "gee whiz" technology of U.S. smart bombs, cruise missiles, and other high-technology hardware. Carefully selected videos of pinpoint attacks on air-defense and command-and-control targets gave the impression that collateral damage to civilians had been minimized or eliminated entirely from coalition air attacks. Briefing presence was also important. Briefers were selected who were very articulate and experienced in dealing with news media professionals (Lt. Gen. Kelly in Washington) or whose military bearing was itself intimidating against hostile questions (Schwarzkopf's briefings in Riyadh).

Most of these briefings were very long on visuals and short on hard information. They provided few clues about those aspects of the war which were not proceeding according to prewar plans. The problem of bomb damage assessment, for example, proved to be far more daunting than planners had supposed. Many targets had to be restruck repeatedly before assurance could be given that they actually had been destroyed, and significant ordnance was expended attacking decoys, including dummy mobile missiles. Very little was said about the nature of Iraq's military strategy other than to characterize it as incompetent. The existence of special forces such as U.S. Task Force 160 or Britain's SAS was not even acknowledged, again on the grounds of operational security.

Briefings never really explained why it was necessary to assemble a force of some 700,000 troops, including the air and offshore naval power assigned to it, in order to defeat a country the size of Iraq. The fact that, after the air campaign, Iraq's army in the KTO was finished as a fighting force within four days suggests that the personnel and firepower, which the Bush administration had declared necessary, were grossly excessive. Military conservatism and caution in providing redundant assets prior to war is both understandable and standard operating procedure. But, even making allowances for tolerable levels of personnel and equipment redundancy, the coalition force assembled against Iraq seemed more suitable in size and military organization for battle against the Soviet Union of the early 1980s. Few noted this apparent discrepancy between end and means, and news briefings seemed to lull potential criticism on this point into complacency.

The third aspect of the Bush news media strategy was the demonizing of Saddam Hussein and his regime. This component was aimed not so much at the professional news media as at the U.S. public: the news media were the conveyor belt on which the desired image of Saddam would travel. Remarkably, the U.S. media showed little interest in melting down this Saddam-as-Hitler analogy—a far cry from their past treatment of some other American adversaries. Few noted, for example, that Saddam's government was a secular regime that was not based on the intolerant Islamic fundamentalism that held sway in Iran. Saddam Hussein had no sustained ideological or cultural hatred of the United States or its way of life. He had been a major recipient of U.S. food aid and military-related technology during the 1980s, when he was thought by Washington to be a useful balancer against Iran in the Gulf region. Nor had Iraq taken American hostages in the visible and dramatic way that Iran had in 1979, or as Iranian minions in southern Lebanon had during the 1980s.

Most mainstream U.S. news media, moreover, were not concerned to point out that Iraq had some legitimate reasons for complaint against Kuwait. The Iran-Iraq War (though, admittedly, started by Saddam) had drained the Iraqi treasury, and a rise in world oil prices was desperately sought in order to make up for years of lost revenue. Kuwait spurned repeated efforts by Baghdad to negotiate this issue seriously. Nor did the Kuwaitis take seriously Iraq's frustration over Kuwaiti slant drilling into oil fields in southern Iraq and over Kuwaiti control of Warbah and Bubiyan islands, potentially strategic points for squeezing Iraqi access to shipments via the Persian Gulf. Saddam's demand to make Kuwait the "nineteenth province" of Iraq was illegitimate but not entirely incomprehensible, given the fact that the boundary between the two states was essentially the creation of a colonial power many years before.

Media memories were also selective concerning U.S. allies in the Gulf War. The Syrians of Hafez al-Assad were suddenly no longer the most irresponsible sponsors of terrorism in the Middle East, but legitimate coalition supporters of the crusade against the usurper in Baghdad. And media memory apparently forgot altogether the stance taken by Saudi Arabia in the aftermath of the October War of 1973. A Saudi-led OPEC boycott sent the United States and other developed economies into a tailspin for nearly a decade. The full story of the economic consequences of that disaster has still to be written. The Saudis' action in 1973 was an explicit and direct retribution against the United States for supporting the Israelis after Israel had been attacked by Egypt. Ironically, two reasons offered by the coalition for going to war against Iraq were (1) to prevent the conquest of Saudi Arabia (whether Saddam actually intended this has never been established) *and* (2) to deter Israel from military intervention.

Another justification offered as part of the demonizing of Saddam Hussein and his regime was the claim that weapons of mass destruction—including large stores of immediately usable chemical weapons and an effort to develop a nuclear capability—made Iraq a unique regional and international menace. Iraq's chemical weapons were a realistic threat: the armed forces were stocked with nerve and mustard gases, and Iraq had used gas during its recent war against Iran and even against its own dissident Kurds. Biological toxins were thought to be in storage for possible use, although lack of experience in using biological weapons without adverse side effects on one's own troops has inhibited many otherwise capable states from going down the road of biomilitarization.

Iraq's nuclear weapons potential was an issue for the Bush administration during the Desert Shield buildup from August 1990 through mid-January 1991. U.S. CIA and military intelligence doubted that Iraq had any deliverable nuclear weapons. The necessary in-flight testing which would be required for deliverable weapons had not taken place. It was thought possible, though, that Iraq was close to developing a crude nuclear device. In fact, U.S. intelligence underestimated Iraq's nuclear potential. Absent its military defeat and the subsequent U.N.-enforced inspections, the Iraqi government probably could have produced within a few years some nuclear weapons deliverable by aircraft or ground-launched missiles, including the notorious Scuds.

The nuclear potential and existing chemical weapons capability of Iraq on the eve of Desert Storm, however, had to be considered against the capabilities of the coalition which opposed Saddam Hussein. The United States was the leading nuclear superpower and could respond in kind to any Iraqi first use of nuclear weapons. The coalition organized against Iraq, moreover, included other nuclear powers, among them Britain and

France. In addition to the obvious possibility of a nuclear riposte to any nuclear first use, the United States hinted that it might use nuclear strikes in response to an Iraqi first use of *chemical* weapons or other nonnuclear weapons of mass destruction. This threat was never stated directly as official Bush policy, but it was alluded to by at least one cabinet official whose allusions had to be taken seriously. Saddam would also have to assume that chemical attacks would certainly be met with coalition chemical responses, and he must also have known that U.S. forces, at least, were well rehearsed and equipped for chemical warfare.

In short, Iraq's threat of nuclear or massive chemical use was a threat of self-destruction in the face of overwhelming military superiority. An especially acute fear on the part of U.S. and Israeli leaders was that Saddam would launch Scuds armed with chemical charges against cities in Israel. Rumors to this effect accompanied the very first Scuds that impacted on Israeli soil, but the alarms were eventually discomfirmed. Thus it seems a safe assumption, since charitable motives on Saddam's part cannot be assumed, that he was deterred from chemical first use by the plausible threat of retaliation in kind, or worse. Saddam did engage in environmental terrorism, igniting Kuwaiti oil fields and arranging for huge oil spills into the Persian Gulf. Neither of these last two tactics was a significant factor in the military outcome or a major concern of Central Command.

Oil was as obvious a motive for the U.S. and allied response to Iraq's invasion as was the concern, to some extent overstated in its military dimensions, about Iraq's weapons of mass destruction. Another motive given by the Bush administration was that this was the first test of the "new world order" made possible by the end of the Cold War. The United States and the coalition had to wage war to show that aggression could not stand and to defend the principle of sovereign independence of states.

This last motive was not entirely insincere on the part of the United States and its allies. The end of the Cold War and the willingness of the Soviet Union to support U.N. resolutions against Iraq did create a window of opportunity for military action authorized by the Security Council. The Cold War conflict between the United States and the Soviet Union had denied this opportunity for U.N. assertiveness. Nonetheless, Desert Storm was a military operation that took place behind an unusual political backdrop. It would be difficult to reproduce the favorable scenario which made possible international support for the prompt use of military force against Iraq.

The Bush news media strategy certainly averted home front demoralization and defeat of American forces by adverse publicity (for which many had blamed the press and the electronic media during the Vietnam War). On the other hand, the rapid termination of the Gulf War and the unwillingness of the mainstream media to ask many of the most probing questions about the rationale for military, as opposed to some other, action against Iraq led to anesthetized coverage of Desert Storm. The American public saw the war, for the most part, through the conceptual lenses of Central Command headquarters, the White House, and the Pentagon. The Bush strategy, predicated on the myth that the news media had served the cause of North Vietnam decades ago, ensured that critical coverage of war aims and methods would be minimized so long as the war remained short and low in friendly casualties.

5

THE NUCLEAR AGE and MILITARY STRATEGY

Nuclear weapons fulfilled one aspect of Clausewitz's vision of future war and, at the same time, disappointed another aspect. Large-scale nuclear war threatened not only governments but entire societies and civilizations with permanent, irrevocable destruction. Clausewitz's hypothetical of absolute war had found its available instrument. On the other hand, nuclear force could not be coupled to reasonable policy: at least, the *use* of nuclear force could not. Therefore, leaders turned to *deterrence*, an experiment in applied psychology, to reestablish the connection between force and policy in the nuclear age. If nuclear war was pointless to wage, especially against another nuclear-armed state, it was under some conditions thought advantageous to be able to threaten war, or to threaten to slide accidentally into a war.

The arrival of the nuclear age with the bombings of Hiroshima and Nagasaki was not at first perceived as a qualitative change in the technological environment for strategy. U.S. theorists and policymakers struggled, during the later 1940s and early 1950s, to adapt simultaneously to the nuclear revolution and to a newly bipolar world. The onset of the Cold War between Washington and Moscow after 1947 was marked on the U.S. side by three primary way stations: the Truman Doctrine, the Marshall Plan, and NATO. All were without precedent in U.S. peacetime history, and the third, NATO, committed the previously unilateralist Americans to an entangling alliance in order to deter Soviet political assertion backed by military power.

U.S. "containment" strategy after 1947 accepted political stalemate between the Sovietized Eastern bloc and the Atlantic alliance. Leaders then had to decide how to fit nuclear weapons into a policy of protracted stalemate. The Truman administration did not quite know what to do with nuclear weapons, which were not plentiful even at the outbreak of war in Korea in June 1950. Under Truman, nuclear weapons were not assigned in peacetime to the forces that would be tasked to use them. The then small number of nuclear weapons available in U.S. and Soviet arsenals suggested to American military planners that a nuclear war might be only the first phase of a global struggle, eventually requiring the mobilization of massive armies and large fleets. World War III would precede a repetition of World War II.

Toward Mutual Deterrence

Under Eisenhower, though, nuclear weapons became much more plentiful, as did long-range bombers for the intercontinental delivery of those weapons. It seemed that technology had at last caught up with such prophets of airpower as Giulio Douhet and Alexander De Seversky. Massive destruction of an opponent's society could be accomplished without the need to defeat his armed forces in battle. The arrival of intercontinental land-based and sea-launched ballistic missiles only confirmed the impression that Clausewitz's absolute war was now not only a philosophical construct but a terrible actuality. Strategy had turned a corner, and military traditionalists struggled to incorporate the unprecedented destructive power of nuclear weapons into the acceptable lexicon of strategy and doctrine.

In the early years of the nuclear age, two positions were staked out in debates about the significance of the new weapons. Military *fundamentalists* acknowledged that nuclear weapons were different from other weapons in their degree of destructive power. On the other hand, fundamentalists denied that strategy had been turned inside out by the new technology. However destructive nuclear weapons might be, they were still instruments of rational statecraft. The issue was to determine how, not whether, to use them.

Opposed to the fundamentalists were the *revisionists*. Much as did Marxist theorists with regard to prevailing notions about capitalism, nuclear revisionists contended that nuclear weapons had changed military strategy fundamentally and forever. The destructive power of nuclear weapons, the speed with which that destruction could be accomplished, and the number of weapons on each side of the Cold War stressed fatally the connection between military instruments and political objectives. Strategy, from the revisionist perspective, had been stood on its head.

These polar positions lent themselves to compromise within the U.S. policy debate. Budgets and available technology determined the size and character of the U.S. and, arguably, the Soviet arsenals more than theory did. Nevertheless, the theoretical perspectives of military fundamentalists and revisionists on the relationship between nuclear weapons and war policy were themselves important political forces. The U.S. arms control community adopted an almost entirely revisionist perspective and, from that, deduced strategic policy positions supportive of mutual deterrence or deterrence based on assured retaliation. Advocates of this position later adopted the nomenclature first pinned on them by critics: mutual assured destruction, or MAD. By the arrival of the Kennedy administration, mutual deterrence based on offensive retaliation had become U.S. strategic orthodoxy.

Part of the reason for the orthodoxy of U.S. deterrence based on offensive retaliation was that defensive antimissile technology lagged considerably behind the technology for missile attack. ABM (antiballistic missile) or BMD (ballistic missile defenses) would have to perform at nearly perfect levels under untried conditons in order to meet the protective standard for defenses expected in U.S. strategic culture. The Soviets were more willing in the 1960s to experiment with early-generation BMD systems, but by the end of the Johnson administration it had become clear to them that the defenses of that era were not on the same plateau as the offenses. The SALT I agreement in 1972 included the ABM Treaty, which limited both the United States and the Soviet Union to missile defenses at two sites (later reduced to one) and precluded attempts to deploy nationwide territorial defenses.

It was thought by some U.S. arms control advocates that SALT I meant Soviet acceptance of mutual deterrence based on offensive retaliation. This optimism was premature, for Soviet research and development on defenses continued in the 1970s along with modernization of their offenses. The ABM Treaty signified that the Soviet Union saw the futility of an immediate arms race with the technologically unpredictable Americans. Détente allowed for some diminution in U.S.-Soviet political competition, including final resolution of the Cold War status of Berlin and the two Germanys. A 1974 protocol later reduced the allowable ABM sites for each side to one: the Soviet Union maintained its Galosh system around Moscow; the U.S. Congress shut down the single American site at Grand Forks, North Dakota, in 1975.

Thus, although both Washington and Moscow gave lip service to mutual deterrence, the superpowers' military research establishments hedged their bets against the unlikely but forbidding possibility that the other side might achieve a breakthrough in defenses. Such a breakthrough would overturn the nuclear revolution and restore traditional strategy by means of victory in combat. President Reagan sought to take this aspiration for the rebirth of strategy from dream to reality when he declared into existence, on March 23, 1983, the Strategic Defense Initiative (SDI—"Star Wars" to its critics).

SDI and Missile Defense

The fury of the reaction to Reagan's announcement was something to behold. The president had not staffed the recommended research-and-development program through the national security bureaucracy. Caught flat-footed, Reagan bureaucrats stoically applied themselves to defending SDI and finding a rationale for missile defenses within the Reagan military strategy. Since the president and his secretary of defense, Caspar Weinberger, had also emphasized the modernization of offensive nuclear weapons, it was problematic that the sword and shield aspects of U.S. strategy could be reconciled. Reagan strategy sought a world gradually disarmed of nuclear offenses and replaced by nonnuclear defenses. The problem was that a "defense transition" of this sort could not be accomplished rapidly: in the interim between mutual deterrence, based on offenses, and mutual survival, based on defenses, a great many thorny political and military minefields lay in wait.

One problem for Reagan's SDI was that many of his own Pentagon bureaucrats, uniformed as well as civilian, doubted the possibility of serious defenses against nuclear weapons. Those skeptical of SDI made several criticisms that, to a point, were valid. First, a U.S. system that was "too good" would intimidate the Soviets by promising to deny them their second-strike retaliation, on which present and near-term deterrence had to rest. Second, the cost–exchange ratio between newly developed and deployed defenses and incrementally improved offenses, intended to offset those defenses, seemed unfavorable to the defenses. Third, competent U.S. defenses might provoke suspicious Soviets into a new and more dangerous arms race in offensive *and* defensive weapons. Fourth, even less-than-competent BMD might serve as useful antisatellite weapons (ASATs) capable of knocking down the other side's warning and communications satellites prior to a first strike.

Reagan's departure from government and the demise of the Soviet Union completely changed the terms of the strategic debate about the relationship between offenses and defenses. Interest in a comprehensive "peace shield" for the U.S. homeland gave way to the more attainable objective of protection against limited strikes, whether rogue launches or terrorist attacks. The Bush administration's version of accidental/terrorist attack protection was more expensive and ambitious than the scaled down Clinton version, but the use of Patriot defensive missiles against Iraqi Scuds (with debatable effectiveness) ensured that antitactical missile defense would remain on the U.S. defense agenda. What was again off the agenda by the time of Clinton's inaugural was any revival of territorial defense of the U.S. homeland. Among nuclear systems, offenses still seemed preeminent in the 1990s.

The Stability–Instability Paradox

Classical strategy survived, however, below the threshold of nuclear deterrence. If offense-dominated nuclear strategies led to cautiously defensivist policies during the Cold War, a "stability-instability" paradox permitted planners to contemplate victory by use of conventional military arms. Then, too, limited war was a feature of the nuclear age on account of the risks and costs of total war and on account of the plethora of contested areas between Soviet ambitions and NATO interests. A conventional war in Europe was planned for by both sides but was gradually perceived, well before the end of the Cold War, as potentially suicidal. This was so for two reasons. First, the possibility for escalation from conventional to nuclear war in Europe was very likely. Second, this likelihood of nuclear escalation became an indispensable element in NATO strategy by the 1950s and remained so, despite subsequent efforts to lengthen the fuse. What is now known about Soviet military doctrine for most of the Cold War is that it emphasized early nuclear use in order to blast corridors through NATO defenses for attacking Warsaw Pact forces.

War was also possible below the threshold of conventional war, in the form of insurgency and counterinsurgency. Insurgency and revolutionary war presented a major challenge to U.S. military thought, of which more will be said in Chapter 7. The present issue is that insurgency and revolutionary warfare were perceived by U.S. policymakers as specialized communist tools for overturning governments sympathetic to the West. The communists of the Cold War had somehow found a set of magic keys for destabilizing Third World governments: they had only to use those keys without Western opposition and the dominoes would fall into the socialist camp from Latin America to Southeast Asia.

Unconventional wars shared with conventional wars in the nuclear age the fact that they could be fought under circumstances in which nuclear weapons were irrelevant. The likelihood that either the United States or the Soviets would employ nuclear weapons in counterinsurgency was small, and the probability that nuclear weapons would accomplish anything useful in that context was zero. Unconventional wars were unlike conventional wars and more like nuclear deterrence in one respect, however. Unconventional wars helped to delegitimize the confidence of leaders in statist warfare, under the control of accountable governments and professional armed forces for clearly articulated political purposes.

For Clausewitz, the substructure of state policy was the base on which the superstructure of military preparations and operations was erected. The state was the sole source of meaningful and legitimate policy guidance for war. Unconventional wars attacked the very legitimacy of the state and undermined the self-image of its officer corps as heroic fighters against foreign adversaries. Many officers were forced by their governments into "dirty wars" of assassination and oppression against their own citizens. Unconventional war, especially when it seemed to succeed, threatened the connection between state and army at both ends. The state became less the consensual arbiter of the use of force, and the army less obviously the symbol of state unity and public authority.

Nuclear Soldiering

Like unconventional conflicts, the mission of nuclear deterrence attacked the "soul force" of developed Western and Soviet armies.[1] Nuclear soldiers were sentinels who hoped never to have to demonstrate the effectiveness of their weapons. The more successful deterrence was, the less frequently force needed to be used. A competition in risk taking replaced the traditional preparedness for combat as the preferred method of soldiering. Nuclear soldiers, sailors, and air personnel were unable to demonstrate their competency without nullifying the very social contract between state and army on which their concept of service was based. Nuclear war would mean the end of the state, and thus the contract.

Theorists tried ingeniously to get around this problem by substituting deterrence for defense. This substitution was equivalent to the substitution of apples for oranges. Deterrence and defense were both necessary components of a sound military posture, but nuclear armaments seemed to completely displace defense missions with deterrent missions. In addi-

---

1. I admit the imprecision of this metaphor and welcome improvements.

tion, nuclear powers and their militaries began to think more like deterrers and less like defenders, even under conditions of conventional war with no possibility of nuclear escalation. For example, the model of gradual escalation used for the management of nuclear crises was extended to the conduct of conventional and counterinsurgency war, as in the U.S. involvement in Vietnam.

The new nuclear strategists in the United States were for the most part not military professionals. To a greater degree than in the Soviet system or in European armed forces, U.S. nuclear strategic thinking bypassed the experience and historical focus of the officer corps. Civilian experts in psychology, economics, and political science transferred their concepts to the management of nuclear crises and to the arrangement of arms control negotiations. However useful these unmilitary worldviews may have been in those realms, they proved problematic as explanatory models for the conduct of war.[2] Game theory, perception theory, rational-choice models, and the like were all very well for the classroom or the academic study; only infrequently, though, did they offer useful substantive advice to harried policymakers or commanders.

U.S. nuclear strategic thinking, like a great deal else in American military strategy, is afflicted with an excessive dependence on technology. Contractors, government bureaucrats, and their congressional allies promote the latest wonder weapon as the solution to current strategic problems. Reagan's SDI suffered more from the lack of a convincing strategic rationale than it did from the arguments, unprovable in any event, that defensive technology could never be competitive with offensive technology. The shifting sands of U.S. congressional policy debate provided poor guidance for the sorting out of military-strategic issues. For example, liberals accepted the MX ICBM as a Carter program but found it incompatible with arms control as a Reagan program. Some conservatives insisted that the United States was so needful of missile defenses that it ought to deploy them immediately (in the 1980s) with off-the-shelf technology, despite considerable evidence that vulnerable defenses of that kind would invite attack.

Gorbachev and Deterrence

Mikhail Gorbachev, having ascended to the Soviet party chairmanship in 1985, borrowed from the U.S. arms control book of deterrence stability

---

2. For pertinent illustrations and critique, see Colin S. Gray, *Weapons Don't Make War: Policy, Strategy and Military Technology* (Lawrence: University Press of Kansas, 1993), esp. 122–45.

and increased the bidding. Gorbachev's requirement was to reduce Soviet threat assessment of Western hostility in order to restrain his military while he emphasized domestic political and economic reform. Much to the surprise of U.S. policymakers, the Soviets agreed in 1987 to "double zero," or removal of all INF (intermediate nuclear force) missiles from Eurasia. Gorbachev separated this issue from other arms control agendas, including the ongoing discussions about arms control for strategic nuclear weapons and for space. He astutely recycled U.S. arms control assumptions back to Washington and within his own national security bureaucracy, which was invigorated by demarches from politico-military think tanks that were taken much more seriously in the era of *glasnost.* From mutual deterrence it followed that there was a "reasonable sufficiency" of armaments, including nuclear weapons, beyond which Soviet new thinkers judged the piling up of additional weapons to be irrelevant.

Worse still for Soviet conservatives, Gorbachev unveiled his new political thinking on security and asserted that security was a condition to be obtained with the cooperation of former enemies. In his widely circulated manifesto *Perestroika,* published in 1987, the Soviet leader assigned both Marx and Clausewitz to the intellectual ash heap of history. The class struggle was over as Marx had understood it, according to Gorbachev, and Clausewitz "belongs to the libraries." The two pillars of Soviet Cold War military thinking prior to 1985—Marxian dialectic and Clausewitz's understanding of the relationship between war and politics—now assumed the status of provisional theorems subject to dispute.

Gorbachev's versions of mutual deterrence, sufficiency of arms, and common security caused him to oppose without qualification the Reagan version of missile defense. The Soviet leader could not control his generals' appetite for modernization if it appeared that the United States was pushing weapons development onto an entirely new plateau. It was ironic that the Soviet leadership was clinging to mutual deterrence based on offensive retaliation at the very time, in Reagan's second term, that the U.S. government was promoting a defense transition. In 1967, when U.S. Secretary of Defense Robert McNamara had confronted Soviet Premier Alexei Kosygin at Glassboro, New Jersey, the positions had been reversed. Kosygin asserted the right of Moscow to deploy defenses and denied that defenses were destabilizing to mutual deterrence, as McNamara insisted at the time.

McNamara then, and Gorbachev later, had recognized correctly the inability of states to use nuclear weapons to military or strategic advantage. Relative advantage in numbers or types of weapons or launchers of a particular kind did not translate, for either side at any stage of the Cold War, into political advantage. Thus McNamara anticipated, and Gorbachev reaffirmed for the Soviet Union decades later, that essential parity existed once both sides had survivable retaliatory forces sufficient to inflict unacceptable damage on the other. It also seemed clear that this essential parity would be maintained during the post–Cold War period, throughout the various phases of mutual arms reductions (START I and START II). To show this, I have performed simulations of U.S. and Russian/Commonwealth of Independent States forces at three levels: (1) the forces as they actually stood in April 1994; (2) deployments of both sides consistent with the START I agreement of 1991; and (3) deployments of both sides consistent with the START II agreement of 1993. The results are summarized in Table 7.

A Security Partnership

The collapse of the Soviet Union and the reappearance of a Russia declared friendly to the West changed the context for U.S. and allied nuclear strategymaking. The immediate challenges for U.S. policy were (1) to es-

Table 7. Stability in Three Simulated Nuclear Force Exchanges

	April 1994	START I	START II
Total Russian/CIS deliverable wh	1,654	1,306	1,159
Total Russian/CIS deliverable emt	839	576	477
Deliverable Russian/CIS reserve wh	673	541	504
Deliverable Russian/CIS reserve emt	324	227	188
% Deliverable Russian/CIS reserve wh	.4068	.4138	.4349
% Deliverable Russian/CIS reserve emt	.3862	.3946	.3949
Total U.S. deliverable wh	2,316	1,457	1,263
Total U.S. deliverable emt	1,030	652	435
Deliverable U.S. reserve wh	770	667	605
Deliverable U.S. reserve emt	289	290	193
% Deliverable U.S. reserve wh	.3322	.4579	.4792
% Deliverable U.S. reserve emt	.2807	.4441	.4443
Correlation of deliverable wh (U.S. to Russian/CIS)	1.40	1.11	1.08
Correlation of deliverable emt	1.22	1.13	0.91
Correlation of reserve wh	1.14	1.23	1.20
Correlation of reserve emt	0.89	1.27	1.02

NOTE: Simulations use a model developed by James J. Tritten, formerly Associate Professor, U.S. Naval Postgraduate School, Monterey, Calif. Dr. Tritten is not responsible for the application here; data on the precise force characteristics available from Stephen J. Cimbala. CIS = Commonwealth of Independent States; wh = warheads; emt = equivalent megatonnage.

tablish a new security partnership with Russia, (2) to integrate Russia and the former Soviet republics into a Pan-European or larger security community, and (3) to disarm the former Soviet nuclear arsenal according to the START I and START II agreements signed in 1991 and 1993. START I had been negotiated prior to the collapse of the Soviet Union, and Russia had assumed the role of stand-in for former Soviet obligations. However, the breakup of the Soviet Union left strategic nuclear weapons in three non-Russian republics as well as in Russia. The weapons of Belarus, Kazakhstan, and Ukraine had somehow to be included in the START regime.

Under the Lisbon protocol to START I, it was assumed that Belarus, Kazakhstan, and Ukraine would assign to Russia or destroy their nuclear weapons. Ukraine, feeling nationalistic and distrustful of the intentions of Boris Yeltsin's Russia, balked at removal of its strategic nuclear weapons even after its tactical nuclear weapons had been returned to Russia. In 1992 and 1993, Ukrainians and Russians also argued about the status of the Black Sea Fleet, divided for a time between the two states. This raised the additional and nuclear-related issue of what to do with nuclear-capable launchers or warheads assigned to the fleet. Finally it was agreed that the fleet would revert to Russia in its entirety, in return for Russian guarantees of economic aid and other concessions to Ukraine.

The presidents of the United States, Russia, and Ukraine met in Moscow on January 14, 1994, and issued a "Trilateral Statement" reflecting various points of agreement.[3] Ukrainian President Leonid Kravchuk reaffirmed his state's commitment to adhere to the Nuclear Nonproliferation Treaty (NPT) as a nonnuclear country in the shortest possible time. Presidents Clinton and Yeltsin recognized that Ukraine, Belarus, and Kazakhstan would receive "fair and timely compensation" for the value of highly enriched uranium in their nuclear warheads as those warheads were sent to Russia for dismantling. Clinton and Yeltsin informed the Ukrainian president that they were prepared to provide security guarantees to Ukraine once the START I Treaty entered into force and Ukraine became a party to the NPT as a nonnuclear weapons state. The United States and Russia reaffirmed their commitment not to use nuclear weapons against any such state, "except in the case of an attack on themselves, their territories or dependent territories, their armed forces, or their allies" by such a state in alliance or association with a nuclear power.[4]

Other guarantees given to Ukraine at the January 1994 summit included commitments (1) to respect the sovereignty and existing borders of OSCE

---

3. For the text, see *Arms Control Today*, no. 1 (January/February 1994): 21.
4. Ibid.

member states (Organization on Security and Cooperation in Europe, expanded from its Cold War membership of thirty-five bloc and nonaligned states to more than fifty); (2) to refrain from the threat or use of force against the territorial integrity or political independence of any state; and (3) to forgo the use of weapons except in self-defense or otherwise in accord with the U.N. Charter. Presidents Yeltsin and Clinton also agreed to support Ukrainian requests for Security Council assistance if a denuclearized Ukraine were to become the victim of an attack or threat in which nuclear weapons were used. President Clinton underscored U.S. willingness to provide financial and technical assistance for the safe dismantling of nuclear forces and the storage of fissile materials. Under the Nunn–Lugar program, the United States had already agreed to provide Russia, Belarus, Kazakhstan, and Ukraine with about $800 million of such financial and technical assistance. Ukraine would receive a minimum of $175 million of these funds.[5] The full implementation of SALT II would leave the United States and Russia with 3,000 or so strategic nuclear weapons on each side. The arithmetic would allow for some revamping and modernization of the two states' forces, and the political relationship between Moscow and Washington had evolved by 1994 to the point at which detargeting of each side's missiles against the territory of the other had been agreed to. The detargeting agreement was symbolic of the larger issue of the relevancy of Cold War planning approaches to the post–Cold War relationship between the United States and Russia. U.S. defense strategy under Presidents Bush and Clinton recognized that regional conventional wars, not global wars inevitably involving nuclear weapons, were the drivers of Pentagon force and contingency planning. A detoxified U.S.-Russian political relationship opened the door to reductions even below the levels of SALT II and toward truly "minimum deterrent" levels. For minimum deterrence to appeal either to Russia's or America's war planners, however, the arsenals of Britain, France, and China would have to be constrained. It would also follow that some agreed-upon deployments of limited BMD against rogue or accidental attacks would be proposed for negotiation among the major nuclear powers.

Whether strategic nuclear "deterrence" was the appropriate way even to consider the future military relationship between the United States and Russia was debatable. Military partnership appealed on a variety of is-

5. Some argue that preserving a Ukrainian nuclear deterrent (one over which Ukrainian armed forces have both physical custody and operational control) could be stabilizing rather than destabilizing. See William C. Martel and William T. Pendley, *Nuclear Coexistence: Rethinking U.S. Policy to Promote Stability in an Era of Proliferation,* Studies in National Security no. 1 (Maxwell AFB, Ala.: Air War College, April 1994), 49–66, esp. 60.

sues, including space exploration, nonproliferation, transparency of military deployments and exercises in Europe, and U.N. peacekeeping missions supported by both. The U.S. Single Integrated Operational Plan for nuclear war seemed anachronistic by the time President Clinton assumed office. Based on elaborate and precise calculations about the timing and character of attacks on the Soviet Union, the SIOP was a nuclear version of the Schlieffen Plan. It included strikes against Soviet nuclear and conventional forces, command-and-control systems, and economic infrastructure contributory to war recovery. As the U.S. Cold War arsenal of strategic nuclear weapons grew, targets were added to the National Strategic Target List (NSTL) and incorporated into the SIOP master nuclear war plan. The SIOP was constructed so that, under any conditions of surprise attack against U.S. forces, a coordinated and massive response would destroy the sinews of Soviet military and economic power.

In the context of a cooperative U.S.-Russian security relationship, the entire concept of a SIOP will almost certainly be rethought. Instead of a single war plan emphasizing massive response, the United States will in all likelihood move toward a cafeteria of nuclear options and toward emphasis on a more delayed and selective response. Of particular importance is that a nonthreatening relationship with Russia allows the United States to disinvest in forces poised for immediate retaliation on a "hair trigger" (so-called prompt launch). U.S. force structure in the 1990s and in the next century should shift away from systems that depend upon prompt launch for survival or for the fulfillment of strike plans. Instead, sea-launched ballistic and cruise missiles and air-delivered weapons should receive the most emphasis in U.S. strategic modernization.

Deciding on force postures or weaponry mixes in a less threatening environment will require that U.S. leaders make fundamental choices among policies. Policy decisions postponed by Cold War drift must now be confronted. David W. Tarr has summarized the five kinds of "regimes," or rules and procedures that define the limits of acceptable behavior, for the nuclear weapons policies of nuclear states.[6] These regimes have specific attributes that can be compared: each has a preferred power ratio, a core strategy, representative offensive and defensive force levels, and implications for extended deterrence and arms control. These options are summarized in Table 8.

The second regime, superiority, was excluded by U.S.-Soviet political agreement even before the end of the Cold War. Besides, the destructiveness of even small numbers of nuclear weapons makes superiority a will-

6. David W. Tarr, *Nuclear Deterrence and International Security: Alternative Nuclear Regimes* (London: Longman, 1991), 5.

Table 8. Alternative Nuclear Regimes by Attributes

	First Regime (Parity)	Second Regime (Superiority)	Third Regime (Minimum Deterrence)	Fourth Regime (Nuclear Disarmament)	Fifth Regime (Defense Dominance)
Power ratio[a]	Equal	Superior/inferior	Equal	Equal	Equal
Core strategy	MAD	Defensive deterrence	Minimum deterrence	Conventional deterrence[b]	Defense dominance
Force level[c]					
Offense	High	High	Low	Zero	Low
Defense	Low	High	Zero	Marginal	High
Extended deterrence	Secure	Credible	Untenable	Untenable	Uncertain
Arms control	Moderate	Weak	Strong	Dominant	Strong
Transition from first regime		Unstable	Stable	Unstable	Unstable

SOURCE: David W. Tarr, *Nuclear Deterrence and International Security: Alternative Nuclear Regimes* (London: Longman, 1991), 199.

[a]Balance between U.S. and Russian forces.
[b]David Tarr uses the term "weaponless deterrence," but I prefer "conventional."
[c]Nuclear arms only.

o'-the-wisp unless Russia undergoes total political and military collapse. Minimum deterrence, nuclear disarmament, and defense dominance all assume strong to dominant international arms control, including stringent controls against nuclear technology and missile proliferation.

Continuing Controversy

Nonproliferation or Counterproliferation?

Should U.S. policy emphasize the prevention of nuclear weapons spread, as emphasized in the Nuclear Nonproliferation Treaty, or the neutralization of states' nuclear capabilities after they have been acquired or deployed? The question is timely. Experts now anticipate that the number of states aspiring to obtain or actually obtaining nuclear weapons or other weapons of mass destruction (including chemical and biological weapons) is sufficient to destabilize the international order in the aftermath of the Cold War. As crucial as the prevention of nuclear proliferation is, the effort may be futile. Even in the comparatively constrained nuclear competition of the Cold War, arms control had (at best) a mixed record of success.[7]

The Clinton administration, amid some controversy, announced that *counterproliferation* would become part of its policy to prevent the threat or use of nuclear weapons by hostile powers against American or allied interests.[8] Clinton Pentagon documents now use the locution "non/counterproliferation" to refer to the spectrum of activities that might be undertaken before, during, or after states have acquired nuclear weapons under conditions judged to be adverse to U.S. interests. U.S. Assistant Secretary of Defense for Nuclear Security and Counterproliferation Ashton B. Carter reportedly favored measures to deal with proliferation after it had occurred instead of export control and diplomatic suasion to prevent proliferation. During a briefing for congressional aides in September 1993, the assistant secretary was said to have proposed giving U.S. technology for the prevention of accidental or unauthorized nuclear release (e.g., electronic locks, or permissive-action links, making warheads inoperable without special codes) to aspiring nuclear powers. Some nonproliferation experts were thus wary of the appointment of William Perry as secretary of defense in 1994. Perry admittedly had doubts about the efficacy of efforts to control the export of so-called dual-use technologies from industrialized nations to Third World and other nuclear aspirants. A Pentagon arms control specialist is quoted by one critic of Clinton's proliferation policy to the effect that "we are now trying to figure out how to bomb the things the United States is now exporting."[9]

Saddam Hussein's progress toward the development of an Iraqi nuclear arsenal, assisted by export of "dual use" technology from the industrialized West, is cited by critics of the Clinton proliferation policy. On the other hand, this example could also support the case for counterproliferation. The debate between Clinton and his critics is about "necessary" versus "sufficient" conditions for making a world of potentially ten to fifteen nuclear-armed states avoidable or, if not avoidable, safer. Few would disagree that export controls and other measures of nuclear prevention are desirable: they have a proven track record. The issue is

7. Colin S. Gray offers the skeptical appraisal that the pursuit of peace with security through arms control "may be likened to the toil of a medieval alchemist seeking to transmute base metal into gold." Gray, *House of Cards: Why Arms Control Must Fail* (Ithaca, N.Y.: Cornell University Press, 1992), 4.

8. Office of the Deputy Secretary of Defense, *Report on Nonproliferation and Counterproliferation Activities and Programs* (Washington, D.C.: DOD, May 1994).

9. Gary Milhollin, "The Perils of Perry and Co.," *Washington Post,* February 6, 1994.

whether prevention is both necessary *and* sufficient to control the dangers associated with the spread of nuclear weapons. A sufficient policy might reasonably embrace, *in addition to measures of prevention,* measures of moderation once prevention has failed. Harvard University political scientist Steven E. Miller categorizes the kinds of assistance that the United States or others might provide to new nuclear states in order to enhance safety (preventing accidents), security (preventing unauthorized use), and stability (minimizing nuclear vulnerability).[10]

No one doubts, for example, that India has the capability to manufacture nuclear weapons, and India has already deployed ballistic missiles capable of carrying conventional or other warheads several thousands of kilometers. India's archrival in South Asia, Pakistan, is allegedly working toward a nuclear weapons capability. Saudi Arabia has acquired long-range ballistic missiles from China (CSS-2s). Israel has ballistic missiles and an unacknowledged nuclear capability. Iran seeks a nuclear weapons capability, as does Libya. The number of countries which by the year 2000 will have nuclear weapons or ballistic missiles, or both, is sufficient to raise legitimate concern over whether "prevention only" will suffice for international security (see Chapter 9 below).

Before critics disparage the transfer of nuclear-safety technology from the United States to other countries, they should consider the effect of such sharing that occurred during the Cold War between the two nuclear superpowers. The Soviet Union adopted U.S. nuclear-safety and crisis management ideas and procedures, to the benefit of both sides. Two of the most notable were the use of Soviet versions of permissive-action links (PALs) and the U.S.-Soviet Direct Communications Link, or "hot line," established in the aftermath of the Cuban missile crisis. The Soviet use of PALs contributed to Moscow's ability to prevent accidental or inadvertent nuclear war and to U.S. confidence in the security of the Soviet deterrent against unexpected political developments within the Soviet Union. These electronic locks and other procedural controls over unauthorized or accidental nuclear use were especially important during the abortive coup in Moscow during August 1991. An aspiring junta of communist retrogrades and opportunists attempted to depose President Gorbachev and to install a reactionary cabal in the Kremlin. Senior military leaders in the former Soviet armed forces chose not to go along. An illegitimate seizure of power was thus averted, but the appearance of a "near miss" hastened the downfall of the Soviet Union in December of that year.

---

10. Steven E. Miller, "Assistance to Newly Proliferating Nations," ch. 5 in Robert D. Blackwill and Albert Carnesale, eds., *New Nuclear Nations: Consequences for U.S. Policy* (New York: Council on Foreign Relations, 1993), 97–134, esp. 115–19.

It was of prime importance that the United States and its NATO allies had confidence during the coup attempt that some 30,000 Soviet nuclear weapons, including 11,000 or so strategic nuclear charges, were under firm political and military control against usurpers. This confidence in NATO capitals was a result of discussions between Soviet and Western military representatives over the years which yielded an understanding by Western experts of Soviet security controls over their nuclear arsenal. Had it been otherwise, and had Washington in particular been uncertain about whether "General Tolstoy" or "Private Dostoevsky" could fire a missile on his own, U.S. nuclear alerts might have been both necessary and unsuitably provocative of Soviet alerts.

The "hot line" is a related but distinct kind of reassurance against nuclear usurpation. Whereas PALs and other mechanical or procedural controls help to prevent accidental or unauthorized nuclear release, the hot line between Washington and Moscow is a crisis management tool. U.S. and Soviet heads of state discovered, during the Cuban missile crisis of 1962, that their ability to communicate rapidly, with high fidelity, and directly was inadequate. Originally established as a teletype link between Washington and Moscow, the hot line is now a primary satellite connection with other backups. It is designed for direct communication between heads of state, allowing person-to-person contact unfiltered by the diplomatic or military bureaucracies of either side.

In addition to the Washington–Moscow hot line, the United States and Russia have pursued the possibility of direct communications between their military establishments. The purpose of such communications would not be policymaking in times of crisis, but the ability to send verifiable information about troop movements, alerts or alert stand-downs, and other military indicators which intelligence services use to estimate friendly or hostile intent. The Reagan administration began to explore the possibility of direct U.S.-Soviet military links between the two states' national command authorities, and discussions continued under Bush and Clinton. The Russian concept was at some variance with the American notion. The latter version was to have Russians serving in the U.S. command center (hosted by Americans) and Americans serving in the Russian center (hosted by Russians). The Russians preferred to keep personnel in their own country but approved of plans to send messages between the high commands.

Direct military links between superpower high commands would also be useful for monitoring global events, including rogue launches of missiles and other unexpected events of mutual concern. A presumably positive U.S.-Russian political relationship would favor joint, space-based surveillance connected to the direct-military-link facilities: namely, some version of NORAD (North American Aerospace Defense Command) for combined warning and space tracking. Not all direct military-to-military connections need be high-speed or dedicated to emergency response, however. Ongoing capabilities to transmit pictures and data related to problems of interest to both the United States and Russia, such as nuclear and missile proliferation, would be sensible components of any direct military-to-military connection.

The preceding prognosis is a hopeful one which assumes Russia's own ability to get its nuclear house in order, including the dismantling of nuclear warheads acquired from former Soviet republics as well as of those no longer considered necessary for the future Russian arsenal. Thus, the control of intra-Soviet technology diffusion or nuclear materials diversion is related to Russia's ability to assume a leading role in nonproliferation, or counterproliferation, agendas. The Soviet Union's performance on this issue during the Cold War was judged by most U.S. experts to be first-rate. The Soviets were perhaps even less likely than some U.S. NATO allies to export "dual use" technologies or nuclear materials to aspiring nuclear states, such as Israel or Iraq.

Russia's post–Cold War government is in theory willing to be as supportive of nonproliferation as was the Soviet regime, but in practice Russia faces a different incentive structure. Post-Soviet Russia is required to destroy nuclear weapons according to arms control treaties and to demilitarize its economic and industrial base in order to free resources for investment and private-sector growth.[11] The United States has indicated that it is willing to help Russia's transition toward disarmament and democracy, but the decision rests ultimately within the politically active circles of Russia itself. Russia's present situation is a confused mixture of authoritarianism, pluralism, and anarchy.[12] As for U.S. assistance, the Congress has authorized financial support for Russia's demilitarization and denuclearization, under the Cooperative Threat Reduction (CTR) program cosponsored by Senators Sam Nunn (D–Ga.) and Richard Lugar (R–Ind.). Congress authorized the program in 1991 from Defense Department funds in order to help the states of the former Soviet Union: (1) destroy weapons of mass destruction, including chemical and biological weapons; (2) provide for safe and secure storage and transportation of such weap-

---

11. Russia's current dilemmas are well covered in Daniel Yergin and Thane Gustafson, *Russia 2010: And What It Means for the World* (New York: Random House, 1993).

12. Zbigniew Brzezinski, "NATO and Russia," ch. 7 in Stephen A. Cambone, ed., *NATO's Role in European Stability* (Washington, D.C.: Center for Strategic and International Studies; Brussels: North Atlantic Treaty Organization, 1995), 44–50.

ons pursuant to their ultimate destruction; and (3) reduce the proliferation risk of weapons of mass destruction.[13] Congress later added assistance for defense conversion in the former Soviet Union as another objective of the program. By June 1995, the Defense Department had initiated some thirty-eight projects to implement agreements with Russia, Belarus, Kazakhstan, and Ukraine. Funding for the CTR program through May 1995 is summarized in Table 9.

U.S. funding support was directly and indirectly useful for the denuclearization of Russia and Ukraine, for example. Russia had eliminated more than 400 strategic missile launchers by July 1994 even though CTR dismantlement-assistance deliveries to Russia did not begin until September of that year.[14] Russia's willingness to proceed even prior to receiving assistance reflected the encouragement given by the promise of U.S. aid. Ukraine was an even more critical case: without external assistance, destruction and dismantlement of nuclear weapons delivery systems there could not proceed. CTR aid played a critical role in allowing Ukraine to move toward completion of its START I compliance objectives. As of January 1995, all 46 of the MIRVed SS-24 ICBMs deployed in Ukraine had their warheads removed (10 per launcher), and 40 SS-19 MIRVed ICBMs had been removed from their silos. Ukraine stated that, as of April 1995, 40 percent of its strategic nuclear warheads (700 or so) had been returned to Russia. (All nuclear weapons, according to agreements signed by Ukraine with Russia and the United States, were to be removed from Ukrainian territory by mid-1966).[15]

There was less good news, although some, with regard to the problems of control over nuclear weapons and materials. Russia does not have adequate safe-and-secure storage for the components of the thousands of nuclear weapons scheduled for relocation or destruction. U.S. CTR funds, however, will help to build improved storage facilities. The news is less good with regard to Russia's ability to protect and account for civilian nuclear materials that carry a high risk of proliferation. The United States has sought to improve Russia's accounting for direct-use material (enriched uranium and plutonium) and is working on a long-run program to improve controls at eighty to a hundred civilian, naval nuclear, and nuclear-weapons-related facilities.[16] Unfortunately, within the former Soviet

13. U.S. General Accounting Office, *Weapons of Mass Destruction. Reducing the Threat from the Former Soviet Union: An Update,* GAO/NSIAD-95–165 (Washington, D.C.: GAO, June 1995). The report appendixes include a good deal of back-and-forth between GAO and DOD on the extent to which CTR assistance has, or has not, succeeded to date.
14. Ibid., app. 2, p. 13.
15. Ibid., app. 2, p. 14.
16. Ibid., app. 3, p. 23.

Table 9. Funding for Cooperative Threat Reduction, 1992–1995
(Millions of Dollars)

Projects	Notifications to Congress	Obligations	Disbursement
Destruction and dismantlement			
Chemical weapons and lab, Russia	55.000	22.182	7.336
Communications link			
Belarus	2.300	.974	.457
Kazakhstan	2.300	.614	.134
Ukraine	2.400	.650	.131
Environmental restoration: Project Peace	25.000	14.772	1.831
Nuclear infrastructure elimination			
Belarus	5.000	0	0
Kazakhstan	17.000	0	0
Ukraine	10.000	0	0
Strategic offensive arms limitation			
Belarus	6.000	0	0
Kazakhstan	70.000	.324	.049
Russia	150.000	112.083	19.639
Ukraine	205.000	89.536	19.279
SUBTOTAL	550.000	241.135	48.856
Chain of custody/nonproliferation			
Armored blankets, Russia	5.000	3.244	2.905
Emergency response			
Belarus	5.000	4.288	3.604
Kazakhstan	5.000	2.045	.302
Russia	15.000	12.857	11.182
Ukraine	5.000	2.002	.179
Export controls			
Belarus	16.260	3.073	1.237
Kazakhstan	2.260	1.117	.137
Russia	2.260	.044	.011
Ukraine	7.260	3.337	.254
Fissile material containers, Russia	50.000	44.944	10.086
Material control and accountability			
Kazakhstan	5.000	4.923	.364
Russia	45.000	20.333	.568
Ukraine	12.500	11.504	.129
Nuclear reactor safety, Ukraine	11.000	11.000	.046
Railcar safety upgrades, Russia	21.500	21.500	17.649
Storage facility design	15.000	15.000	12.886
Storage facility equipment	75.000	27.356	2.511

Table 9. *Continued*

Projects	Notifications to Congress	Obligations	Disbursement
Weapons security, Russia	20.000	0	0
SUBTOTAL	318.040	188.567	64.030
Demilitarization			
Defense conversion/industrial partnerships			
Belarus	20.000	19.607	8.098
Kazakhstan	15.000	14.860	.105
Russia	40.000	17.218	3.681
Ukraine	50.000	38.286	4.280
Defense enterprise fund	27.670	7.670	7.670
Research and development foundation, Russia	10.000	0	0
Science and technology center			
Belarus	5.000	0	0
Kazakhstan	6.000	0	0
Russia	35.000	22.853	20.889
Ukraine	15.000	.414	.307
SUBTOTAL	223.670	120.908	45.030
Other programs and support			
Arctic nuclear waste, Russia	30.000	19.520	5.270
Military-to-military contacts			
Belarus	7.524	.301	.098
Kazakhstan	.900	.074	.014
Russia	11.548	7.761	3.844
Ukraine	5.900	.869	.321
Other assessment costs	24.400	19.720	9.221
SUBTOTAL	80.272	48.245	18.768
TOTAL	1,171.982	598.855	176.684

SOURCE: U.S. General Accounting Office, *Weapons of Mass Destruction. Reducing the Threat from the Former Soviet Union: An Update*, GAO/NSIAD-95-165 (Washington, D.C.: GAO, June 1995), 34–35.

Union are hundreds of tons of highly enriched uranium or plutonium that invites illegal diversion by thieves, terrorists, and others. Russian facilities as of June 1995 lacked modern physical-protection systems and automated tracking systems for prompt identification of losses. The U.S. Department of Energy has signed a letter of intent to cooperate with Russia's nuclear regulatory agency (GAN) in order to implement a national material-control and accounting system. However, Russia's atomic energy ministry, MINATOM, has in the past resisted expansion of GAN's role.[17]

17. Ibid., app. 3, p. 24.

Even if advocates of nonproliferation can be persuaded to accommo-date some modicum of assistance to potential nuclear proliferators on grounds of safety, security, and stability, differences remain among poli-cymakers and scholars on the issue of what sort of military threats or responses can be used against recalcitrant proliferators? The "Continuing Controversy" section of Chapter 9 takes up this specific question.

6

INTELLIGENCE and FOREIGN POLICY

COLD WAR AND HOT PEACE

Well before the end of the Cold War, it was clear that the politically effective use of force had shifted to those wars which fell well below the threshold of large-scale, interstate conventional war, and even further from the almost inconceivable destruction of nuclear war. Armies used on behalf of policy would now have to grapple with less conventional, and therefore less menu-driven, agendas. Among these was the need for continuing peacetime intelligence about an ever more complicated mosaic of state and nonstate actors. For example, U.S. armed forces suddenly tasked to invade Grenada in October 1983 found themselves without accurate maps or knowledge of where American medical students were housed on that island.

The end of the Cold War was not the end of intelligence wars. Intelligence is frequently referred to as the "second oldest profession" for good reason. States have sought to obtain intelligence about enemies and friends since antiquity. The roads of ancient Rome were constructed with the needs of military intelligence in mind. The Byzantine Empire was justifiably famous for the depth of its intelligence practice, and Machiavelli's writings testify to the importance of intelligence in Renaissance Florentine diplomacy. The American Revolution would have been hard put to succeed without various kinds of military and political intelligence about British intentions and capabilities. Napoléon was famous for his insatiable appetite for information about all things pertinent to opposing forces, including the personalities of their rulers and the tempers of their citizenry. The great Chinese philosopher of war, Sun Tzu, emphasized the significance of intelligence for the conduct of war; Clausewitz, a Prussian philosopher of equal renown, regarded most of the operational intelligence of his day as unreliable, transient, and false.[1]

The significance of intelligence for security, in short, has received a great deal of historical documentation. Despite this, the management of intelligence policy and the conduct of political and military intelligence activities continue to generate great controversy, and nowhere is intelligence more controversial than in the United States. The Second World War imposed upon the United States a need to rethink its entire approach to intelligence, especially with respect to espionage. The British tradition of tradecraft carried over into the founding of the U.S. Office of Strategic Services (OSS) by General William ("Wild Bill") Donovan, an admirer of the British way of intelligence practice. Although much of Donovan's wartime empire was dismantled and scattered among other agencies at war's end, the idea that a permanently attentive peacetime intelligence apparatus was part of the U.S. national security tool kit could no longer be denied.

CIA and U.S. Strategic Culture

The U.S. CIA, a creature of the National Security Act of 1947, was a product of American strategic culture as much as it was the inheritor of the OSS tradition. From the very beginning, the CIA was assumed to operate under a degree of administrative oversight that was atypical even for other democratic intelligence services. However, only the executive branch chose to exercise its oversight options, and even these were employed sparingly for the first several decades. The result was the development of a separatist mentality in the clandestine services, supported by a "can do" spirit and a sense of Cold War competitiveness with Soviet intelligence.

The National Security Act opened the door for assignment to the CIA of responsibilities other than intelligence collection and analysis. Covert action, including paramilitary covert actions, gravitated toward the CIA dur-

---

1. Sun Tzu, *The Art of War,* trans. and commentary Samuel B. Griffith (New York: Oxford University Press, 1971), and Carl von Clausewitz, *On War,* ed. and trans. Michael Howard and Peter Paret (Princeton, N.J.: Princeton University Press, 1976), esp. 198–203. For comparison of the two strategists on this and other points, see Michael I. Handel, *Sun Tzu and Clausewitz Compared* (Carlisle Barracks, Pa.: Strategic Studies Institute, U.S. Army War College, Spring 1991), and Michael I. Handel, "Intelligence in Historical Perspective," ch. 9 in Keith Neilson and B.J.C. McKercher, eds., *Go Spy the Land: Military Intelligence in History* (New York: Praeger Publishers, 1992), 179–92.

ing the Eisenhower administration. Allen Dulles, Eisenhower's CIA director, operated with a great deal of autonomy and drew additional support from his brother, Secretary of State John Foster Dulles. Allen Dulles, a legendary World War II OSS operative from Switzerland, moved into territory that the U.S. armed forces regarded as too politically problematic. There was a perceived need to support friendly governments and to overthrow unfriendly ones, and the U.S. military was inclined neither by training nor by temperament to do so.

CIA successes in Operation Ajax, against Iran in 1953, and in Operation PB Success, against Guatemala in 1954, created an aura of invincibility about CIA covert action which passed from Eisenhower to the Kennedy administration. Kennedy inherited from Eisenhower a plan for the invasion of Cuba that was to become infamous as the Bay of Pigs disaster in 1961. Persuading itself that Cuba was a "soft target," the CIA persuaded others. Kennedy had set the stage by dismantling the interagency oversight upon which Eisenhower had relied to review proposed CIA covert actions. The aftermath of Bay of Pigs left the CIA with a tarnished image and a greater unwillingness to take on paramilitary covert action in lieu of the Department of Defense.

Covert action was never the main function of U.S. or other modern intelligence agencies, in any case. Collection of information and the analysis (or "analysis and estimation") of that information was the principal responsibility of foreign intelligence services. It was up to policymakers to decide how to use that information, within the context of foreign and national security objectives. On the other hand, the line between policy and administration was frequently difficult to draw in intelligence work. Policymakers often asked for the details and the raw data in order to form their own judgments about events. And CIA estimates were sometimes politically charged, carrying weight for or against the views of presidents, defense secretaries, and other principals in the policy debate.

Two illustrations of the politically charged character of CIA estimates are provided by the Johnson administration's debates over Vietnam and the Nixon administration's efforts to reach strategic arms control agreements with the Soviet Union. During the Vietnam escalation, CIA estimates were consistently more pessimistic about the likelihood of U.S. and South Vietnamese military success than were those of the Pentagon. Intense interagency disputes arose, for example, over the North Vietnamese–Viet Cong "order of battle," with CIA estimates significantly larger than those of the Pentagon on account of CIA decisions to include many irregular forces. CIA Director Richard Helms eventually capitulated to the Pentagon on this issue despite the misgivings of his analysts, who were subsequently proved correct.

The Nixon administration in its preparations for SALT I, concluded in 1972, was concerned about Soviet potential to deploy MIRVs (multiple, independently-targeted reentry vehicles) on their large SS-9 ICBMs. Secretary of Defense Melvin R. Laird contended that the Soviets were planning to MIRV the SS-9 and that they were undoubtedly going for a first-strike capability against the U.S. land-based missile force. The CIA doubted that the Soviets had a MIRV capability and identified the SS-9 warhead as an MRV (a multiple reentry vehicle without the capability to direct individual warheads at separate targets). Again the CIA was right on the scientific merits but incorrect politically and therefore forced to compromise with the insistent Laird (who was also supported on this issue by National Security Adviser Henry A. Kissinger).

These examples of order of battle and MIRV have to do with "point" estimation as opposed to the more contextual "what if" questions often posed to intelligence by political leaders. In 1976, CIA Director George Bush agreed to set up a "Team B" counteranalysis to the prevailing CIA estimates on the Soviet military buildup. Team B was stacked with luminaries from the Committee on the Present Danger and others suspicious in principle of Soviet intentions. The areas of disagreement between CIA mainstream analysts and Team B had more to do with estimates of future *intentions* than with past Soviet accomplishments in strategic modernization. A government's intentions are notoriously difficult to fathom, for different reasons in democracies compared with authoritarian systems. In democracies, political pluralism may mean that there is no consensual "government mind" to tap, or elections may throw out of office the existing government and substitute one of uncertain convictions. In totalitarian or authoritarian systems, the government mind may reduce itself to the temporary, and unsteady, whims of the dominant party leadership or dictator. Stalin's mind was a difficult predictive variable in the best of times, and Hitler's volatility is equally well documented.

With respect to war, policymakers want to know from their military and intelligence bureaucracies one thing: "Can we win at an acceptable cost?" The answer is not always apparent prior to the actual engagement of combat forces. In Vietnam, the United States found that it was unable to create a viable polity in South Vietnam or to sustain U.S. public support for military escalation despite what was arguably an adaptive performance by many field forces. Former Defense Secretary Robert McNamara now says that he and other advisers to Presidents Kennedy and Johnson misjudged the international system by assuming that U.S. credibility would suffer a drastic decline if America capped its Vietnam commitment. McNamara now argues that with a more realistic perception of relations between China and Vietnam, on one side, and China and the Soviet Union, on the other, the United States could have withdrawn from Vietnam as early as 1963–65 without affecting American credibility elsewhere in the world.[2] McNamara's refocused conceptual lenses, shed of the Cold War paradigm assuming unity of views among all states hoisting the communist banner in Asia, enumerates acceptable U.S. exit stations as summarized in Table 10.

Intelligence and Policy

Common sense might suggest that authoritarian systems are better organized to carry out long-range intelligence collection and estimation. Historical evidence from the First World War, however, does not suggest that this is so. The autocracies (tsarist Russia, Austria-Hungary, and Imperial Germany) did not do noticeably better than the democracies (Britain and France) in estimating the capabilities and intentions of their probable opponents.[3] Russia's prewar intelligence on Austria-Hungary was the exceptional case of a high-level penetration of the Austro-Hungarian high command, from which Russia learned a great deal about Austrian military weaknesses. The problem with prewar estimation was not so much in the quantitative or order-of-battle aspect at the outset of war; the much more fundamental issue was the combat potential of the various sides for a longer war.

In their preparations for World War I, the great powers for the most part assumed a short war that would be decided by a climactic battle, as in the termination of the Franco-Prussian War in 1870. This mistaken assumption drove analysis and planning toward the collection of information about rapidly mobilizable forces and logistics that would be ready immediately upon the outbreak of war. Less effort was dedicated to estimation of the military and economic staying power of the various sides. Wishful thinking dictated some classically notorious errors in estimation. Germany's naval planners decided that they could risk unrestricted submarine warfare and the possible enmity of the United States. They *assumed* that unrestricted submarine warfare would knock Britain out of the war before America could come to the rescue. The assumption that Britain would collapse before the United States could become compe-

---

2. Robert S. McNamara with Brian VanDeMark, *In Retrospect: The Tragedy and Lessons of Vietnam* (New York: Random House, 1995), 320.

3. Ernest R. May, "Cabinet, Tsar, Kaiser: Three Approaches to Assessment," ch. 1 in May, ed., *Knowing One's Enemies: Intelligence Assessment before the Two World Wars* (Princeton, N.J.: Princeton University Press, 1986), 11–37.

Table 10. Possible Vietnam Exits without Loss of U.S. Credibility
(McNamara's Reconstruction)

Withdrawal Date	U.S. Force Levels, South Vietnam	U.S. Personnel Killed in Action	Reason for Withdrawal
November 1963	16,300 advisers	78	Lack of political stability and collapse of Ngo Dinh Diem regime
Late 1964 or early 1965	23,300 advisers	225	Clear evidence of inability of SVN to defend itself, despite U.S. training and logistical support
July 1965	81,400 troops	509	Additional evidence that SVN cannot defend itself despite U.S. assistance
December 1965	184,300 troops	1,594	Evidence that U.S. military training and tactics were not suited for the guerrilla war being fought
December 1967	485,600 troops	15,979	CIA reports indicate bombing of North Vietnam will not force NVN to desist; inability to turn back enemy forces in SVN

SOURCE: Robert S. McNamara with Brian VanDeMark, *In Retrospect: The Tragedy and Lessons of Vietnam* (New York: Random House, 1995), 321. Adapted by Stephen J. Cimbala, who is solely responsible for its use here.

NOTE: SVN = South Vietnam; NVN = North Vietnam.

tently mobilized for war was not based on any careful study of U.S. mobilization potential or British staying power. Rather, the basis for the German projection of British collapse was an argument that assumed that a certain quantity of shipping losses would bring about a demoralized, and therefore defeated, Britain.

The Japanese made a similar error in planning their surprise attack against the U.S. naval forces at Pearl Harbor. Japanese war planners knew that a prolonged war against the United States could not turn out to Japan's advantage. Japan's prewar estimates of America's formidable wartime production potential proved, in the event, to be better than those done in the United States. Nonetheless, perception of need created the drive toward opportunity. Slapped with numerous U.S. diplomatic demarches in the spring and summer of 1941, and faced with an American oil embargo which threatened to retract Japan's imperial reach into China and South Asia, Japanese leaders invented a U.S. motivation suitable for their fears. They assumed that a series of lightning victories early in the war would discourage U.S. leaders and persuade Roosevelt to settle for half a loaf in the Pacific, allowing for Japanese and U.S. spheres of interest. The reaction of the American public to any attack on U.S. forces or territory was not considered in framing this assumption of a U.S. willingness to settle for war termination based on partial defeat.

Japanese assumptions might seem absurd, but they were no more insensitive to prevailing conditions than those made by the British leaders who sought to break the World War I stalemate on the western front. The Gallipoli campaign to force the Dardanelles was at first based on the assumption that Turkish resistance would be so weak that naval forces alone could accomplish the mission. British planners assumed that the Turkish government would flee or promptly capitulate as British ships sailed through the straits and neared Constantinople. It was later decided to send ground forces also. Turkish resistance once landings had taken place was expected to be token, so a smallish force of British and dominion troops was employed in the initial assaults. Intelligence about the actual capabilities of Turkish forces was insufficient, and reliable maps of the local terrain were not available to British war planners. Turkish forces, stiffened by the leadership of the German Liman von Sanders, cut down waves of attacking infantry from entrenched defensive positions, and the British operation became a Marne on the Mediterranean until it was terminated in 1916.

The overwhelming evidence from the experience of twentieth-century warfare, despite the many resources devoted by armies and states to intelligence, is that surprise attacks almost always succeed. At least, they almost always succeed in the initial period of a war.[4] Hitler's thrust into the Soviet Union in 1941 and Japan's attack on Pearl Harbor that same year were large tactical successes in the short term. But neither attacker was able to convert tactical victory into strategic victory. Military effectiveness is thus not of a piece: as the performance of German armies in the two world wars of this century shows, tactical excellence can be com-

4. Richard K. Betts, *Surprise Attack* (Washington, D.C.: Brookings Institution, 1982).

bined with strategic imbecility. Germany's World War II insistence in taking on the United States and the Soviet Union at the same time made the
attacker's defeat inevitable. U.S. conventional tactical operations in Vietnam were, according to expert military accounts, proficiently conducted
and rarely opposed by enemy regulars with any success. U.S. strategy did
not provide, however, for a way to win "hearts and minds," or the psychological and social war, in South Vietnam. Nor could the U.S. endow its
South Vietnamese ally with political legitimacy in the midst of insurgency.
Most telling, U.S. strategy could not rally the American home front behind
the war.

Intelligence estimates of the willingness of noncombatants to support
their armed forces have been, in this century at least, embarrassingly
wide of the mark. The point applies not only in insurgencies but in conventional wars. The British World War II bomber command under Sir Arthur Harris anticipated that "dehousing" the civilian working-class population of German cities would cause that country's war effort to grind to a
halt. The argument was based on assumptions about the probable effects
of airborne devastation on civilian morale. German air raids against London partook of the same rationale, though with less enthusiasm. The relationship between physical destruction and collapse of civilian resistance
was simply assumed, not demonstrated, in military estimates. In the case
of Britain's air war against Germany, until the Normandy invasion, air
power was the only way for Britain to strike directly at German territory
and pay back the losses Germany had caused British civilians. Therefore,
what was possible became, in the event, necessarily strategic.

The air power theorists are only one illustration of a widespread twentieth-century phenomenon. Although intelligence frequently mistakes the
military capabilities of armies and the political intentions of governments,
it does even worse when it attempts to fathom the intricacies of unfamiliar societies. U.S. expectations about Japan before World War II were that
Japanese military technology was inferior and that Japanese society
would be unable to provide state-of-the-art weapons for naval and air
warfare. Needless to say, the events of 1941 destroyed this assumption
utterly. Japan's fighter aircraft were the best in the skies during the initial
months of the war. The range of Japan's carrier-based fighter-bombers
was much greater than U.S. planners had anticipated, a partial cause of
the disaster at Pearl Harbor. Nor did American planners anticipate that
Japan would make torpedoes that could ride in the shallow water that
surrounded Pearl Harbor and which was thought to make it invulnerable
to torpedo attack.

Hitler's cultural and racial stereotypes of Slavs drove him toward the
attempted conquest of Russia when he was unable to subdue Britain.

There was no reason to believe that Russia was conquerable by any invader, as Napoléon had learned in 1812. Germany's blitzkrieg tactics were designed for war in a theater of operations very different from that presented by the vastness of Russia. Russia could retreat to the very spires of Moscow while wearing out Hitler's troops in the process. Nor had Hitler reckoned with the fact that he would be waging war against an aroused group of Soviet nations. However much those nations, such as the Ukrainians, hated Moscow's tyranny, they despised equally or more Hitler's treatment as his forces moved through their territory. There were not many things worse than Stalin, but Hitler offered an exception to the rule, and Soviet citizens of diverse nationality suddenly found in Mother Russia a holy cause.

U.S. inability to deal with the fall of the shah of Iran and the ensuing hostage crisis of 1979–80 was in no small way owing to flawed perceptions of Iranian society and of the intrasocietal constellation of Iranian political forces. The political significance of the Islamic clergy had been dismissed as a factor in the maneuvering to oust and then to replace the shah. Ayatollah Khomeini was at first misperceived by Western analysts and political leaders as a moderate with whom normal diplomatic business could be pursued. The fanatical character of the regime became clear only as Revolutionary Guards obtained military cachet and attempted to impose a new political order, based on the Koran, on Iranian society at large.

Intelligence is hampered not only by ignorance about the target state, army, or society, but also by an alerted enemy attempting to deceive. Intelligence and deception are inseparable disciplines. Tactical deception usually accompanies armies, fleets, and air forces into battle. Strategic deception is practiced by heads of state and their intelligence services in order to mislead the enemy about one's own intentions and capabilities. The protection of one's own secrets from exposure is a necessary condition for strategic success, but this is a more complex process than people outside the intelligence world suppose. Putting up fences such as compartmentation, unbreakable codes, and the like around classified information can help to protect sources and methods, but the denial of adversary access to one's vital secrets requires more. It also requires that one spy on oneself, through the adversary's eyes.

Counterintelligence

Our ability to spy on ourselves through enemy eyes is one fact of counterintelligence. Both the FBI and the CIA in the United States have counterintelligence responsibilties. The FBI is responsible for the detection and apprehension of American citizens engaged in treason. The CIA role in counterintelligence comes from its charter to protect its own sources and methods. The CIA and other foreign intelligence organizations, toward this end, are charged with the penetration of other states' intelligence services. We can accomplish this in two ways. The first is to persuade key enemy operatives to defect permanently to the United States, bringing their knowledge with them. The second way, having much greater potential, is to get another state's officials to "defect in place." A defector-in-place is someone who continues to hold an important position in a foreign intelligence organization but who is actually working in behalf of one's own national interests, or vice versa.

The advantage of a defector-in-place is that he or she continues unknown within the other side's camp as a trusted confidante. This arrangement can pay huge dividends. During the 1970s, for example, Günther Guillaume, secretary to former West German Chancellor Willy Brandt, was unmasked as a traitor under the control of East German intelligence. As Brandt's confidential aide, Guillaume was able to provide comprehensive information on the status of NATO war plans against the Warsaw Pact to his East German controllers. They, in turn, passed on this information to the Soviet KGB, or Committee for State Security.

Perhaps the most prominent Soviet military defector-in-place during the Cold War was Soviet Military Intelligence (GRU) Colonel Oleg Penkovskiy. Penkovskiy provided very sensitive information about the status of Soviet missile programs and other strategic data in the early 1960s to his British and American controllers. For example, although the United States could rely upon photographic satellites to take pictures of planned medium-range and intermediate-range missile sites in Cuba, there was uncertainty about some of the performance parameters of these missiles. How long would it take once they were assembled and mated with launchers for them to be fueled and fired? What, if any, was the refire capability using stored missiles? If a Cuban missile crisis erupted into a U.S.-Soviet nuclear exchange, what were the actual capabilities of Soviet ICBMs targeted on U.S. national territory and flying along polar trajectories? Some of the information provided by Penkovskiy about the probable performance characteristics of Soviet strategic forces was probably reassuring to U.S. political leaders attempting to stare down Khrushchev in October 1962.

The most widely publicized high-level penetration of the British Secret Intelligence Service (MI-6) was that accomplished by the "Cambridge spies" during and after the Second World War. The case of Harold ("Kim") Philby is probably the best known. Working his way up the ladder of

British intelligence with a winsome personality, Philby ultimately became responsible for British foreign intelligence activity against the Soviet Union. He had been recruited by the Soviets at Cambridge University in the 1930s along with other, and later almost equally notorious, British spies for the Soviet Union. This circle of ex-Cambridge, Soviet-controlled British spies also included Philby contemporaries Donald Maclean and Anthony Burgess.[5] Maclean probably did more serious damage than Philby. Serving from 1944 to 1948 in Washington, D.C., Maclean became the youngest counselor in the British diplomatic service and had access to the most sensitive political and military information passing between London and Washington, including communications between the U.S. president and the British prime minister.

During the 1960s and 1970s, the CIA and their British cousins were in turmoil about the possibility that their organizations had been penetrated by Soviet "moles," or controlled-agent defectors-in-place. The British handled things with less embarrassing public fanfare, but their concern was just as real as that of the U.S. counterintelligence community. The latter, headed by the legendary James J. Angleton, operated on the working hypothesis that there *must be* one or several high-level penetrations of the CIA by Soviet foreign intelligence. The Angletonian method was to cast doubt on the bona fides of Soviet defectors, from whom the CIA and FBI obtained much of their information about Soviet intelligence, and to suspect any information coming from the USSR until it had been proved exhaustively as to its sources and authenticity. Angleton's pursuit of counterintelligence purity became such a nuisance within the agency that he was sacked by CIA Director William Colby in the 1970s. By then, Angletonianism had demoralized the CIA's Soviet division and broken a number of promising careers.

On the other hand, Angletonian paranoia seemed justified when, in February 1994, it was revealed that Aldrich Ames had spied for the Soviet Union (before the Cold War ended) and for Russia (after the Cold War) while serving in the CIA Soviet counterintelligence division and in other slots. Turning around the other side's counterintelligence as a defector-in-place is the summum bonum of intelligence. By leaving Ames in place to operate as a Soviet agent and with knowledge of the CIA's Soviet sources and methods, Moscow was able for a time to put out of business the entire U.S. spy network in the Soviet Union. Undoubtedly a number of Soviet citizens lost their lives as a result of Ames's unknown treason. The

---

5. Numerous accounts of these activities exist. See, for example, Verne W. Newton, *The Cambridge Spies: The Untold Story of Maclean, Philby, and Burgess in America* (Lanham, Md.: Madison Books, 1991).

Ames case was a reminder that a person need not be a highly ranked intelligence operator or administrator in order to be valuable to enemy intelligence. All that matters is that he or she has consistent access to important information, regardless of his or her rank.

Intelligence after the Cold War

As the above discussion shows, the perennial functions of intelligence must be performed by a state regardless of time and circumstance. These perennials are collection, analysis and estimation, counterintelligence and, more controversially, covert action. The end of the Cold War does not change the basically anarchic character of interstate relations, but it may change the tasking priorities for U.S. and allied intelligence agencies.

The vanished Soviet threat that dominated U.S. Cold War intelligence gathering permitted policymakers to avoid fundamental questions about intelligence priorities. A more unstructured international political system raises unfamiliar issues, some outside the context of traditional military security. These issues, and their implications for intelligence, include the following: the proliferation of weapons of mass destruction; the spread of ballistic and cruise missiles throughout the Third World; economic competitiveness extended into the realm of intelligence, including industrial espionage; and, last but not least, the organization of the intelligence community itself.

The threat posed by the spread of nuclear, biological, and chemical weapons requires that collection priorities be reoriented to the monitoring of activities related to acquisition of such weapons. The same point applies to the global dissemination of ballistic and cruise missiles which could be used to deliver weapons of mass destruction. There are at least two parts to this threat as an intelligence problem. One is to verify that a certain country is attempting to acquire dangerous technologies or facilities. Another is to determine the character of a state's intentions with regard to mass-destruction weapons or long-range missiles.

The CIA has already adapted the machinery used to monitor Soviet nuclear weapons and missile developments during the Cold War to the mission of monitoring weapons spread in the Third World. Photographic, ELINT (electronic intelligence), and other satellites can detect telltale emissions or signatures of suspect activities. Spies on the ground can then investigate for additional details. The procedure can also work in reverse. Spies "in place" can call attention to a suspect facility or pattern of technology imports. Overhead reconnaissance and surveillance can then be tasked to zero in for additional verification. During the months preceding the Cuban missile crisis of 1962, numerous sightings of equipment suspected of being Soviet missile shipments were made by ground observers and reported to Washington contacts. Some of these sightings were erroneous; others were accurate but without the proper context. For example, some observers noted equipment components for Soviet-made surface-to-air missiles. Since SAMs are air-defense and not offensive missiles, these reports were not judged as especially alarming. On October 16, when U.S. photointerpreters saw the SAM complexes in their proper context, deployed for the protection of planned offensive-missile sites, the significance of the original SAM sightings grew in retrospect.

Among the most significant taskings for future U.S. and other Group of Seven intelligence services are the detection of proliferation and the provision of support for counterproliferation missions. The Nuclear Non-Proliferation Treaty and the Missile Technology Control Regime (MTCR) are designed, respectively, to limit the spread of nuclear weapons and advanced missiles. The NPT has been far more successful than MTCR, a collective effort among industrialized countries to restrain technology transfer. One problem with missile proliferation is that short-range tactical ballistic missiles are now widespread throughout Third World militaries. The Soviet Scud-B, made available to Iraq by arms transfers, was given an extended range and a new payload by Iraq and used for attacks on cities during its war against Iran in the 1980s. Countries outside Europe can now manufacture missiles and rockets having tactical range (several hundred kilometers) or greater. Major ballistic missile capabilities are already in the hands of states harboring regional grievances, including India, Iran, Israel, and North and South Korea. Counterproliferation may be highly dependent upon the synergy between intelligence support and special operations, discussed below in Chapter 9.

Continuing Controversy

Should the CIA Engage in Covert Action?

During the Cold War, especially during the 1950s, the U.S. Central Intelligence Agency was often given its head to engage in plausibly deniable covert operations. The bulk of these did not involve military action but consisted of all sorts of undisclosed involvement in the internal politics of foreign countries. These involvements included sponsorship of friendly political parties, support for radio stations and newspapers having pro-U.S.

biases, socializing with important politicians under diplomatic cover, and other activities that the U.S. government preferred not to engage in openly.

Most covert actions during the Cold War were uncontroversial, but the paramilitary actions became the stuff of political upheaval in the 1970s and subsequently. The Watergate investigations spilled over into investigations of the U.S. intelligence community by several congressional committees (the Pike Committee in the House of Representatives, the Church Committee in the Senate). These investigations revealed that the CIA had engaged in assassination plots, coups, and other activities that members of Congress and observers in the news media regarded as inappropriate for intelligence agencies. In addition, the investigations raised the issue of intelligence community accountability to policymakers. Finally, the charge was made that the CIA had violated its original charter by straying into domestic spying on U.S. citizens, a role reserved by statute for the Federal Bureau of Investigation.

We shall pass only momentarily over the first of these three issues: involvement of the CIA in activities which might be judged as intrinsically unprofessional, dishonorable, or inappropriate. The issues of accountability and CIA involvement in domestic spying are related issues of process and are usefully treated together. Having discussed those, we can return to consider the problem of value judgments about the kinds of activities which are appropriate for U.S. intelligence, or for any democratic intelligence service.

A key difference between the intelligence services of democracies and those of authoritarian systems is that the latter are accountable only to the head of state. Stalin's intelligence services served the Soviet dictator first, the state and party second. The same pattern was followed by the Iraqi leader Saddam Hussein in the 1980s, who made certain that trustworthy close relatives occupied positions of the greatest sensitivity. Sometimes, when a ruler's mistaken intuition is substituted for sound intelligence estimation, such a pattern of personally rather than institutionally accountable intelligence services can threaten the state. Thus, Germany invaded the Soviet Union in June 1941 despite Stalin's insistence that Hitler would not invade in that year, an insistence that flew in the face of the many indicators provided to Moscow by Soviet field operatives (and foreign intelligence) that attack was imminent.

Not all foreign-intelligence services in autocracies or totalitarian systems serve only the head of state, but the most important ones receive the leader's careful attention and nurturance for the most basic reason: self-protection. Leaders have approach–avoidance conflicts with their intelligence services as with their militaries when no constitutional order of succession discourages the illegal seizure of power. It follows, therefore, that the separation of domestic from foreign intelligence, characteristic of democratic political systems, does not obtain in authoritarian systems. The Soviet KGB, for example, was the "eyes and ears of the party." It had the largest share of responsibility for gathering nonmilitary intelligence in foreign countries, and it was also responsible for the political surveillance of Soviet citizens and foreign visitors.

Democracies recognize that divided power is important and that this concept works in two directions. First of all, the military, intelligence, and other security organs must be accountable to elected politicians. Second, the military and intelligence community must itself be a divided house. Much of the apparent anarchy and overlapping responsibility found within democratic military and intelligence services results from the recognition that a single, all-powerful General Staff or central intelligence organ is a threat to pluralism. Of course, not all democracies have taken pluralistic competition and bureaucratic politics to the extreme that Americans have, but this extremism in the pursuit of pluralism reflects U.S. political culture.

In Britain, the responsibility for domestic counterintelligence is assigned to MI-5, and that for foreign intelligence to MI-6, the Secret Intelligence Service. This division of labor is followed in many democracies, including those outside Western Europe and North America: Israel's Shin Bet is tasked for domestic security, Mossad for foreign intelligence. In Britain, neither MI-5 nor MI-6 is responsible for routine police work; and the United States also follows this pattern (although, again, with more decentralization across fifty states). Similarly, French Cold War foreign intelligence (SDECE) and domestic counterintelligence were separate functions, although we have less documentation about their activities compared with the English and the American services.

Despite these institutional separations between domestic and foreign intelligence in democracies, the two functions are interdependent and the performance of assigned duties often requires interagency collaboration. This is the case, for example, when a CIA case officer is exposed as a Soviet or Russian defector-in-place, à la Aldrich Ames in 1994. The case against Ames was built by cooperation over a period of years between the CIA and FBI. The FBI retained functional jurisdiction because Ames was a U.S. citizen spying for a foreign government. The CIA was an interested party because it was CIA secrets that Ames was compromising. The FBI, in other words, called the prosecutorial shots, reporting to the U.S. Department of Justice.

Foreign counterintelligence is a mission within the intelligence services, including CIA, with the objective of preventing enemy penetration of our own sources and methods for obtaining intelligence. Foreign counterintelligence thus involves a "wilderness of mirrors" in which counterintelligence officers are by nature inclined to see everything upside down. If the Soviet KGB says that they had nothing to do with Lee Harvey Oswald's assassination of President Kennedy, for example, then suspicious U.S. counterintelligence must wonder whether a real connection is being obscured. The legendary U.S. counterintelligence operative James J. Angleton drove his CIA colleagues crazy during the Cold War by suspecting virtually everyone in the foreign counterintelligence division of spying for Moscow. Angleton would undoubtedly feel vindicated by the Ames case; others would say that his suspicions were analogous to those of the soothsayer who predicted a world war every year of the twentieth century, saying in 1914 and in 1939, "I told you so."

One way to control this wilderness of mirrors is to separate as cleanly as possible the domestic and foreign intelligence-gathering functions. This includes denying to foreign-intelligence gatherers any juridical or police powers on home territory. Thus, in the U.S. case, the CIA may not detain or arrest American citizens nor prosecute them in court. Nor can its larger and more heavily funded cousin, the National Security Agency, which is responsible for communications security and other highly classified missions. The Department of Defense, which has an intelligence arm within each service and an interservice Defense Intelligence Agency, is empowered to discipline its own uniformed personnel but has no power over U.S. civilians (except under conditions of martial law, which must be put into effect by politicians).

When the boundaries between democratically accountable foreign and domestic intelligence break down, then intelligence agencies have every incentive to define for themselves the appropriateness of their missions. The CIA was willing and able in the 1950s and 1960s to overthrow governments and to plot assassinations of Fidel Castro and other leaders. It was not made clear that there was any outside accountability for its day-to-day operations: accountable politicians in the executive and legislative branches were content not to know. It followed that the line between foreign and domestic intelligence activity was vulnerable to erosion. Presidents Johnson and Nixon both wanted the CIA to spy on American citizens who were thought to be influenced by foreign governments to oppose the Vietnam War. The CIA went along with Johnson but sensed in Nixon an even more paranoid temperament, and so demurred. Richard Helms's unwillingness to take the fall for Watergate (by agreeing to tell investigators that it had been a covert CIA national security operation) cost him his job in the Nixon administration and helped to oust Nixon from the White House as Watergate unraveled.

Under J. Edgar Hoover, the FBI became convinced that Martin Luther

King, Jr., and other civil rights leaders were communists with ties to foreign governments. King was wiretapped, and the Southern Christian Leadership Conference was hounded by politically motivated surveillance in the 1960s. Hoover's conviction that many American liberals and radicals were communist dupes gave him immense power within Washington policymaking circles during the Cold War. In effect, he was playing the communist card in order to expand the juridical and political reach of his agency.

Until his death Hoover was politically untouchable. When, for example, President Nixon's White House aides John Ehrlichman and H. R. Haldeman decided that Hoover ought to retire, they wrote out for Nixon a breakfast meeting script in which he praised the FBI director's many years of service and then asked for Hoover's resignation. The day after the meeting between Nixon and Hoover, Ehrlichman called Haldeman to ask how things went. Haldeman's response was, "Don't ask." Not only had Nixon avoided asking Hoover to resign, but he had offered to increase the FBI budget and to resolve a number of administrative issues in Hoover's favor.

Hoover's is an exceptional case within the U.S. experience, but the "exception" covered so much of the Cold War (and may have contributed to its prolongation) that it recalls the relationship between accountable foreign and domestic intelligence. With an FBI operating under its own assumptions about foreign communist-directed left-wing politics, U.S. policy was unaccountably being pulled toward an antidétente foreign policy stance. In addition, Hoover became not only a watchdog against treason but judge and jury of politically correct behavior. When the CIA was induced under President Johnson to maintain files on U.S. citizens who might be connected to a foreign subversive sponsor, the path for this transgression had already been made clearer by Hoover's worldview.

The third issue that created difficulties for the CIA in the 1970s was the charge of engaging in activities that were inappropriate for intelligence, inherently unethical by American standards, or both. These activities included overthrowing governments by sponsoring coups in which foreign leaders were killed or by "hands on" planning of assassination attempts (e.g., against Cuba's Fidel Castro). Congressional investigations also discovered that the CIA had engaged in suspect research into drugs thought to be useful for mind control. These and other revelations covered the front pages of U.S. newspapers with lurid headlines for many months and, in the minds of many intelligence critics, called into question the relationship between U.S. intelligence and democracy.

It turned out on closer examination that the fault lay not only, though perhaps mainly, with the intelligence agencies. Policymakers in the executive and legislative branches had failed to supervise intelligence and to enforce on intelligence personnel those standards of conduct which were acceptable. Presidents winked as the CIA plotted assassinations in the 1950s and 1960s, and Congress did not look into the details of clandestine operations. The Bay of Pigs operation produced some temporary furor, but that was mostly about the failure of Kennedy to authorize a backup full military invasion of Cuba after the original operation failed on the beaches. No one asked fundamental questions about CIA methods and purposes, and the shifting sands of executive-branch supervision (the making and unmaking of intelligence community bodies of "wisemen" and interagency task forces, for example) ensured that the intelligence community would be largely self-directed.

As in the American automobile industry, so too in U.S. intelligence: the workers received the blame and paid the price for the failures of management. Charged by Congress with perjury, Richard Helms pleaded "no contest" in order to bring an end to the proceedings and paid a fine. He had been accused of being evasive about CIA operations in Chile during 1970s, especially about the "Track Two" program to topple Marxist President Salvador Allende Gossens by any means, including if necessary a U.S.-supported coup. The orders had come directly from the Nixon White House. Helms, accustomed to the rules under which Congress had quizzed CIA directors in earlier decades, followed the tradition of telling as little as he had to. He told Congress that there was no CIA program to overthrow the government of Chile by coup or other illegal means. His statement was true of the officially acknowledged "Track One" diplomatic and economic assistance programs, but misleading with regard to the unacknowledged "Track Two" destabilization program.

Helms was not the first CIA director to take the fall for presidential follies in covert operations. The Bay of Pigs cost Allen Dulles and Richard Bissell their CIA jobs. Dulles and Bissell (head of the Directorate of Plans, responsible for clandestine operations) were the two most important CIA figures of the exuberant 1950s. Bissell was the father of the famed U-2 reconnaissance plane and, later, of U.S. satellite reconnaissance programs for CIA. Bissell may have been the smartest person to serve in the U.S. government since Thomas Jefferson. Nevertheless, he and Allen Dulles convinced themselves of (to use Alice in Wonderland's phrase) a thousand impossible things before breakfast about the likelihood of overthrowing Castro by exile invasion. The most improbable assumption was that the entire Cuban people disliked Castro as much as the U.S. government did. It followed that, according to CIA assumptions, the exile landing on the beaches would be followed by a home-grown uprising that would topple Castro and install a U.S.-dominated, "user friendly" government in Havana.

Had such a program worked out, the U.S.-friendly government in Havana would probably have been controlled by organized crime. In the least defensible aspect of CIA Cold War covert operations, the agency enlisted the aid of mobsters in assassination plots and other efforts to topple Castro. These mobsters included some of the leading lights in the U.S. national crime syndicate, several of whom were simultaneously under investigation by the U.S. Department of Justice. As Hoover had influenced foreign policy through the back door of domestic counterintelligence, the CIA had now influenced domestic policy by using the targets of criminal investigations in overseas operations. The adverse byproducts of commingling foreign and domestic policy could not have been worse.

There was a danger, after the revelations about CIA and FBI accountability lapses, that the accomplishments of those and other intelligence agencies would be overlooked or forgotten. U.S. allies were shocked at the hammering administered to the CIA and other security agencies by public investigations which seemed to ridicule the need for any clandestine operations. The 1980s witnessed a decline in the level of congressional and news media hysteria about CIA "rogue elephant" activities. Eventually a balance was struck by congressional legislation which provided for continuing oversight of CIA operations, including requirements to report promptly any presidential desire to undertake covert actions.

Under President Reagan, CIA Director William Casey exploited a more favorable public and congressional climate for intelligence community assertiveness and for struggle against the "evil empire" in Moscow. Casey was given carte blanche by the White House to undertake clandestine operations against the Soviet-supported regime in Afghanistan and the Cuban-supported government in Nicaragua, among others. Casey had no difficulty getting bipartisan congressional support for arming the Afghan rebels, but on U.S. efforts to support the anti-Sandinist rebel Contras Casey told Congress as few details as he could get away with. Casey was, in all likelihood, the puppet master who suggested the Iran-Contra connection by which Oliver North and other White House operatives sold arms to Iran and plowed the profits back into support for the Contras.

The guns for Iran were not illegal, just embarrassing, for President Reagan's State Department had labeled Iran a terrorist state for its prior seizures of U.S. hostages. The spillback of Iranian arms-sales profits to the Contras *was* illegal, according to the congressional legislation known as the "Boland amendments" which forbade U.S. intelligence agencies from aiding the Nicaraguan rebels for about two years. Subsequently repealed, the Boland legislation had to be got round while it was in force, or the administration had to abandon at least temporarily its war against the Sandinistas. Since the CIA could not be the legal conduit for Contra funds, an off-the-shelf operation run from the White House served the purpose.

The subsequent "Iran-Contra scandal" was an inferior soap opera compared with the dramatic revelations of the 1970s, but it raised again the ugly issue of intelligence accountability. In effect, the Reagan administration had transferred an intelligence function—covert action—to an arm of the government that was not accountable to Congress for the day-to-day peformance of its duties. Cynics would say that is exactly why Reagan and Casey had put it there. But end runs around Congress were no longer possible, and hardly desirable, in the world of U.S. intelligence policymaking of the 1980s. The Congress insisted on foreknowledge of covert operations (not necessarily the right to disapprove, although the threat of adverse investigations and ill-timed leaks was always present).

A U.S. intelligence service without a capability for covert action seems almost a contradiction in terms, although paramilitary covert actions might better be assigned to the Department of Defense. Covert operations are the exception, not the norm, and they deserve prior scrutiny by executive and legislative supervisory channels. The CIA is better prepared to carry out its missions and better protected against critics' second guessing if it informs policymakers in advance about its important operations and their intended objectives. In intelligence as in war, getting Congress to sign on is the practical equivalent of public approval, which then closes arguments about "why" or "what" so that intelligence can concentrate on "how."

7

SPECIAL OPERATIONS and UNCONVENTIONAL WARFARE

The American way of war has traditionally assumed, as did Clausewitz, that armed forces tasked by responsible governments are given missions that are clearly set apart from political and social variables. The contamination of military operations by nonmilitary aspects of conflict drives generals and admirals to despair and confounds the Clausewitzian universe of force and policy. Today, more than ever, the "exception" of specialized and politicized military operations is becoming the norm for U.S. and other armed forces. But this "renorming" of expectations about depoliticized war flies in the face of military service traditions. The U.S. Army's military staff culture, for example, is still dominated by the branch cultures of infantry, armor, and artillery and, therefore, by the conventional military–Clausewitzian perspective on the separation of politics and operations.[1]

Special operations come in many variations. The designation "special" can stand for special mission, special insignia, and special tradition. In the contemporary U.S. military, special operations forces (SOF) are composed of designated Army, Navy, and Air Force personnel trained for specific missions. Each military department of the U.S. armed forces contributes a service-component command to the joint U.S. Special Operations Command (SOC) at MacDill Air Force Base, Tampa, Florida. The Army Special Operations Command is some 30,000 strong, including active and reserve Special Forces, Special Operations Aviation, Rangers, Psychological Operations (PsyOps), and Civic Affairs units. The U.S. Naval Special Warfare Command numbers about 5,500 active and reserve operational

1. Carl H. Builder, *The Masks of War: American Military Styles in Strategy and Analysis* (Baltimore: Johns Hopkins University Press, 1989), 185–93, esp. 188.

and support personnel. These naval special forces include the Sea-Air-Land (SEAL) teams depicted in popular adventure films. The Air Force SOC includes an active Special Operations Wing and two special operations groups, plus reserve and National Guard forces.[2] The growth of special operations forces between 1981 and 1991 (roughly the Reagan-Bush years) is charted in Table 11.

The Department of Defense Reorganization Act of 1986 (the so-called Goldwater–Nichols legislation), as amended in 1987, established the position of Assistant Secretary of Defense for Special Operations and Low-Intensity Conflict and directed the creation of a unified U.S. Special Operations Command (USSOCOM). The issue of command and control was fundamental. The Goldwater–Nichols legislation was prompted by congressional sentiment that the Department of Defense was overtaxed with servicism. Each arm of service was looking out for itself, and missions requiring interservice collaboration (joint missions) were falling between the cracks.

Command and Control

The issue of command and control for U.S. special operations was important for another reason. U.S. special operations forces are the inheritors

Table 11. Growth of U.S. Special Operations Forces, 1981–1991 (No. of Units)

	1981	1988	1991
Special forces groups	7	8	9
Ranger battalions	2	3	3
Psychological Operations battalions	3	4	4
Civic Affairs battalions	1	1	1
SEAL teams (elite Navy commandos)	3	6	7
SEAL delivery-vehicle teams	0	2	2
Special boat units	6	7	7
Special Operations Wing	1	2	3
Special Operations Aviation Group	0	0	1
TOTAL	23	33	37

SOURCE: Michael A. Cuddihee and John W. Schmidt, *Special Operations Forces—Responsive, Capable and Ready* (Maxwell Air Force Base, Ala.: U.S. Air War College, May 1990), 44; cited in Claude C. Sturgill, *Low-Intensity Conflict in American History* (Westport, Conn.: Praeger Publishers, 1993), 104.

2. Hon. James R. Locher III, Assistant Secretary of Defense for Special Operations and Low-Intensity Conflict, and Gen. Carl W. Stiner, USA, Commander-in-Chief, U.S. Special Operations Command, *United States Special Operations Forces, Posture Statement 1993* (Washington, D.C.: DOD, 1993), 5.

of a long tradition of controversy. Within Western militaries the role of irregular or unconventional forces, and the significance of the kinds of conflicts they have been tasked to fight, are justifiably matters of military-technical and high political dispute. They are matters of military-technical dispute because roles and missions assigned to special operations, and the equipment and training required to support those roles, can be seen as detracting from the purposes and programs of conventional units. The political controversiality of special operations has several sources, but one important source is that the missions for which special operations forces are tasked can be explicitly political and diplomatic.

According to U.S. Assistant Secretary of Defense for Special Operations and Low-Intensity Conflict James R. Locher III, the U.S. Special Operations Command on October 23, 1992, had 4,300 special operations personnel in forty three countries and sixteen states participating in 114 missions.[3] The "traditional" missions of U.S. special operations forces, according to the Department of Defense, are summarized in Table 12.

The missions typically assigned to special operations forces differ from those undertaken by conventional forces in important ways, although special forces may also support conventional military operations. First of all, special operations require very precise timing. There is usually no opportunity for correction if the initial operation goes off course. Second, special operations often involve the use of exceptional training, atypical equipment, and unorthodox approaches to warfare. Third, the political sensitivity of special operations often demands a lower-profile operation, using specialists in the language and culture of the host or target country. Fourth, and last, special operations are highly dependent on timely and accurate intelligence.

According to the U.S. Special Operations Command: "SO missions are intelligence-driven and intelligence-dependent. They require immediate and continuous access to information from traditional as well as non-traditional sources. SO generally relies on formal intelligence structures, but, for certain sensitive missions, tactical and operational information must be developed using SOF assets such as advanced or reconnaissance forces."[4] Special operations forces are one kind of elite force, and elite forces (paratroops in most armies, panzer units in the World War II German armed forces) tend to rub up against conventional forces and missions, creating potential friction and jealousy. The British Special Operations Executive (SOE) was created in 1940 as a small, secret fighting force to organize resistance and to undermine in other ways Hitler's Reich. It immediately became contentious in Whitehall whether a single organiza-

3. Ibid., 10.
4. Ibid., 4.

Table 12. U.S. Special Operations Forces: Traditional Missions

Mission and Purpose	Activities
Unconventional warfare Conduct various military and para-military operations in enemy-held, enemy-controlled, or politically sensitive territory	• Indirect activities of long duration, including guerrilla warfare and other offensive, low-visibility or clandestine operations • For the most part, conducted by indigenous forces trained, organized, and equipped by SOF, who provide direction for indigenous troops
Direct action Seize, damage, or destroy a target; recover or capture personnel or material in support of strategic or operational objectives or conventional forces	• Small-scale, offensive actions of short duration • May include ambushes, raids, direct assaults, mine emplacement, or standoff attacks from air, ground, or maritime platforms • May also require support for cover and deception operations, or the conduct of independent sabotage operations, usually inside enemy territory
Special reconnaissance Collect information about enemy intentions and capabilities to support conventional forces	• Reconnaissance and surveillance • Collection of data, including meteorological, hydrographic, and other • Provide target acquisition and post-strike reconnaissance data
Foreign internal defense Assist other governments against subversion, insurgency, or lawlessness	• Promote internal development of economic, political, social, and military structures • Provide training and assistance to host-state military and paramilitary forces
Counterterrorism Preempt or resolve terrorist incidents	• Interagency activities, using specialized capabilities
Psychological operations (PsyOps) Induce and reinforce foreign attitudes favorable to U.S.A.	• Influence attitudes and behaviors of foreign governments, individuals, groups, and organizations
Civil affairs Maintain, establish, and influence relations among civil government, military, and civilian population to expedite military operations	• May be a stand-alone operation or in support of larger forces • Military forces may assume some of the normal responsibility of local government

SOURCE: Hon. James R. Locher III, Assistant Secretary of Defense for Special Operations and Low-Intensity Conflict, and Gen. Carl W. Stiner, USA, Commander-in-Chief, U.S. Special Operations Command, *United States Special Operations Forces, Posture Statement 1993* (Washington, D.C.: DOD, 1993), 8.

NOTE: SOF = special operations forces.

tion could be responsible for propaganda and military subversion. Eventually, responsibility for propaganda was moved to the newly created Political Warfare Executive (PWE) because the Ministry of Information opposed lodging the mission in SOE. Agents of the British Secret Intelligence Service (MI-6) were usually forbidden to have anything to do with SOE.[5]

The rivalry between SOE and British intelligence or military services was not unexpected, and charges of amateurish bungling have been laid at the door of SOE by its critics. SOE was partly intended by Churchill and the cabinet as a psychological boost for a British public that wanted to see some action taken against Hitler's expanding imperium. The practical effectiveness of this action, however slight, was not necessarily its only purpose. Of course, if the action backfired, as in the raid against Dieppe by commando forces, it cast doubt on the entire value of commando and other special operations. The social and psychological value of SOE was also felt abroad. It served to involve persons, including nonmilitary resisters in occupied lands, in some sense of belonging to a collective resistance against Hitler's tyranny.

SOE came under fire after World War II not only for its apparently limited effectiveness but for its political incorrectness in regard to which anti-German, anti-Japanese, and anti-Italian groups it chose to support. For example, where communist movements had the strongest possibility of expelling Axis forces or costing them great sacrifices, SOE was prepared to work with those communist forces despite their red taint. SOE supported communist insurgents in Burma and Malaya, in addition to the strategically more important Yugoslav case. One difficulty was that many of these civil wars or insurgencies, overlain with the conventional warfighting among the major World War II combatants, created a complicated mosaic.

Yugoslavia during the Second World War provided an example of a conflict with many faces. Croatia had been set up as an independent, sovereign state under the control of the dictator Ante Pavelic. The remainder of the Yugoslav territory was divided among Germany, Italy, Hungary, and Bulgaria. Rival guerrilla organizations within these two territories competed for the mantle of sole legitmate revolutionist. The Cetniks were loyal to the exiled king and his government; the Partisans, a self-styled national liberation movement, were working closely with the Soviet Comintern. Cetniks and Partisans fought against one another in addition to their separate battles against Germans and Italians.[6]

In 1943, during his mission for Churchill as liaison to Tito's partisans,

5. M.R.D. Foot, *SOE: An Outline History of the Special Operations Executive, 1940–46* (London: British Broadcasting Company; University Publications of America, 1986), esp. chs. 2 and 3.

6. Ibid., 153–54.

Fitzroy Maclean earnestly warned the prime minister that Tito was openly communist and that, if triumphant, he would establish a postwar system in Yugoslavia that would be pro-Soviet. Churchill, ever the pragmatist, asked Maclean: "Do you intend to make Yugoslavia your home after the war?" "No, Sir," Maclean replied. "Neither do I," Churchill responded. "And, that being so, the less you and I worry about the form of Government they set up, the better. That is for them to decide. What interests us is, which of them is doing the most harm to the Germans?"[7]

Misgivings about Elite Forces

Among the charges made by critics against elite forces, including special operations forces and elite units within conventional forces, is that they confound an orderly chain of command. Another criticism is that their elitism is discouraging to regular troops: the morale of the rank and file can be adversely influenced by official stroking of elites. It is argued also that elite forces drain off some of the best enlisted talent from the regular forces. All of these complaints are likely to be made against very visible and politically powerful elite forces within the larger military establishment, such as the French paratroops in Algeria, the British SAS, Israel's Palmach, and the U.S. Green Berets.[8]

On the other hand, specially trained forces have their own bill of particulars to present against regulars. The armed services in Western democracies are, no less than their imperial predecessors or their authoritarian contemporaries, predisposed to bureaucratic sclerosis and institutional mindlessness. Sometimes regulars have to think of themselves as irregulars in order to maintain their psychological harmony. William Manchester's *Goodbye Darkness: A Memoir of the Pacific War*, tells movingly of his experiences in the U.S. Marines attempting to roust the Japanese from Pacific island strongholds.[9] He served in an intelligence section tasked for reconnaissance patrol, mapping, prisoner of war interrogation, estimates of enemy strength, and related duties. Manchester's descriptions of the Pacific war bring out several things. First, his "raggedy ass Marines" became seasoned combat veterans and had no time for spit and polish: they smoked, stank, swore, and otherwise behaved in many

7. Ibid., 155.
8. Eliot A. Cohen, *Commandos and Politicians: Elite Military Units in Modern Democracies* (Cambridge, Mass.: Center for International Affairs, Harvard University, 1978).
9. William Manchester, *Goodbye Darkness: A Memoir of the Pacific War* (Little, Brown & Co., 1980).

unmilitary ways. Most were regarded in boot camp as military misfits. Second, what kept them in training and in combat was their feeling of shared fate and obligation toward their squad and platoon buddies. Inept officers were ignored and eventually got themselves killed by careless behavior under fire. Third, too many Marines were sacrificed in the assaults on account of poor operational intelligence, bad planning, and downright incompetent high command.

The architect of Guadalcanal was U.S. Admiral Ernest King, Chief of Naval Operations, who picked Vice-Admiral Robert Ghormley as his campaign commander. Ghormley, however, felt that the situation in the Solomon Islands was hopeless. So did Admiral Frank Jack Fletcher, chosen by Ghormley to direct the assault. As the task force prepared to sail, Fletcher called a conference and asked how many days would be needed to put the Marines ashore. He was told five days. Nonetheless, Fletcher said, he would leave after two days "because of the danger of air attacks and because of the fuel situation. . . . [I]f the troops can't be landed in two days, then they should not be landed."[10] The Marine commander, General Alexander A. Vandegrift, was so desperate for intelligence, especially mapping information, that he had his staff study seventeenth-century sailing charts and interview missionaries, traders, schooner captains, and other refugees from the Solomons. In the European theater of operations, Bastogne became memorable because the 101st Airborne was surrounded by enemy forces for eight days; at Guadalcanal, the Marines were isolated for fourth months. Commanders, though, should not get all the blame. Politicians deserve their share:

> One reason the struggles in the Pacific constantly teetered on the brink of disaster is that they were shoestring operations. At one point the United States was spending more money feeding and housing uprooted Italian civilians than on Americans fighting the Japanese. The navy let the Marines on the Canal down because Washington was letting the navy down, devoting nearly all its resources to Eisenhower's coming invasion of North Africa. We knew that our theater was a casualty of discrimination . . . because our government, appealing to its national constituency, which was almost entirely composed of former Europeans and their descendants, boasted of it.[11]

The point is overstated, but the perception of a front-line fighter who later became a noted author is understandable. The uneasy relations be-

10. Ibid., 168.
11. Ibid., 175–76.

tween regular and elite forces is not only a matter of personal or professional jealousy. It is also very much embedded in competing theories of war. Those soldiers who prefer a sharp line of demarcation between the sphere of politics and the art of war are more comfortable with conventional military engagements fought by regular units. Those officers who assume that the dividing line between war and politics is less distinct are more comfortable with the activities of special forces and other irregular units. When conventional and unconventional wars are being fought at the same time by the same country, as with the United States in Vietnam, there is considerable confusion in perspective.

Revolution and Insurgency

French colonial experience led to the development of several national schools of thought on revolution and counterinsurgency warfare.[12] Mao Zedong developed his own theories of guerrilla warfare on the basis of a unique case: China's modern revolution.[13] Che Guevara based his own theory of revolution on the important concept of the *foco*, or focal military unit, capable of harassing government forces and holding key economic assets while expanding its social base.[14] These and other theories of revolution and counterrevolution showed various faces of the problematic relationship between war and politics.[15] As the new nations of the developed world proliferated after 1960, so too did unstable authoritarian and democratic governments resting on weak political legitimacy. Revolution and insurgency followed almost automatically.

Competing theories of military effectiveness against insurgency strug-

12. John Shy and Thomas W. Collier, "Revolutionary War," ch. 27 in Peter Paret, ed., *Makers of Modern Strategy: From Machiavelli to the Nuclear Age* (Princeton, N.J.: Princeton University Press, 1986), 815–62. For a critique of French counterinsurgency theory, see D. Michael Shafer, *Deadly Paradigms: The Failure of U.S. Counterinsurgency Policy* (Princeton, N.J.: Princeton University Press, 1988), 138–65.

13. D. Michael Shafer shows that U.S. counterinsurgency theorists almost always read writers like Mao Zedong and Che Guevara out of historical context, as master theorists of a universal method for guerrilla warfare. U.S. counterinsurgency strategy has reflected this misreading: if there is a universal method for insurgency, there must be a universal solution to it. See Shafer, *Deadly Paradigms*, 107–11.

14. Ernesto Che Guevara, *Guerrilla Warfare* (New York: Vintage Books, 1961), is an important source on his revolutionary theory.

15. See Douglas Blaufarb, *The Counterinsurgency Era: U.S. Doctrine and Performance* (New York: Free Press, 1977); Sam C. Sarkesian, *America's Forgotten Wars: The Counterrevolutionary Past and Lessons for the Future* (Westport, Conn.: Greenwood Press, 1984); and Anthony James Joes, *Modern Guerrilla Insurgency* (Westport, Conn.: Praeger Publishers, 1992) for additional theoretical perspective and case studies.

gled for supremacy within U.S. policymaking circles in the early and middle 1960s, with obvious implications for the character of America's Vietnam commitment. We might summarize these lines of argument as follows: (1) revolution is the by-product of social change and political modernization; (2) revolution is the result of forces external to the state, including foreign ideologies and revolutionary organizational forms, imported into the indigenous situation. One line of theory thus saw the communist challenge as a competing model of social and political modernization. The U.S. and Western response, according to this diagnosis of the source of revolutionary impulses within developing societies, should be to offer a preferred model over the communist model. This preferred model should have political-social as well as military aspects, according to proponents. The challenge of modernization was to "grow" pluralist democratic societies that would thwart communist aspirations to power, and the United States needed to ally itself with indigenous rulers who accepted that prescription as a fact of life.

A second line of argument within U.S. policymaking during the early and middle 1960s dismissed internal social and political forces as the basis for revolution and placed the blame on the influence of communist outsiders. According to this second theory, wars would continue to be won or lost on the battlefield and in almost exclusively conventional military engagements.[16] Social modernization was not the task of armed forces, especially not of foreign military advisers. The United States could usefully train other countries' armed forces according to proven American tactics and standards, in this view, but we could not transplant democracy to infertile political soil.

By and large, adherents to these two schools of thought ended the U.S. involvement in Vietnam with different sets of historical memory. Those favoring political and social modernization prior to successful military commitment contended that the United States did well, in Laos and in Vietnam, with its civic action and irregular self-defense programs run by special forces, especially by the Green Berets under CIA direction.[17] In

16. D. Michael Shafer's insightful critique of U.S. and French counterinsurgency theory (see nn. 12 and 13 above) assumes too readily that perspectives emphasizing modernization as a primary source of revolution were logically consistent with arguments holding that external revolutionary ideologies (and ideologues) were responsible for revolution. His overall argument is correct despite this minor point. U.S. modernization theorists and military theorists of revolution both failed to understand the essentially *political* character of revolution.

17. Andrew F. Krepinevich, Jr., *The Army in Vietnam* (Baltimore: Johns Hopkins University Press, 1986), 70–71, discusses the success of U.S. Special Forces in 1961–62 in pacifying villages employing counterinsurgency doctrine and under CIA control. Under Operation Switchback, Civilian Irregular Defense Groups (CIDG) operations were subsequently transferred to Defense Department control under U.S. Military Assistance Command, Vietnam, with less satisfactory results.

this view, the turning over of the Indochina war to the regular U.S. Army chain of command (that transition having been officially accomplished with the creation of the Military Assistance Command, Vietnam, or MACV, during the Kennedy administration) was a fateful step in the wrong direction. The regular U.S. Army mindset attacked the problem as a conventional war with unconventional sidebars, oblivious to its social and political roots. The result was to alienate the very people whose allegiance the South Vietnamese government needed for its survival.

According to the "war first" school of thought, on the other hand, by 1965 the North Vietnamese had established firm control over the insurgency in the south. A military defeat of that insurgency and a blooding of its military sponsors in Hanoi were necessary conditions before the government and population of South Vietnam would be interested in social and political development. The U.S. commitment to "search and destroy" operations and the eventual removal of Green Berets from the theater of operations were two signals that the conventional military paradigm of warfare had won out in Washington, if not in the field. Support for the conventional model was provided, according to its adherents, by the virtual destruction of the Viet Cong infrastructure after the Tet offensive in 1968. Thereafter, North Vietnamese regular units were required to assume the major burden of fighting in the south, and the final triumph of North Vietnam in 1975 was the result of the South Vietnamese collapse in the face of a major conventional military offensive.

One difficulty with theories of revolution and insurgency (and their opposite strategies, counterrevolution and counterinsurgency) is that they abstract across cases of such diversity and nonconformity that generalizations tend to be vapid. Another deficiency is that such theories often fail to link the results desired in the field with the professional proclivities and ethos of the armed forces sent into the conflict. For example, it matters a great deal whether the U.S. Army that was sent to Vietnam conceived of itself as a voluntary, elite professional force favoring flexible tactics or as a mass machine designed to fight a war of attrition. Related to an army's self-concept is the priority it gives to different instruments of warfare. Thus General Bruce Palmer, Jr., reflecting on the American experience in Vietnam, writes:

> And so the allegation is frequently made that the U.S. Army pins its hopes for battle success on heavy, massed firepower rather than on the professional skill and tenacity of its infantry, who in the final analysis must close with the enemy and finish him off. This

explains why the Army tends to put its more highly educated and qualified personnel into artillery and armor units rather than infantry, and traditionally has looked upon the artillery as the elite combat arm. . . . [S]uch attitudes are seriously flawed.[18]

Today there is continuing disagreement within the academic and military professional communities over the future of warfare and, therefore, over the dominant model for relating force to policy. My concluding chapter shall say more about this issue, but here we need to mention one aspect. If conventional wars like Desert Storm are the wave of the future, then the dominant role of special forces will to act as adjuncts, however important their missions, to regular theater commanders and in support of very traditional missions. On the other hand, if the future lies in small-scale operations such as hostage rescue and counterterrorism, then special forces will be able to set apart their special training and ethos with more clarity. Counterinsurgency falls somewhere between the two paradigms (conventional and unconventional) of future war.

Even the "conventional" or traditional roles for special forces seem to have expanded in the new world disorder of the 1990s. Peacekeeping, counternarcotics, disaster relief, and other missions which are not strictly combat have crowded the calendar of the United Nations and its leading member states in recent years. (Peace Operations are considered in more detail in Chapter 8.) Nor have U.S. commanders been reluctant to use special forces in essential support for otherwise-conventional military operations. In 1989, for example, in Operation Just Cause, U.S. special forces performed various critical tasks in Panama. Navy SEALs neutralized Panamanian naval capabilities. Air Force SOF units in Spectre gunships destroyed General Manuel Noriega's Panamanian Defense Force (PDF) command-and-control facilities and suppressed enemy fire.[19] Army Rangers seized Torrijos/Tocumen and Río Hato airfields, and Army Special Forces secured the Pacora River Bridge. In Operation Promote Liberty in 1990, special operations forces helped rebuild Panama's infrastructure and assisted local governments in the restoration of public services.[20]

18. Gen. Bruce Palmer, Jr., *The 25-Year War: America's Military Role in Vietnam* (Lexington: University of Kentucky Press, 1984), 205.

19. The training of Navy SEAL and Air Force SOF units, among other elite forces, is discussed in Douglas C. Waller, *Commandos: The Inside Story of America's Secret Soldiers* (New York: Simon & Schuster, 1994).

20. *U.S. Special Operations Forces, Posture Statement 1993*, 19 (see n. 2 above).

Special Forces as Peacekeepers

The receding of the Cold War glaciers has opened the way for a new assertiveness by the United Nations in peacekeeping and peacemaking operations. Roughly, the distinction between the two is in the degree of voluntary cooperation provided by the disputant or combatant parties with outsiders who are attempting to terminate the conflict. In *peacekeeping*, the combatants have more or less decided to stop fighting and want the United Nations to establish a presence that will make it more difficult for either side to restart combat. *Peacemaking*, or peace enforcement, is more ambitious. A peace enforcement operation allows external forces to impose war termination on warring parties, whether or not they have all decided to quit fighting.[21] An example of peacekeeping is the United Nations Emergency Force sent to patrol the Sinai between the Arab-Israeli wars. An example of peace enforcement is the U.N. Congo Organization (ONUC, by its French initials) which, following Congolese independence in 1960 and the breakdown of civil order, forcibly suppressed the effort by Katanga province to secede from the country and disarmed Katanga's mercenary forces.

Peacekeeping forces are by definition special operations forces of a kind. They are armed missionaries with a pacification mission, although they may have to defend themselves if attacked. For peacekeeping operations to succeed, it is necessary that the forces receive some cooperation from the disputants in winding down the war. If the war is a civil war and not one between sovereign states, then the cooperation of the surrounding population is indispensable. In Bosnia and in Somalia during the early 1990s, U.N. peacekeeping forces encountered difficulty in obtaining cooperation from the combatants, and in both cases the United Nations ultimately authorized a change in mission from peacekeeping to what we have called peacemaking (or peace enforcement). The results were different in the two cases. In Bosnia, the United Nations authorized NATO air strikes if Bosnian Serb forces failed to comply with a directive to move artillery and mortars at least twenty kilometers back from the hills overlooking Sarajevo. NATO aircraft also downed Serb fighter planes engaged in tactical bombing missions that violated the "no fly zone" declared by the United Nations and implemented by NATO beginning in 1992.

In the case of Somalia, U.S. forces were sent in December 1992 to create secure zones in which food relief for starving Somalis could be maintained. The Clinton administration inherited this commitment and a United Nations anxious to restore civil order in Somalia. The U.N. objective soon became the U.S. objective, and U.S. combat forces clashed with

21. These are not the official U.N. definitions, but my own.

Somali warlords. In October 1993, a U.S. Army Ranger raid on a suspected headquarters of the warlord General Muhamed Farah Aideed resulted in significant U.S. casualties and much political embarrassment for the Clinton administration. Press reports accused Defense Secretary Les Aspin of bad judgment, for not having sent tanks requested months earlier by U.S. field forces—tanks that might have permitted a rescue of the outnumbered Rangers. It was apparent that the U.S. position had taken a turn from peacekeeping to peace imposition, but without the sanction of the U.S. Congress or the American public. President Clinton, recognizing this, ordered a change in policy which would guarantee the departure of most U.S. forces by the end of March 1994.

It is clear that the kinds of missions for which U.S. special forces are trained were more appropriate in the Somali context than the missions for which conventional forces are prepared. The problem in Somalia was rooted in the lack of any indigenous political authority. No political center could impose its will on dissident and fractious clans, nor could any center obtain consensus on the rules of the game for political decision-making. The Somali case was important as a test of peacekeeping because conditions there, albeit in exaggerated form, were not unique in Africa. West Africa in 1993 was a tinderbox, marked by breakdowns in civil authority and by internal wars that invited the attention, for better or for worse, of outside forces.

There is a danger that, caught up in post–Cold War hubris, the United Nations may oversell peacekeeping and peace enforcement. The hard work must still be done by nation-states, and the combatants must sooner or later prefer peace to war. The track record for outside forces imposing order on regional wars or civil strife since World War II (apart from the Sovietization imposed by the now defunct USSR) is not favorable. The United Nations cannot muster the firepower that the Americans used in Vietnam, nor that expended by the Soviets in Afghanistan. Today's media-conscious world paradoxically makes the bacillus of ethnic nationalism more contagious. The technology allows instant communication of information from the most remote corner of the globe to the major industrialized capitals of the Group of Seven. On the other hand, telecommunications have a significant imitative impact, whether on consumers of clothing and automobiles or on consumers of revolutionary nationalism. "If they can do it, why can't we?" is a question that discontent and destitute people in the Third World are likely to ask even more frequently at the end of the twenty-first century than now.

Faced with internationally imitative rebellion based on ethnic nationalism, religion, or other primordial values, the "establishment" of the existing international order might wish to turn to peacekeeping as an expedient solution. It would seem to do no harm to provide specially trained,

U.N.-assigned, and multinational forces for this purpose. However, peace-keeping and peace enforcement remain much more controversial among U.N. members and within the various constituencies of the developed democracies. There is also the risk that U.N. peacekeeping may come to be seen by indigenous forces as a new form of imperialism. After all, it is the great powers with permanent seats on the Security Council who decide whether and where the United Nations can use peacekeeping or other force on behalf of international order. Another concern about runaway peacekeeping is whether the various state members of regional and universal organizations will be amenable to placing additional national force components under multinational command. Armies tend to be difficult enough to control under the command of a single state.

The pairing of peacekeeping functions and special operations forces is not as paradoxical as it might at first seem. Psychologically, U.S. audiences are somewhat inclined to associate special operations with Green Berets and Vietnam. Yet special operations are a part of almost any conventional military operation, including Desert Storm in 1991, that draws from more than a single branch of service and involves high cost and risk. Special forces in Desert Storm performed vital missions. For example, U.S. "Pave Low" helicopter teams crossed into Iraq on January 17, 1991, and flew low across the desert in order to drop markers for Army attack helicopters. Army SOF also performed specialized night reconnaissance, infiltration behind enemy lines, and other necessary missions in support of conventional air and ground forces.[22]

The language skills and cultural sensitivity required of peacekeepers are assets for special operations forces performing civil affairs, foreign internal defense, psychological operations, and counterterrorism. Indeed, these hallmark functions of U.S. special forces loom larger in the present and foreseeable menu of politico-military skills expected of peacekeepers. Would it be too farfetched to suggest that, in some situations, peace-keepers are special forces in training, or that special forces are peace-keepers without the U.N. stamp of approval?

Continuing Controversy

Are Covert Operations and Clandestine Warfare Compatible with Democratic Accountability and Military Professionalism?

During the Second World War, the role of special operations forces became extremely controversial. The British experience with Special Opera-

---

22. *U.S. Special Operations Forces, Posture Statement 1993*, 21.

tions Executive and the American experience with the Office of Strategic Services gave rise to fears on the part of diplomats and soldiers in both countries. The fears were of two sorts: (1) that SOE and OSS were not as accountable as they should have been and (2) that they relied on extraordinary methods, and more than one outrageous character, in order to bring about very little of military or strategic value.

These indictments against special operations have also been made against the clandestine services of the Central Intelligence Agency. Problems of accountability and professionalism surfaced during the U.S. congressional investigations of the CIA during the 1970s. The involvement of CIA with organized criminals, allegations of CIA assassination plots, and dubious attempts to destabilize elected governments raised warning flags about activities outside the normal diplomatic and military chains of command. The U.S. political system was especially sensitive to the issue of possible human rights abuses committed by CIA and allied Western intelligence agencies.

Part of the legacy passed from the OSS to the CIA was that it was entirely proper for the same agency to conduct clandestine paramilitary operations and traditional espionage. During the 1940s and 1950s, when many in the U.S. government refused to accept the Cold War stalemate but saw the risks of conventional war in Europe as unacceptable, the alternative of intelligence warfare had a seductive appeal. Using a variety of means in addition to its own assets (e.g., proprietary companies and borrowed armed forces of foreign nationals), the CIA built an extraordinary empire by the time John F. Kennedy had assumed office.

CIA successes in overthrowing the governments of Iran (in 1953) and Guatemala (in 1954) led to hubris about the potential of covert action and clandestine warfare. This became shockingly apparent at the Bay of Pigs. Thereafter, CIA paramilitary operations would never have the same luster of invincibility within the U.S. government, nor the old reputation for infallibility among foreign friends and enemies. Kennedy toyed with the idea of disbanding the CIA but needed it for his administration's own home-grown clandestine war in Laos, and for the possibility that he might have to expand U.S. intelligence and military capabilities in Vietnam. The CIA supervised civic action and parmilitary activities by Green Berets in Laos and in Vietnam during the early 1960s: CIA's army of Meo tribesmen, under several presidents, was one of the principal clandestine operations of the United States in Southeast Asia.

Elections in 1958 were intended to integrate Laos's disparate political factions into a coalition government but failed to quell political disputes among leftist, neutralist, and rightist factions. By 1959 the United States had assigned Green Berets (Project White Star) to mobile training teams for each of twelve battalions of the Royal Laotian Armed Forces (RLAF).

In 1960, paratroop forces under the command of Kong Le overthrew the government in Vientiane and asked the declared neutralist Souvanna Phouma to form a new government. The U.S. position was officially to support Souvanna, but actually to work against him by aiding the CIA-cultivated Colonel Phoumi Nosavan. The United States had decided by the autumn of 1960 that a coalition government influenced by the communist Pathet Lao was too left-leaning and not acceptable to the Eisenhower administration.[23]

The U.S. stake in Laos was judged important because Laos was a conduit for increasing amounts of aid from North to South Vietnam, where another Cold War competition was now heating up. The problem was that the United States could not openly establish a military command in Laos: according to the terms of the Geneva agreement of 1954, only French military personnel were permitted to remain to advise the RLAF. The United States did have a military advisory group, however, under another name: the Program Evaluation Office, headed by a U.S. general officer.[24] Laos, however, remained very much the CIA's hunting ground, unlike Vietnam where intelligence would be more or less subordinated to the U.S. military command.

In Laos, the CIA established armed paramilitary units of hill tribes, called Hmong or Meo. The most important Meo military commander, Vang Pao, formed an alliance with the CIA and developed a secret army (Armée Clandestine) for battle against the neutralist Kong Le and leftist (Pathet Lao) forces. Chased out of the high Laotian plateau in the spring and summer of 1961 by Kong Le and Pathet Lao attacks, Vang Pao's forces were rebuilt by CIA air supply and by siphoning Meo units from the RLAF. Eventually the Vang Pao forces grew to about 30,000, of which some 10,000 were formed into "special guerrilla units," regular partisan battalions with three companies and a headquarters.[25]

Two aspects of the CIA's Meo/Hmong army were controversial in retrospect. The first was its accountability. U.S. support for the Armée Clandestine was scattered across CIA, U.S. AID, and military assistance budgets. When the CIA sought to increase the size of the Armée Clandestine after 1964, it briefed Congress with a request to support more than a hundred secret units under the control of Vang Pao. The forces actually controlled by Vang Pao amounted to no more than several dozen platoons. CIA inflated this figure on paper by reorganizing the platoons of Vang Pao's forces into many more units, each with a small number of

23. See John Prados, *Presidents' Secret Wars: CIA and Pentagon Covert Operations since World War II* (New York: William Morrow & Co., 1986), 262ff.
24. Ibid., 265.
25. Ibid., 272.

men. Impressed by this apparent success in Meo mobilization, Congress approved the budgetary requests as submitted.[26]

The second controversial aspect of the CIA's Meo/Hmong army was its potential incompatibility with U.S. foreign and security policy as explained publicly. The secret army in Laos was working against the constitutional government, which was officially recognized as such by the United States. In addition, even before CIA involvement, the proud and fierce Meo were a state within a state. This created a dilemma: the independent Meo army could thrive only if the central government in Vientiane were weak. But if that government were too weak, it would not be able to prosecute the war against the Pathet Lao successfully.

Further embarrassment came to the CIA when it became clearer to members of Congress that some of the CIA's Laotian allies, including senior officers in the RLAF, were involved in drug smuggling for huge profits.[27] It was also alleged that crews for the CIA's proprietary airline, Air America, were running drugs. In fact, investigations did find individual cases of drug smuggling, presumably without the knowledge of CIA case officers. In the end, the image created of CIA permissiveness toward, or association with, persons smuggling drugs resonated badly on the American home front at a time when drug abuse was a major public policy issue. As one writer about this period has noted: "This points directly to a key weakness of covert operations: Making alliances with indigenous groups inevitably involves buying into the less than wholesome features of such groups. Even if only through guilt by association, this in turn may discredit CIA programs as well as the larger aims of American policy."[28]

Whether covert actions, with or without the involvement of special forces, were compatible with standards of democratic accountability or professionalism was an issue during the CIA's operations in Vietnam as well. CIA assisted, although it did not direct, the Civil Operations and Rural Development Support (CORDS) program to develop resistance to Viet Cong infiltration of the South Vietnamese countryside. One aspect of CORDS was "Phoenix," supervised by the once and future CIA employee William Colby. Phoenix was charged by antiwar critics with responsibility for assassination and terrorism on a large scale. Many of the victims were allegedly innocent of any genuine connection with the Viet Cong. Accord-

26. At this time, the intelligence subcommittees of the House and Senate armed services committees reviewed and approved CIA budgets, which were not made available to the rest of Congress. The procedure was changed in the 1970s. See Prados, *Presidents' Secret Wars,* 274.

27. Alfred W. McCoy with Cathleen B. Read and Leonard P. Adams II, *The Politics of Heroin in Southeast Asia* (New York: Harper & Row, 1972).

28. Prados, *Presidents' Secret Wars,* 287.

ing to John Ranelagh, author of a widely used text on the CIA and U.S. intelligence during the Cold War, Phoenix was "a well-conceived program badly executed."[29]

The concept of Phoenix was in part driven by the sophistication of the Viet Cong infrastructure in South Vietnam. The typical province was organized into a number of major components: the Province Unit (main fighting force); the Medical Service; the Proselytizing Unit; and, most significant for CIA, the Ban-an-ninh, or Secret Police. The Ban-an-ninh were a substantial force of some 25,000 who conducted extensive espionage against the government of South Vietnam and its armed forces. In addition, the Ban-an-ninh were thought to be engaged in terrorism, assassination, and kidnapping. The object of Phoenix was to fight back against the Secret Police and other support organizations, without which the main guerrilla fighting units would have gradually dried up.[30] Telling friend from foe proved to be a more complicated exercise than the CIA planners of Phoenix had suspected. Enemy agents infiltrated the program and used their position to turn Vietnamese against the South Vietnamese government. Many of those marked for interrogation or assassination were so fingered as a result of personal or family feuds.

In the case of Phoenix, the CIA pleaded that its role was planning and analysis, at one remove from the dirty work of torture and assassination being carried out by members of the South Vietnamese government and military. The same plea was entered with regard to the CT (Counterterror) groups, later called "provisional reconnaissance units," first organized by Colby in 1965. The purpose of the CT teams was to use Viet Cong techniques of terror, including assassination and kidnapping, against the enemy leadership.[31] CIA recruited, organized, and supplied the CT teams, which were eventually absorbed into Phoenix. U.S. officials sponsored this program to train South Vietnamese in techniques which many Americans, including influentials in Congress and in the news media, found abhorrent. And, again, some fence-straddling South Vietnamese saw in the CT and Phoenix programs further evidence of a U.S. willingness to enter into terror, and worse, against the South Vietnamese people indiscriminately.[32]

Another instance of dubious accountability and questionable values in covert action occurred during the Nixon administration. A Marxist, Sal-

29. John Ranelagh, The Agency: The Rise and Decline of the CIA (New York: Touchstone Books, 1987), 437. See also John Prados, The Hidden History of the Vietnam War (Chicago: Ivan R. Dee, 1995), 204–20.
30. Ranelagh, The Agency, 438.
31. Ibid., 440.
32. Ibid.

vador Allende Gossens, was elected president of Chile despite efforts of the United States in support of his opponents. President Nixon was determined not to accept the electoral verdict, and his national security apparatus began a two-track program to destabilize Allende's regime. "Track One" was more or less openly acknowledged: cuts in U.S. economic aid and diplomatic overtures critical of Allende's decisions. The second and more important track was clandestine. "Track Two" was an effort to prevent, by military coup or other means, the confirmation of Allende's election.

In a meeting with President Nixon, National Security Adviser Henry Kissinger, and Attorney General John Mitchell on September 15, 1970, CIA Director Richard Helms was told to go all-out to prevent Allende's confirmation (the vote was scheduled for October 24). Helms later told the Senate Select Committee on Intelligence (the Church Committee): "If I ever carried a marshal's baton in my knapsack out of the Oval Office, it was that day."[33] The local CIA chief of station had little enthusiasm for the task, but complied with the orders from higher up. Several conspiratorial Chilean generals were courted by CIA contacts, but none of these anti-Allende conspirators was competent to act decisively and in a timely manner. Allende was confirmed by the Chilean Congress as scheduled, although he would later be overthrown and killed in a coup by the Chilean military.

The United States could not install a preferred government in Chile in 1970 by using the means that it had used successfully in 1964. In the earlier election, the United States had provided political and economic assistance to the Christian Democratic centrists of Eduardo Frei, who won the election. The Nixon administration, however, considered the Christian Democrats to be excessively left-leaning, and in 1970 the United States preferred to support a right-wing alliance under the leadership of Jorge Alessandri. Alessandri, the candidate of affluent business and landed interests, had split the antisocialist vote with the Christian Democrats, allowing Allende to win a plurality in the popular vote.

Out of desperation, the Nixon administration turned to Track Two, involving the CIA in covert support for the military overthrow of a government that was not necessarily detrimental to U.S. foreign policy interests. The decision that any government in Latin America with an elected Marxist at its head was an extension of Moscow's influence seemed odd, given the Nixon-Kissinger détente policy then being pursued toward the Soviet Union. In addition, the entire episode showed some of the difficulties of

33. Thomas Powers, *The Man Who Kept the Secrets: Richard Helms and the CIA* (New York: Washington Square Press, 1979), 300.

arranging military coups by long distance. After several botched attempts, dissident generals succeeded in killing the head of the Chilean armed forces, General René Schneider. These abortive and successful attempts on Schneider, an opponent of any unconstitutional usurpation of power by the military, pointed in an obvious way at U.S. complicity against Allende.

The Chilean case was not the most dubious involvement of the United States in instigating a foreign military coup, however. That honor is reserved for the misguided decision to encourage South Vietnamese generals to overthrow President Ngo Dinh Diem in early November 1963. CIA Director John McCone and his Saigon chief of station in 1962, future CIA Director William Colby, opposed U.S. support for a coup against Diem. McCone and Colby argued that Diem, whatever his faults, was the best available leader from the standpoint of U.S. interests. But the repression of Buddhists in 1963 by Diem and his notorious brother, Ngo Dinh Nhu, prompted a group in the State Department to favor Diem's removal. The counterinsurgency group under General Maxwell D. Taylor also favored U.S. support for a coup against Diem. An August 1963 coup attempt to which the United States had given its nod was called off at the eleventh hour, but the attempt was repeated with official U.S. encouragement and with success on November 1.[34]

The U.S.-supported coup against Diem may be the first case of a video-instigated overthrow of an allied government by paramilitary means. Television coverage of Buddhist pagodas being ransacked by Nhu's special forces, and even more dramatic footage of Buddhist suicides, caused revulsion in the American press, in Congress, and in the administration. The result of Diem's departure, however, was a political and military disaster. Almost all his successors were politically inastute and unable to hold together the various factions into which the South Vietnamese regime had been divided. Prosecution of the war against the Viet Cong and North Vietnamese did not improve. Corruption of the government in Saigon and its penetration by hostile intelligence services only increased. The continuing incompetency of the South Vietnamese government after 1963 made even the most successful U.S. military campaign of doubtful utility. In the last analysis, the United States had staged a coup against itself.

34. Ibid., 207–8.

8

MILITARY PERSUASION

PROMOTING PEACE THROUGH ARMS

The end of the Cold War has increased the number of calls for the use of U.S. armed forces for the mission of military persuasion. In this chapter, I first define the concept of military persuasion, marking it off from other uses for armed forces.[1] I then consider some of the contentious issues surrounding U.S. military persuasion in the Cold War past and post–Cold War present. Those issues include whether the U.S. armed forces are suited for, or institutionally compatible with, various kinds of military persuasion missions, including peacekeeping. The costs of military persuasion in relation to other expected military roles and missions for the U.S. armed forces are also assessed.

The Concept

Military persuasion is the use of armed force for purposes other than destruction. A significant literature exists about the *coercive political uses* of military power. For example, Thomas C. Schelling's studies of bargaining games between states and Alexander George's investigations of "coercive diplomacy" have demonstrated that armed forces can be used to influence the intentions of opposed states in crisis and other conflict situ-

1. See also Stephen J. Cimbala, *Military Persuasion: Deterrence and Provocation in Crisis and War* (University Park: Pennsylvania State University Press, 1994).

ations.[2] Not all uses of military power for political influence apart from destruction are coercive, though. There are a number of noncoercive but significant ways in which military power can be, and has been, used to persuade instead of destroy.

Four examples of the use of armed forces for *noncoercive persuasion* are: civic action and related political or military assistance; tripwire or "plate glass window" functions; military demonstrations and representations; and, of most immediate interest here, military diplomacy. In each category there are borderline behaviors which, one might reasonably argue, partake of coercive and noncoercive influence. I suggest nevertheless that each of these four categories has a center of gravity that is closer to noncoercive than to coercive persuasion. In coercive persuasion, the threat to use force is manifest or apparent, and often involves the credible threat to escalate a crisis or war to a more dangerous or more destructive level. Coercive persuasion is more like Schelling's compellence than it is like deterrence: it is more an active than a passive form of persuasion, and the threat of military action looms in the foreground, not the background. President Kennedy's quarantine of Soviet military shipments to Cuba in October 1962 was an act of compellence, with the objective of forcing Khrushchev to remove the missiles, as well as of deterrence, precluding other missiles from being shipped to Cuba.[3]

Civic action includes a great variety of activities, centered on the development of viable local institutions for health, education, security, and other requisite state functions. Tripwire or "plate glass window" missions interpose one state's forces in the path of possible, though not necessarily imminent, attack. The United Nations Emergency Force (UNEF) interposed between Egypt and Israel from 1956 to 1967 performed this function, as does the U.S. contingent of the U.N. force deployed in Macedonia in 1993. Military demonstrations may include timely and well-placed naval activities to "show the flag," for example, or overhead reconnaissance which the observing state makes little effort to conceal. Military maneuvers that are not actually concealed preparations for a surprise attack, but that signal a defender's readiness for surprise, can also be included among noncoercive military demonstrations.

2. Thomas C. Schelling, *Arms and Influence* (New Haven, Conn.: Yale University Press, 1966); Alexander L. George et al., *The Limits of Coercive Diplomacy: Laos, Cuba, Vietnam* (Boston: Little, Brown, 1971).

3. Alexander L. George, "The Cuban Missile Crisis," ch. 11 in George, ed., *Avoiding War: Problems of Crisis Management* (Boulder, Colo.: Westview Press, 1991), 222–68; Graham T. Allison, *Essence of Decision: Explaining the Cuban Missile Crisis* (Boston: Little, Brown, 1971); Raymond L. Garthoff, *Reflections on the Cuban Missile Crisis*, rev. ed. (Washington, D.C.: Brookings Institution, 1989); James G. Blight and David A. Welch, *On the Brink: Americans and Soviets Reexamine the Cuban Missile Crisis* (New York: Hill & Wang, 1989).

Military diplomacy ranges widely, too, from military-to-military contacts for the purpose of confidence building to the undertaking of explicitly diplomatic missions by uniformed personnel. Peacekeeping and peace enforcement (see below) are forms of military diplomacy. Both peacekeeping and peace enforcement are nonwar operations by intent, although peace enforcement requires the coercive use of military power for ends other than the destruction of a state's military power. A schematic representation of the forms of military persuasion is provided in Table 13.

Peacekeeping and Military Missions

In this book, I treat peacekeeping as a basically noncoercive form of military diplomacy (see Table 13). Different agencies of the U.S. government employ variable terms for peacekeeping, peacemaking, and the like. The terminology of other states and the United Nations adds more variety. The official U.N. terminology distinguishes among peacekeeping, peacemaking, peace building, and peace enforcement:

Table 13. Forms of Military Persuasion

Basically Coercive	Basically Noncoercive
Coercive bargaining/compellence (e.g., Kennedy's imposition of a blockade against Soviet shipments to Cuba in 1962)	Civic action (e.g., construction of roads, schools, and hospitals)
Ultimatums (e.g., Kennedy's insistence upon removal of the Soviet missiles by a certain deadline)	Plate glass window/tripwire (e.g., interposition of noncombatant force between or near combatants to preclude initiation of war or war widening)
Maneuvers accompanied by threat (e.g., United States and Soviet Union during several Berlin crises)	Demonstrations not accompanied by explicit or strong latent threat of actual war (e.g., reconnaissance to which state being observed has resigned itself)
Fait accompli (e.g., incursion of forces into territory previously off-limits, as in Hitler's Rhineland invasion)	Military diplomacy (e.g., confidence-building measures to increase transparency against planning for surprise attack)

SOURCE: Classification by Stephen J. Cimbala; but see Alexander L. George, "Strategies for Crisis Management," ch. 16 in Alexander L. George, ed., *Avoiding War: Problems of Crisis Management* (Boulder, Colo.: Westview Press, 1991), 377–94.

(1), peacekeeping - deployment of UN forces in the field with the consent of all parties concerned, usually including military or police and frequently civilians;
(2), peacemaking - action taken by the UN to bring hostile parties to agreement, using peaceful means such as those foreseen in Chapter VI of the UN Charter;
(3), peace building - action to prevent a relapse into conflict by creating support structures for peaceful settlement;
(4), peace enforcement - action taken by UN armed forces under Chapter VII to restore peace (often termed "collective security").[4]

The U.S. Department of Defense makes a distinction between "traditional" and "aggravated" peacekeeping missions:

(1) *traditional peacekeeping.* Deployment of a UN, regional organization or coalition presence in the field with the consent of all the parties concerned, normally involving UN regional organization, or coalition military forces, and/or police and civilians. Non-combat military operations (exclusive of self-defense) that are undertaken by outside forces with the consent of all major belligerent parties, designed to monitor and facilitate implementation of an existing truce agreement in support of diplomatic efforts to reach a political settlement to the dispute.
(2) *Aggravated peacekeeping.* Military operations undertaken with the nominal consent of all major belligerent parties, but which are complicated by subsequent intransigence of one or more of the belligerents, poor command and control of belligerent forces, or conditions of outlawry, banditry, or anarchy. In such conditions, peacekeeping forces are normally authorized to use force in self-defense, and in defense of the missions they are assigned, which may include monitoring and facilitating implementation of an existing truce agreement in support of diplomatic efforts to reach a political settlement, or supporting or safeguarding humanitarian relief efforts.[5]

4. Boutros Boutros-Ghali, *An Agenda for Peace: Preventive Diplomacy, Peacemaking and Peace-keeping* (New York: United Nations, 1992), defines the first three functions. Peace enforcement is defined in other studies: see Cdr. Martha Bills, USN, et al., *Options for U.S. Military Support to the United Nations* (Washington, D.C.: Center for Strategic and International Studies, December 1992), 3.
5. See John G. Roos, "Perils of Peacekeeping: Tallying the Costs in Blood, Coin, Prestige, and Readiness," *Armed Forces Journal International* (December 1993): 14, for these Defense Department definitions. Donald M. Snow's uses of "peacekeeping" and "peacemaking" are comparable to the above definitions of "traditional peacekeeping" and "aggravated peace-

And according to U.S. Army doctrine, "peace operations"

> is a new and comprehensive term that covers a wide range of ac-
> tivities. These activities are divided into three principal areas: *sup-*
> *port to diplomacy (peacemaking, peace-building and preventive di-*
> *plomacy), peacekeeping, and peace enforcement.* Peace operations
> include traditional peacekeeping operations as well as more force-
> ful activities, such as the protection of humanitarian assistance,
> the establishment of order and stability, the enforcement of sanc-
> tions, the guarantee and denial of movement, the establishment of
> protected zones, and the forcible separation of belligerents.[6]

What military missions follow from these definitional constructs? If we
take the four generic missions identified by the United Nations (peacemaking, peace building, peacekeeping, and peace enforcement), we can
derive many specific military missions, summarized in Table 14.

An additional and frequently used category to describe military activities related to persuasion instead of coercion is "operations other than
war" (OOTW). As used by the U.S. Army, OOTW includes activities that
fall within both "peacekeeping" and "peace enforcement" as listed in Table 14. According to one list provided by expert analysts, OOTW includes
the following: counterinsurgency/insurgency; counternarcotics; counterterrorism; concombatant evacuation operations; arms control; support to
domestic civilian authorities; humanitarian assistance and disaster relief;
security assistance, including training; nation assistance, including civic
action; shows of force; and attacks and raids.[7] The diversity of this list
invites as much confusion as the list of potential missions assigned to
U.N. forces under the "peacekeeping" and "peace enforcement" mandates.

Most of the commentary about U.N. activities has focused on peacekeeping and peace enforcement. Article 42 of the U.N. Charter authorizes
the U.N. Security Council to take collective action to restore peace in the
face of aggression. The United Nations has never acted under Article 42,
however: the Korean and Desert Storm operations were authorized under

---

keeping," respectively: see Snow, *Distant Thunder: Third World Conflict and the New Interna-*
tional Order (New York: St. Martin's Press, 1993), 131.

6. U.S. Department of the Army, *Peace Operations,* FM 100-23, Version #7 (Draft) (Washington, D.C.: Headquarters, Department of the Army, April 1994), ii. I am grateful to Col.
William Flavin, U.S. Army War College, for calling this reference to my attention.

7. U.S. Army, *Operations* (Washington, D.C.: Department of the Army, 1993), cited in
Jennifer Morrison Taw and Bruce Hoffman, "Operations Other than War," ch. 9 in Paul K.
Davis, ed., *New Challenges for Defense Planning: Rethinking How Much Is Enough?* (Santa
Monica, Calif.: Rand, 1994), 224. I assume the citation refers to FM 100-5, *Operations,* al-
though the reference is not so specified.

Table 14. U.N. Military Missions Derived from Peace Support Functions

Peacemaking	Peace Building	Peacekeeping	Peace Enforcement
Assessments	Assessments	Assessments	Assessments
Monitoring	Monitoring	Monitoring	Show of force
	Counterterrorism	Counterterrorism	Counterterrorism
	Observers	Observers	Free passage
	Law and order	Law and order	Blockade
	Humanitarian assistance	Humanitarian assistance	Air/naval campaign
	Disarm/demobilize	Hostage rescue	Hostage rescue
	Organize/train	Prisoner-of-war protection	Limited major regional conflict
	Counterdrug	Noncombatant evacuation	Major regional conflict
	Protect elections	Preventive diplomacy	
	Reconstruction	Buffer force	
	Environmental protection		

SOURCE: Cdr. Martha Bills, USN, et al., *Options for U.S. Military Support to the United Nations* (Washington, D.C.: Center for Strategic and International Studies, December 1992), 3, which provides definitions for each of the derived missions.

Article 52, dealing with collective self-defense.[8] Peace enforcement thus comes about under U.N. responsibility only when peacekeeping or other operations evolve into peace enforcement, and not by means of the designed "collective security" route. The evolutionary pattern is unfortunate, for peacekeeping and peace enforcement are not just points on a continuum. They are different in kind.

Peace enforcement calls for military force sufficient to impose a situation of armistice or disarmament on hostile forces without their consent. This is very difficult to do, even under the best of conditions, for individual governments and their militaries. It is even more demanding for alliances and coalitions. The U.N. Charter envisioned peace enforcement as the collective expression of the great powers (having decisive votes in the Security Council) against aggressive disturbances of the international order. The assumption was that the great powers would agree about what constituted illegal aggression and what would be necessary to combat it. The Cold War belied this assumption of great-power harmony on the issue of peace enforcement; the post–Cold War is still open-ended.

U.N. peacekeeping operations, on the other hand, have been its big business. More than thirty peacekeeping operations have been authorized by the U.N. Security Council and administered through the office of the

8. Bills et al., *Options for U.S. Military Support to the United Nations,* 9.

U.N. secretary-general. Approximately 1,000 U.N. personnel have been killed during peacekeeping operations over the organization's lifetime, including more than 200 in the past few years. About $10 billion has been spent on all peacekeeping operations since the origin of the United Nations, but about half that total has been accumulated within the past two years (1993–94).[9] U.N. peace operations active as of April 1995 are listed in Table 15; compare these with the Cold War peace operations listed in Table 16.

Doubts about Military Persuasion

The end of the Cold War has opened the door to U.N. Security Council peacekeeping or peace enforcement operations backed by both the United States and Russia, among other permanent members. However, the involvement of U.S. forces in multilateral operations will not be uncontroversial on the home front. The commitment of U.S. combat forces under the command of any other government, even under the umbrella of an international organization, creates potential problems of operational integrity and political accountability. These problems did not really arise in Korea or in the Gulf War of 1991 because, though authorized by the United Nations, those operations were essentially U.S.-designed and directed military campaigns.

In a September 1993 press conference, then Chairman of the Joint Chiefs of Staff General Colin L. Powell expressed some of the misgivings of the U.S. officer corps concerning military involvement in operations other than war. Powell did not dismiss the possibility that policymakers might call upon armed forces for peacekeeping or other noncombat missions. He emphasized, however, that the main business of the U.S. armed forces must be war: "Because we are able to fight and win the nation's wars, because we are warriors, we are also uniquely able to do some of these other new missions that are coming along—peacekeeping, humanitarian relief, disaster relief—you name it, we can do it . . . but we never want to do it in such a way that we lose sight of the focus of why you have armed forces—to fight and win the nation's wars."[10] In his testimony

9. Data in this paragraph are from U.S. Congress, Congressional Budget Office, *Enhancing U.S. Security through Foreign Aid* (Washington, D.C.: Congressional Budget Office, 1994), 31–32.

10. Press conference on September 1, 1993, cited in statement by Col. Harry G. Summers, Jr., USA (Ret.), before the U.S. House of Representatives, Committee on Foreign Affairs, Subcommittee on International Security, International Organizations, and Human Rights, September 21, 1993, and repr. in *Strategic Review* (Fall 1993): 70.

Table 15. Active Peacekeeping Operations of the United Nations, 1995

	Date Established	No. Personnel	U.S. Participation?	Estimated 1995 Expenses	Command
U.N. Force in Cyprus (UNFICYP)	March 1964	1,183	No	$44 million	Brig. Gen. (Finland)
U.N. Military Observer Group in India and Pakistan (UNMOGIP)	April 1948	39	No	$8 million	Maj. Gen. (Uruguay)
U.N. Interim Force in Lebanon (UNIFIL)	March 1978	5,146	No	$135 million	Maj. Gen. (Norway)
U.N. Disengagement Observer Force (UNDOF) to oversee cease-fire between Syria and Israel on Golan Heights	May 1974	1,030	No	$32 million	Maj. Gen. (Netherlands)
U.N. Truce Supervision Organization (UNTSO)	May 1948	218	Yes (17 military observers)	$32 million	Col. (New Zealand)
U.N. Assistance Mission in Rwanda (UNAMIR)	October 1993	5,522	No	$240 million	Maj. Gen. (Canada)
U.N. Observer Mission to Liberia (UNOMIL)	September 1993	84	No	$40 million	Maj. Gen. (Kenya)
U.N. Iraq-Kuwait Observation Mission (UNIKOM)	April 1991	1,142	Yes (15 military observers)	$66 million	Maj. Gen. (Nepal)
U.N. Protection Force (UNPROFOR) in former Yugoslavia	February 1992	39,789	Yes (891 troops in Former Yugoslav Republic of Macedonia (FYRM) and Croatia	$1.7 billion (at least)	Lt. Gen. (France)

Mission	Date	Number	U.S. participation	Cost	Commander
U.N. Mission for Referendum in W. Sahara (MINURSA)	April 1991	334	Yes (30 military observers)	$85 million	Brig. Gen. (Belgium)
UN Operation in Mozambique (ONUMOZ)[a]	December 1992	5,062	No	$22 million	Maj. Gen. (Bangladesh)
U.N. Angola Verification Mission II (UNAVEM II)	May 1991	135	No	$290 million	Maj. Gen. (Nigeria)
U.N. Operation in Somalia II (UNOSOM II)[b]	March 1993	9,412	No (although U.S. forces assist in withdrawal of UNOSOM)	$126 million	Lt. Gen. (Malaysia)
U.N. Mission in Georgia (UNOMIG)	August 1993	134	Yes (4 military observers)	$22 million	Brig. Gen. (Denmark)
U.N. Observer Mission in El Salvador (ONUSAL)[c]	May 1991	34	No	$4 million	Col. (Spain)
U.N. Mission in Haiti (UNMIH)	September 1993	74	Yes (5 troops, to increase to 2,200 when UNMIH deployment is complete)	$255 million	Maj. Gen. (U.S.A.)
U.N. Mission of Observers in Tajikistan (UNMOT)	December 1994	17	No	$10 million	Brig. Gen. (Jordan)

SOURCE: U.S. Central Intelligence Agency, *Worldwide Peacekeeping Operations, 1995* (Washington, D.C.: Central Intelligence Agency, April 1995).

[a]All forces were to withdraw by Janurary 31, 1995.
[b]All forces were to withdraw by March 31, 1995.
[c]All forces were to withdraw by April 30, 1995.

Table 16. Cold War U.N. Peacekeeping Operations, 1947–1985

Mission Name, Duration	Mission Description
U.N. Special Committee on the Balkans (UNSCOB), 1947–51	Investigate external support for guerrilla activities in Greece
U.N. Truce Supervision Organization (UNTSO), 1948–	Monitor cease-fires along Israeli border
U.N. Military Observer Group in India and Pakistan (UNMOGIP), 1949–	Monitor cease-fire in Jammu and Kashmir
U.N. Emergency Force (UNEF I), 1956–67	Separate Israeli and Egyptian forces in Sinai
U.N. Observer Group in Lebanon (UNOGIL), 1958	Monitor infiltration of troops and arms from Syria into Lebanon
U.N. Operation in the Congo (ONUC), 1960–64	Provide military assistance to Congolese government; restore civil order
U.N. Temporary Executive Authority (UNTEA), 1962–63	Administer and maintain order in West New Guinea pending transfer to Indonesia
U.N. Yemen Observation Mission (UNYOM), 1963–64	Monitor infiltration into Yemen via Saudi border
U.N. Force in Cyprus (UNFICYP), 1964–	Maintain order; after 1974, monitor buffer zone
U.N. India Pakistan Observer Mission (UNIPOM), 1965–66	Monitor cease-fire in India-Pakistan War of 1965
U.N. Emergency Force II (UNEF II), 1974–79	Separate Israeli and Egyptian forces in Sinai
U.N. Disengagement Observer Force (UNDOF), 1974–	Monitor separation of Israeli and Syrian forces on Golan Heights
U.N. Interim Force in Lebanon (UNIFIL), 1978–	Establish buffer zone between Israel and Lebanon

SOURCE: William J. Durch, ed., *The Evolution of UN Peacekeeping: Case Studies and Comparative Analysis* (New York: St. Martin's Press, 1993), 8.

before Congress in September 1993, Colonel Harry G. Summers, Jr., pointed to the concern among U.S. military professionals that an overemphasis on peacekeeping and other nonmilitary operations would erode the military's sense of its core missions and responsibilities.[11] According to Summers, persons calling for massive involvement of U.S. armed forces in peacekeeping, nation building, and additional operations other than war are "unwittingly turning traditional American civil–military relations

11. Ibid., 69–72.

on its head."[12] Summers is concerned that taking on social or political tasks may displace a military ethos centered on war, to the detriment of the U.S. armed forces and of American society: "Growing out of civilian academic conceits that one can change the world with the tools of social science, this wrongheaded notion that political, social and economic institutions can be built with the sword flies in the face of not only our Vietnam experience, but also the centuries-old American model of civil–military relations."[13]

The civil war in Yugoslavia, leading to the breakup of that country after 1991, provided a case study of the difficulty in obtaining commitments by the great powers to multilateral military intervention. Reports of genocide and the potential for the conflict to escalate beyond the Balkans called for some kind of concerted European or U.N. action, either to separate the combatants or to impose a cease-fire and return to the status quo ante. However, none of the European security organizations seemed able to take the lead. NATO had been designed for an entirely different mission. The West European Union (WEU) was enjoying a welcome rebirth, but it had not yet matured as a center of gravity for preventive diplomacy or for multilateral military intervention. The Conference on Security and Cooperation in Europe, subsequently the Organization for Security and Cooperation in Europe (OSCE), was the most inclusive body capable of taking a stand, but its very inclusiveness precluded harmonious action of a military sort. Sadly, the recognition dawned by 1994 that only a military organization with the capabilities of NATO or the former Warsaw Pact, but without the aura of Cold War illegitimacy either of those organizations would carry, could intervene effectively to put a stop to the slaughter in Croatia and Bosnia.

But even if effective intervention could be obtained, a question remained: On whose side intervention should be undertaken? Collective security, the political umbrella under which multilateral military intervention takes place, presupposes that one can identify an aggressor and a defender, a good guy and a bad guy.[14] In a multinational civil war of the Yugoslav type, the problem of identifying aggressors and defenders would

12. Ibid., 71.
13. Ibid.
14. Comparison of the theoretical principle of collective security with the actual practice is provided by Inis L. Claude, Jr., "Collective Security after the Cold War," ch. 1 in Gary L. Guertner, ed., *Collective Security in Europe and Asia* (Carlisle Barracks, Pa.: U.S. Army War College, Strategic Studies Institute, March 1992), 7–28. Claude notes that excessive optimism about the probable success of collective security frequently follows successful coalition wars (see esp. pp. 14–15).

defy consensus or political objectivity.[15] Prominent U.S. politicians and defense experts called for military interventions of various kinds from 1992 through 1995, and some made compelling cases that the chaos in former Yugoslavia could not be ignored. However strong the imperative, the "how" remained difficult if not impossible to answer until the Dayton peace accord of December 1995.

The evolution of U.N. operations in Somalia in 1992 and 1993 shows some of the difficulty inherent in bringing multinational force to bear on a situation of internal disorder. The original U.N. operation in Somalia, UNOSOM I, was authorized in April 1992 under Chapter VI of the U.N. Charter as a peacekeeping operation. It could not provide adequate security for relief organizations seeking to distribute food to starving Somalis. A stronger force and a broader political mission were called for. The United Nations therefore gave its blessing in December 1992 to a U.S.-led military intervention by a coalition of nineteen states, authorized under Chapter VII, peace enforcement (UNITAF). The transition from peacekeeping to peace enforcement called for a more sophisticated political strategy on the part of the United Nations than it was able, in the event, to put together. So long as the sizable UNITAF force held sway in Mogadishu and other major cities, warlord-led clan violence diminished. But this meant that the United Nations, in the absence of any central Somali government, was the de facto government of the country.[16]

In the mind of the U.N. secretary-general, therefore, this peace enforcement mission also entailed a U.N. contribution to nation building by bringing about reconciliation among competing Somali warlords. However, despite the initial military successes of UNITAF, the United Nations had no political agenda or strategy for handling the warlords. Warlord Muhamed Farah Aideed's forces, the strongest among the contending Somali factions, waited out the transition from UNITAF to UNOSOM II in early May 1993. Aideed exploited UNITAF and UNOSOM'S political weakness, manipulating events in Mogadishu and playing off one member of the UNOSOM coalition against another. As one expert writer warned, "In future peacemaking or peace enforcement operations, the United States and its coalition allies must develop a strategy for meeting the terms of their mandate that integrates military end states with effective political action. Failure to do so will invariably provide local Rambos the oppor-

15. For an analysis of possible uses of ground forces and air power in Bosnia and the degree to which the use of force can or cannot satisfy U.S. or U.N. objectives, see Capt. Brett D. Barkey, USMC, "Bosnia: A Question of Intervention," *Strategic Review* (Fall 1993): 48–59.

16. My appreciation of this issue owes much to Col. William Flavin, USA, formerly of the U.S. Army War College, Carlisle Barracks, Pa. He is not responsible for my arguments here.

tunities they seek to get inside UN and coalition decision processes and turn events to their own advantage."[17]

The questions concerning the operational feasibility of post–Cold War contingency operations, whether for U.S. or for multinational military forces, are the same. What is the political objective? What are the military objectives which follow from this political objective? Are these military objectives attainable with the forces that the United States or the United Nations are willing to commit? Similar questions, in the case of U.S. unilateral operations or a U.S. commitment of troops to multistate operations, must be answered with regard to American domestic politics and its unavoidable connection to foreign policy.

Conventional or Unconventional Wars?

An accurate assessment of future peacekeeping requirements is only as good as a correct forecast about the nature of future war. Experts offer no consensus. Future war is likely to be marked by a mixture of high-technology equipment and low-technology strategy. Reconnaissance-strike complexes using satellite or airborne detection, rapid data processing, and precision-guided weapons will make deep strategic attack possible without nuclear weapons.[18] At the same time, terrorists and other nonstate actors will challenge states and their militaries for the monopoly of war-related information. The electronics and communications revolutions of recent years empower small groups of clandestine warriors by giving them access to global communications networks and the potential for spoofing or otherwise interfering with military command, control, and communications networks.[19]

Futuristic technology thus enables both the big battalion armies and the flea warriors to reduce uncertainty and to minimize friction. In addi-

17. Walter S. Clarke, "Testing the World's Resolve in Somalia," *Parameters* (Winter 1993–94): 42–58.

18. Of particular importance in high-technology conventional warfare are reliable intelligence systems, including prompt feedback of tactical intelligence. Deficiencies in U.S. performance with respect to providing current target imagery for tactical air operations is noted in Rep. Les Aspin and Rep. William Dickinson, *Defense for a New Era: Lessons of the Persian Gulf War* (Washington, D.C.: GPO, 1992), esp. 36. See also William J. Perry, "Desert Storm and Deterrence in the Future," ch. 10 in Joseph S. Nye and Roger K. Smith, eds., *After the Storm: Lessons from the Gulf War* (Lanham, Md.: Aspen Strategy Group, 1992), 241–64.

19. Alvin and Heidi Toffler, *War and Anti-War: Survival at the Dawn of the 21st Century* (Boston: Little, Brown, 1993).

tion, even without high technology, some unconventional wars may fill Clausewitz's prescription, about the relationship between policy and force, better than conventional war. Few who experienced the Vietnam War would now argue, even if they had prior to U.S. involvement in that conflict, that counterrevolutionary wars are more military than they are political.[20] As Sam C. Sarkesian notes, in revolutionary wars "the people of the indigenous area compose the true battleground. Clausewitzian notions and high-tech military capability are usually irrelevant in unconventional conflicts. Conventional military capability and the 'largest' battalions rarely decide the outcome. The center of gravity is in the political-social milieu of the indigenous populace, rather than in the armed forces."[21]

The need to fight syncretic wars which are simultaneously conventional and unconventional drives U.S. military historians and planners back to the Revolutionary War roots of American military practice. As the historian Russell Weigley has noted, General George Washington preferred to model the Continental Army along the lines of eighteenth-century European military forces.[22] Washington feared that irregular forces could not be counted on against British regular forces, and he also remained wary of the potential costs of guerrilla warfare to the American social fabric. Even his postwar efforts to shape the peacetime U.S. armed forces favored a small regular army supported by a compulsory-service

20. Harry G. Summers, Jr., *On Strategy: A Critical Analysis of the Vietnam War* (New York: Dell Publishers, 1984) argues that the United States should have followed a conventional military strategy in Vietnam, leaving counterinsurgency, civic action, and the like to the South Vietnamese. In his view, U.S. strategy failed in Vietnam because it strayed from military traditionalism into politico-military amateurism, especially into graduated escalation and counterinsurgency. Sam C. Sarkesian, *America's Forgotten Wars: The Counterrevolutionary Past and Lessons for the Future* (Westport, Conn.: Greenwood Press, 1984), 194–218, provides a different assessment, contending that the military aspects of the war were especially complex and involved an unusual mixture of conventional and unconventional campaigns.

21. Sarkesian, "U.S. Strategy and Unconventional Conflicts: The Elusive Goal," ch. 10 in Sarkesian and John Allen Williams, eds., *The U.S. Army in a New Security Era* (Boulder, Colo.: Lynne Rienner, 1990), 199. See also Leslie H. Gelb with Richard K. Betts, *The Irony of Vietnam: The System Worked* (Washington, D.C.: Brookings Institution, 1979), for an argument that bad foreign policy resulted from a U.S. domestic policymaking process that worked as it was designed to. For a counterpoint to the Gelb–Betts arguments, see D. Michael Shafer, *Deadly Paradigms: The Failure of U.S. Counterinsurgency Policy* (Princeton, N.J.: Princeton University Press, 1988), 240–75, esp. 260–61.

22. Russell Weigley, "American Strategy from Its Beginnings through the First World War," in Peter Paret, ed., *Makers of Modern Strategy: From Machiavelli to the Nuclear Age* (Princeton: Princeton University Press, 1986), 410–12, and id., *The American Way of War: A History of United States Military Strategy and Policy* (New York: Macmillan, 1973).

and federally regulated militia.[23] On the other hand, America's revolutionary war against Britain also included successful unconventional campaigns against British regulars, such as the guerrilla attacks on General Burgoyne's lines of communication and flanks contributory to his defeat at Saratoga.[24] The U.S. professional military heritage from the War of 1812 was also a mixed estate. On one side stood the Battle of New Orleans, suggesting that citizen-soldiers could fight with distinction against regular British forces. On the other side stood the battles of Chippewa and Lundy's Lane, in which American regulars acquitted themselves well against their British counterparts in open field battles without use of unconventional tactics.[25]

Antithetical views on the issue have been stated by the military historian Martin Van Creveld and by Colonel Harry G. Summers, Jr., USA (Ret.), a noted military analyst of the Vietnam and Gulf wars. According to Van Creveld, large-scale conventional war is mostly obsolete. The future of warfare lies in low-intensity conflict, terrorism, and the like.[26] The reasons for the purported eclipse of large-scale conventional war amount to an affirmation that this kind of conflict does not pay political and military dividends relative to its costs. Van Creveld argues that this trend represents a dismantling of the Clausewitzian paradigm which dominated military strategy formation from the Peace of Westphalia until the end of the Second World War. In Clausewitz's model of the relationship between war and policy, a trinitarian unity among people, government, and army supported the conduct of war on behalf of state interests. War was something done on behalf of the state, and only on behalf of the state. This was an important marker in Western military and political history, for it made possible, along with the political theories of Machiavelli and Hobbes, the "realist" tradition in international politics which informed generations of scholars and students.

Van Creveld argues, in essence, that the realist-statist model is no longer very realistic. The state can no longer assert its monopoly over the resort to violence. If he is correct in this argument, the implications are profound. Once we relax the assumption that trinitarian war is the normative model for all armed struggle, all intellectual hell breaks loose in military studies. We return to the pre-Westphalian environment in which tribes and tribunes resorted to war with the same assumption of political legitimacy as governments. The contemporary civil strife within the for-

23. Weigley, "American Strategy from Its Beginnings through the First World War," 412.
24. Ibid., 410, and Sarkesian, *America's Forgotten Wars,* 107.
25. Sarkesian, *America's Forgotten Wars,* 110.
26. Martin Van Creveld, *The Transformation of War* (New York: Free Press, 1991).

mer Soviet Union, as in Georgia and as between Armenia and Azerbaijan, may be normative for the future of warfare. So, too, may the upheavals in the Balkans which have pitted ethnic and nationality groups against each other in a holy war of satanic proportions.

Harry Summers argues, in contrast to Van Creveld's view, that low-intensity conflict cannot be normative for the U.S. armed forces.[27] Given U.S. political culture and military traditions, the Gulf War of 1991 is more representative of the kinds of wars that the American people and the U.S. Congress will support: high-intensity warfare in which U.S. manpower is spared, technology is exploited to the fullest, and war termination is obtained in the shortest possible time.[28] Undoubtedly the Gulf War was one of a kind, but Summers's argument holds more broadly that high-technology, conventional war is the kind of war that the United States has traditionally waged with great effectiveness. The U.S. track record for low-intensity warfare, on the other hand, is dismal. Scholars also note that the United States has even failed to learn very much about low-intensity conflict from its own historical involvement in wars of this type, including the Revolutionary War against Britain, nineteenth-century Indian fighting, and early twentieth-century pacification of the Philippines.[29]

There are some cautions that we can derive from Cold War history. One such is that forces which are optimized for high-intensity conflict against industrial-strength armies cannot simply be reduced in size and reassigned to low-intensity warfare. During the 1960s and before the Vietnam escalation, for example, it was assumed by planners that forces adequate for war between NATO and the Warsaw Pact would easily brush aside smaller and less heavily armed foes.[30] The result of applying models of mid-intensity, conventional warfare to counterguerrilla warfare was indiscriminate killing of noncombatants and alienation of the rural population in South Vietnam. Neil Sheehan recounts the reflections of Colonel John Paul Vann on U.S. tactics in that war:

> Vann had initially found it difficult to believe the utter lack of discrimination and capriciousness with which fighter-bombers and artillery were turned loose. A single shot from a sniper was enough to stop a battalion while the captain in charge called for an air

27. Summers, *On Strategy: A Critical Analysis of the Vietnam War.*

28. Summers, *On Strategy II: A Critical Analysis of the Gulf War* (New York: Dell Publishers, 1992).

29. Sarkesian, *America's Forgotten Wars,* esp. 155–94, and Andrew F. Krepinevich, Jr., *The Army and Vietnam* (Baltimore: Johns Hopkins University Press, 1986), 5.

30. See the discussion of the U.S. Army "concept" for warfare in Krepinevich, *The Army and Vietnam,* esp. 4–8.

strike or an artillery barrage on the hamlet from which the sniper had fired. Vann would argue . . . that it was ridiculous to let one sniper halt a whole battalion and criminal to let the sniper provoke them into smashing a hamlet. Why didn't they send a squad to maneuver around the sniper and scare him off or kill him while the battalion continued its advance?[31]

It is now acknowledged that low-intensity conflict or unconventional warfare, including counterinsurgency and counterterrorism, is qualitatively different from larger-scale warfare.[32] Another caution derived from the Cold War is that low-intensity conflicts involve ambiguous political missions for which U.S. popular support cannot be assumed and must be assiduously built. A third lesson is that the U.S. armed forces' sense of military professionalism is compromised by missions outside the competency of military training and experience.[33] Assigning to military forces the mission of "nation building" confuses a military mission with a broader political one, to the probable detriment of the military as well as the political objectives.

Robert S. McNamara's belated "memoir" about his role in the U.S. decisionmaking process for Vietnam is brutally candid in its indictment of the high-level U.S. civilian and military failure to understand what kind of war was being fought. According to McNamara, he and other principals made at least the following major conceptual mistakes about the war: (1) misunderstood the geopolitical intentions of North Vietnam, the Viet Cong, China, and the Soviet Union; (2) viewed the leadership and people of South Vietnam in terms of the American experience and, as a result, "totally misjudged the political forces within the country;"[34] (3) underestimated the power of nationalism to motivate the opponent; (4) reflected "profound ignorance" of the history, culture, and politics of the people in the region; (5) failed to recognize the limitations of modern, high-technol-

31. Neil Sheehan, *A Bright Shining Lie: John Paul Vann and America in Vietnam* (New York: Random House, 1988), 107–8 (see also p. 11 on Vann's view of U.S. attrition strategy in Vietnam).

32. Sam C. Sarkesian suggests that the term "unconventional conflict" is preferable to "low-intensity conflict." Unconventional conflicts are nontraditional and not in conformity with the American way of war. These kinds of conflicts emphasize social and political variables, especially the problem of revolution and counterrevolution, instead of the military dimensions of conflict. See Sarkesian, "U.S. Strategy and Unconventional Conflicts," 195–216.

33. Sam C. Sarkesian, *Beyond the Battlefield: The New Military Professionalism* (New York: Pergamon Press, 1981), chs. 4–6.

34. Robert S. McNamara, *In Retrospect: The Tragedy and Lessons of Vietnam* (New York: Random House, 1995), 322.

ogy military forces, equipment, and doctrine in conflict with an unconventional people's movement based on high motivation.[35] These are the
kinds of mistakes that preclude instant replay regardless of the efficiency
of the forces battling at the tactical level.

Some sociologists believe that demography is destiny. If so, the complexity of military persuasion, especially in the use of armed forces for
"operations other than war," grows with increased urbanization in the
developing societies of Asia, Africa, the Middle East, and parts of Latin
America. Mass migration caused by famine, deforestation, and other factors has brought millions of displaced persons across or within borders
from rural into urban areas. Much of the developing world is made up of
agrarian societies in their first generation of significant decrease in mor-
tality rates. As a result, the population base in those countries, predominantly poor, is growing exponentially. For example: in 1950, the population of Africa was half that of Europe; in 1985, the populations of Africa
and Europe were approximately equal (about 480 million in each case);
and by the year 2025, Africa's population is expected to be about three
times that of Europe.[36]

Slums and shantytowns from Monrovia to Mogadishu provide ample
opportunities for insurgency and entrapments for the conduct of OOTW.
Classic insurgencies were rooted in the peasantry and based in the countryside, following the Maoist and Maoist-derived models based on the
successful Chinese (and, later, Vietnamese) experiences.[37] Today's insurgents can follow migrations into the growing numbers of large cities in
the Third World, many located within territorial states that are themselves unable to provide security for much of their urban population.
Concealment of insurgents and terrorists within a large urban population
is easily accomplished. Sometimes entire sections of urban slums and
shantytowns belong not to the authorities but to the warlords or rebels
who actually hold control there. As two experts on OOTW have noted
about the opportunities for insurgents in urban parts of the developing
world:

> Even if insurgents choose not to base their operations in urban
> areas, they can nonetheless take advantage of urbanization. Rural-
> based insurgencies are finding cities increasingly attractive and lu-

35. These and other lessons are listed ibid., 321–23.
36. Paul Kennedy, *Preparing for the Twenty-first Century* (New York: Random House,
1993), 24.
37. Donald M. Snow, *Distant Thunder: Third World Conflict and the New International
Order* (New York: St. Martin's Press, 1993), 67–71. Mao's concepts of revolutionary warfare
are derived from Sun Tzu. See Sun Tzu, *The Art of War,* trans. and ed. Samuel B. Griffith
(Oxford: Oxford University Press, 1963).

crative targets. Whereas cities were once the culmination of a revolution, with the new proliferation of urban areas—and the inability of governments to defend them all—cities have become relatively simple targets that yield high dividends for low cost.[38]

The tactics open to insurgents in the more urbanized environment of the developing world, and in some of the less well protected cities of the developed world, include the disruption or destruction of electrical power and other energy supplies, of communications, of water and sewage and, most important, of security. To use an economic analogy: when the demand for security can no longer be supplied by the responsible state authorities, as in Somalia in 1992, then sources other than the state will supply security, with or without international approval. These sources may be Somali warlords or narcoterrorists in Peru. People will seek whatever protection they can find from sources that they consider dependable and over which they presume to have some influence.

Continuing Controversy

Can the U.S. Armed Forces Sustain "Operations Other than War"?

In the strictest sense, collective security implies a virtually unanimous coalition of law-abiding states precommitted to wage war against any state judged to have aggressed against the peace. Thus, most U.N. peacekeeping and peace enforcement operations during the Cold War were not true expressions of collective security theory.[39] The post–Cold War world has already found the U.S. military involved in a number of peacekeeping, peace enforcement, humanitarian assistance, and other nontraditional operations. Those taking place within a mere two-year period since the end of the Cold War are noted in Table 17.

Peace operations may combine irregular warfare, a mixture of conventional and unconventional forces shooting at one another, along with civic action and nation building. The cognitive complexity of peacekeeping or peacemaking objectives adds to the difficulty of obtaining a good fit between policy objectives and politico-military means. For example,

38. Taw and Hoffman, "Operations Other than War," 228.

39. For perspective on the theory of collective security and its implications for present U.S. and U.N. options, see Inis L. Claude, Jr., "Collective Security after the Cold War," ch. 1 in Gary L. Guertner, ed., *Collective Security in Europe and Asia* (Carlisle Barracks, Pa.: U.S. Army War College, March 1992), 7–28.

Table 17. Selected U.S. Military Post–Cold War Nontraditional Operations, 1990–1992

Location	Date	Mission	Involvement
U.S.A. borders ("JTF Six")	June 1990–	Drug interdiction	100 military plus civilian law enforcement
Kurdistan (Operation Provide Comfort)	April–June 1991	Refugee relief	12,000 U.S. forces with 11,000 partners
Bangladesh (Operation Sea Angel)	May–June 1991	Flood relief	8,000 U.S. Marines and Navy
Philippines (Operation Fiery Vigil)	July 1991	Mt. Inatubo volcano rescue	5,000 U.S. Navy and Marines
Western Sahara	September 1991	Observer force	U.N. military with U.S. officers
Zaire	September 1991	Rescue foreign nationals	French and Belgian troops with U.S. airlift
Cuba	November 1991– May 1992	Haitian refugee relief	U.S. military
Russia (Operation Provide Hope	December 1991– February 1992	Food relief	Western and U.S. airlift
Former Yugoslavia ("U.N. Protection Force")	March 1992–	Peacekeeping	NATO and WEU naval deployments offshore; NATO AWACS monitor "no fly" zone over Bosnia
Italy (Operation Volcano Buster)	April 1992	Mt. Etna volcano rescue	Small force of U.S. Navy and Marines
California ("Joint Task Force L.A.")	May 1992	Restore domestic order	8,000 U.S. Army and Marines; 12,000 National Guard
Florida ("JTF Hurricane Andrew")	August–September 1992	Disaster relief	21,000 U.S. Army, Air Force, and Marines; 6,000 National Guard

Table 17. *Continued*

Location	Date	Mission	Involvement
Iraq (Operation Southern Watch)	August 1992–	Surveillance	U.S. Air Force and Navy
Hawaii	September 1992	Hurricane Iniki disaster relief	National Guard and small U.S. Marines/Air Force
Somalia (Operation Restore Hope)	December 1992–	U.S. "invasion" and pacification for famine relief, restoration of order	All branches of service plus allied U.N. forces

SOURCE: Adapted, by permission, from John Allen Williams and Charles Moskos, "Civil–Military Relations after the Cold War," a paper prepared for delivery at the annual meeting of the American Political Science Association, September 2–5, 1993, pp. 5a and 5b.

NOTE: JTF = joint task force; WEU = West European Union; AWACS = Airborne Warning and Control System.

the United States chose to intervene in Somalia in December 1992 in the face of the collapse of a militarily undersubscribed U.N. relief mission. President George Bush declared that the objectives of the U.S. military commitment were to restore a sufficient degree of order for the shipment of food to the places where it was needed. In 1993 it soon became clear that the maintenance of order in Somalia required pacification of Mogadishu and other areas against the terrorist potential of various warlords, especially Muhamed Farah Aideed. Ultimately the United States became engaged in major combat operations against Aideed's forces, culminating in a firefight on October 3, 1993, which cost the lives of 18 U.S. soldiers. The same battle caused a domestic political flap in Washington and prompted President Clinton to do two things: (1) to send 17,000 U.S. troops immediately to the region and (2) to announce that the United States would withdraw all but a few hundred of its forces from Somalia by the end of March 1994.

The disastrous engagement of October 3, 1993, between U.S. and warlord forces resulted in part from problems of U.N. and U.S. command-and-control interoperability. Another issue forcing congressional scrutiny of the U.S. commitment to peacekeeping or peace enforcement operations was that of cost, both in treasure and in impaired readiness of U.S. combat forces to meet national policy requirements.

The case of Somalia illustrates the potential complexity of "military operations on urban terrain" (MOUT) taking place in a political context that mandates "operations other than war." Operations in urban terrain are difficult enough under the comparatively simple political conditions of conventional warfare between states. Traditional U.S. and other military doctrine for fighting in built-up areas, especially in large cities, has consistently advised: Avoid it. Large-scale mechanized and motorized infantry and armored forces, of the kind deployed by the principal combatants in World War II, were trained to bypass large cities and starve them out. German and Soviet experiences in the Second World War reinforced this traditional propensity for the avoidance of urban warfare. The Germans used encirclement and starvation tactics against Leningrad with more success than they were able to obtain by storming Stalingrad (although Leningrad was eventually liberated). And the Germans lost more than manpower and equipment in the house-to-house fighting at Stalingrad: they lost their reputation for invincibility. The successful storming of Berlin by Stalin's armies in 1945 came at a terrible price. Marshals G. K. Zhukov and I. S. Konev were ordered to take Berlin at all costs, according to Stalin's preset timetable. They did so, at a cost in Soviet combat deaths then acknowledged as around 100,000. Russian archives now reveal that the true number was about 600,000 killed in action. The two Soviet fronts commanded by Zhukov and Konev liberated the city only by physically destroying everything in their path, including any friendly forces that happened to get in their way.

Obviously, use of overwhelming firepower of the kind brought to bear in the 1945 Berlin operation would not be appropriate for OOTW against Third World urban terrorists or insurgents. One cannot combat an insurgency by blowing up the very people and their resources that one has been invited to save from anarchy. Therefore, a political strategy for conciliation of opposed and conflicting forces is as necessary to peace operations in urban areas as is a capability for disarming those who deliberately remain outside the framework of negotiations. Two expert analysts note: "As they learn the specialized skills required by each environment (urban and rural), forces must also be trained to treat the civilian population with respect, so as to prevent popular alienation and to improve the conditions for gathering human intelligence. They may also have to coordinate police and military responsibilities with the civilian government's political countermeasures, if any, as well as efforts by other agencies."[40]

40. Taw and Hoffman, "Operations Other than War," 230.

The Clinton national military strategy required that U.S. combat forces be capable of fighting in two major regional contingencies, say the Gulf and Korea, almost simultaneously. Members of the U.S. Congress well informed about military affairs, among them Representative Ike Skelton (D–Mo.), warned that the United States would have to draw forces away from their peacekeeping missions in order to fulfill the wartime requirements of the national military strategy. According to Congressman Skelton, there are five Army contingency divisions that are supposed to be war-ready at a moment's notice. Three of them—the 10th, 24th, and 101st—were, as of October 1993, partially committed to peacekeeping operations, from Somalia to the Sinai.[41]

Former Army Chief of Staff General Carl E. Vuono, during congressional hearings in October 1993, discussed the impact of U.S. commitments to peacekeeping operations. He noted that in autumn 1993, available U.S. Army forces were committed in part to the following peacekeeping/peace enforcement or humanitarian operations:

1. Somalia. Major elements of three Army divisions, one corps, plus theater Army logistical support.
2. Sinai. Major elements of two brigades in two Army divisions plus associated logistical support.
3. Macedonia. Major elements of two brigades and two Army divisions plus associated logistical support.
4. Bosnia. Forces held in readiness to meet possible NATO peacekeeping/peace enforcement requirements (about triple the force requirements for Somalia).

Overall, according to General Vuono, Army forces in autumn 1993 prepared for commitment, committed, or recovering from commitments to peacekeeping or humanitarian operations constituted a force equal to the major elements of about two corps, for a strength (including rotation base) of about 150,000 troops.[42]

The U.S. Congress in 1993 was also interested in the financial and the readiness costs of peacekeeping operations to U.S. forces. In FY 1993, the armed services reprogrammed about $953 million from other accounts, usually operations and maintenance, to support the unfunded costs of peacekeeping and humanitarian operations. During that same fiscal year, Congress increased the funds designated for peacekeeping by more than $1 billion. According to some congressional sources, however, this fund-

41. Roos, "Perils of Peacekeeping," 13–16.
42. Testimony of Gen. Vuono cited ibid., 17.

ing did not cover all of the services' additional expenses related to peace-keeping operations. For example, Representative Norman Dicks (D–Wash.) claimed in October 1993 that the U.S. Army currently faced a shortfall of more than $600 million in its operations and maintenance accounts by dint of its support for activities in Somalia, Southwest Asia (Iraq), and domestic crisis response.[43] A summary of peacekeeping and humanitarian mission costs and of congressional appropriations by service for FY 1993 appears in Table 18.

In addition to the readiness and financial costs of U.S. involvement in peacekeeping operations, there are the potentially dysfunctional strategic costs. The skepticism of Harry Summers and others about the suitability of nation building as a mission for armed forces, not to mention the well-documented U.S. aversion to protracted low-intensity conflicts, raises notes of caution for presidents and planners alike. The U.N. flag can legit-imize an operation which otherwise might be doubtful of support in the U.S. Congress or in public opinion. But approval in the Security Council does not translate directly into military preparedness for, or public acceptance of, the strategic risks inherent in peacekeeping or peace enforcement. U.S. experience from Korea to Somalia seems to show that operations under one national command, though nominally under the aegis of multinational bodies, enjoy a higher probability of success than military interventions commanded by multinational forces. The Gulf War experience was not really normative in this regard, since U.S. and allied NATO experience provided ready-made interoperability and planning guidance for tactical operations.

The likelihood of success for U.N. peacekeeping or peace enforcement operations without U.S. support and participation is admittedly suspect. Nevertheless, important constraints and risks for U.S. strategy and policy are apparent in present and foreseeable commitments to multinational peacekeeping. First of all, the ability of U.S. armed forces to meet the requirements of national military strategy for two nearly simultaneous

Table 18. U.S. Service Costs for Peacekeeping and Humanitarian Operations, FY 1993 (Millions of Dollars)

	Army	Navy	Air Force	Other	Total
Added funds sought	201.1	222.4	240.2	288.9	952.6
Approved by Congress	201.1	197.5	340.2	311.9	1,050.7

SOURCE: John G. Roos, "Perils of Peacekeeping: Tallying the Costs in Blood, Coin, Prestige, and Readiness," *Armed Forces Journal International* (December 1993): 17.

43. Roos, "Perils of Peacekeeping," 16.

major regional contingencies may be compromised. Second, the lapse of command between multinational policy directives and individual state armed forces makes peacekeeping operations potentially more difficult than traditional combat. Third, financial costs of U.S. participation in peacekeeping may be temporarily swallowed in service operations and maintenance accounts, to the possible detriment of wartime readiness.

9

THE SPREAD of NUCLEAR WEAPONS AFTER the COLD WAR

In late November 1994 the U.S. government announced that it had just completed a most unusual "purchase" from the government of Kazakhstan, a former Soviet republic. Kazakhstan had agreed to let the United States purchase some 600 kilograms of highly enriched uranium that might otherwise have fallen into the hands of nuclear terrorists. With the concurrence of the Russian government, a U.S. team of technical experts oversaw the storage and shipment of the dangerous materials to Oak Ridge, Tennessee, for storage and conversion. The nuclear material could have been used by knowledgeable persons to fabricate as many as fifty weapons.[1]

The U.S. purchase of enriched uranium from Kazakhstan was part of the Cooperative Threat Reduction (CTR) program authorized by the U.S. Congress in 1991. The aid provided under this program, colloquially known as "Nunn–Lugar" after its Senate cosponsors, supported a variety of arms limitation and nonproliferation objectives, including the following: destruction and dismantlement of nuclear weapons and launchers; demilitarization of the scientific and technical establishment of the former Soviet Union (FSU); and improved accounting, monitoring, and protection for direct-use nuclear materials (highly enriched uranium and plutonium) located at some eighty to one hundred FSU civilian, nuclear, and naval facilities.

Portions of this chapter also appear in Stephen J. Cimbala, "Proliferation and Peace: An Agnostic View," *Armed Forces and Society* 22, no. 2 (Winter 1995/96): 211–34.
  1. *Philadelphia Inquirer,* November 23, 1993.

The U.S. concern about the fate of former Soviet nuclear weapons, materials, and supporting personnel and infrastructure was based not only on anticipation of problems but on recent history. The worst nuclear accident ever took place in 1986 at Chernobyl, a city in north-central Ukraine (then part of the Soviet Union). About twenty-five miles from this previously obscure city was the V. I. Lenin Nuclear Power Plant. During a test on April 26, 1986, the obscurity of Chernobyl became notoriety when reactor number 4 exploded, releasing thirty to forty times the amount of radioactivity of the atomic bombs dropped on Hiroshima and Nagasaki. The Soviet government initially revealed nothing about the incident. Monitoring stations in Western Europe first detected radioactivity drifting from the accident, confirmed later by other sources, including satellite photography. The consequences of the accident were enormous: thirty-one lives were lost immediately, hundreds of thousands had to abandon entire cities and villages within a thirty-kilometer zone, and 3 million people may still be living in contaminated areas. Chernobyl became a symbol of Soviet managerial and technical incompetency. It also became a symbol of the risks of nuclear proliferation in countries even less capable of maintaining safe and secure nuclear production and storage.[2] Nor is complacency justified with respect to the problem of nuclear material diversion in the FSU, as Table 19 shows.

Many are justifiably skeptical that nuclear proliferation can be compatible with international political or military stability.[3] However, some experts contend that a controlled process of proliferation would support stability instead of detracting from it.[4] Debates between optimists and

2. Information on the Chernobyl accident is summarized and adapted from Texas A & M University Gopher Server, Russian Historical Archives, transmitted in June 1995. I am solely responsible for its use here.

3. Lewis A. Dunn, *Controlling the Bomb: Nuclear Proliferation in the 1980s* (New Haven, Conn.: Yale University Press, 1982). For more recent assessments, see Leonard S. Spector and Virginia Foran, *Preventing Weapons Proliferation: Should the Regimes Be Combined?* (Warrenton, Va.: Stanley Foundation, October 1992); George H. Quester, *The Multilateral Management of International Security: The Nuclear Proliferation Model* (College Park: Center for International and Security Studies at Maryland, March 1993); John Hawes, *Nuclear Proliferation: Down to the Hard Cases* (College Park: Center for International and Security Studies at Maryland, June 1993); and Andrew J. Goodpaster, *Tighter Limits on Nuclear Arms: Issues and Opportunities for a New Era* (Washington, D.C.: Atlantic Council of the U.S., May 1992). All provide analysis suggestive of proliferation pessimism.

4. Kenneth N. Waltz, *The Spread of Nuclear Weapons: More May Be Better,* Adelphi Paper no. 171 (London: International Institute for Strategic Studies, 1981). See also Kenneth N. Waltz, "Nuclear Myths and Political Realities," *American Political Science Review* (September 1990): 731–45; John J. Mearsheimer, "The Case for a Ukrainian Nuclear Deterrent," *Foreign Affairs* (Summer 1993): 50–66; and Martin Van Creveld, *Nuclear Proliferation and the Future of Conflict* (New York: Free Press, 1993) among the more widely cited optimists. An argument for making a distinction between stabilizing and destabilizing cases of proliferation

Table 19. Selected, Known Nuclear Material Diversions, 1992–1994

Date of Diversion	Seizure Location and Date	Amount of Material	Kind of Material	Origin of Diversion
May–September 1992	Podolsk, Russia, October 9, 1992	1.5 kg	HEU (90% enrichment) in uranium dioxide powder	Podolsk, Russia (Scientific Production Association)
July 29, 1993	Andreeva Guba, Russia, August 1993	1.8 kg	HEU (30% enrichment)	Andreeva Guba, Russia (naval base storage facility)
November 27, 1993	Polyarny, Russia, June 1994	4.5 kg	HEU (20% enrichment)	Sevmorput, Russia (naval base storage facility)
?	Tengen, Germany, May 10, 1994	5.6 g	Pu-239 (99.78% pure)	?
?	Landshut, Germany, June 13, 1994	800 mg	HEU (enriched to 87.7% in uranium dioxide form)	?
?	Munich, Germany, August 10, 1994	560 g (363 g of Pu-239)	MOX fuel	?
?	Prague, Czech Republic, December 14, 1994	2.72 kg	HEU (enriched to 87.7% U-235, in uranium dioxide form)	?

SOURCE: Adapted from William C. Potter, "Before the Deluge? Assessing the Threat of Nuclear Leakage from the Post-Soviet States," *Arms Control Today* (October 1995): 10.

NOTE: HEU = highly enriched uranium; MOX = mixed oxide (of plutonium and uranium).

---

and for emphasizing safety and security of force operations in stabilizing cases is presented in William C. Martel and William T. Pendley, *Nuclear Coexistence: Rethinking U.S. Policy to Promote Stability in an Era of Proliferation* (Montgomery, Ala.: U.S. Air War College, April 1994). The urgency of denuclearization of existing arsenals, especially those in former Soviet republics other than Russia, is emphasized in Graham T. Allison, Ashton B. Carter, Steven E. Miller, and Philip Zelikow, "Cooperative Denuclearization: An International Agenda," in id., eds., *Cooperative Denuclearization: From Pledges to Deeds* (Cambridge, Mass.: Center for Science and International Affairs, Harvard University, 1993), 1–25. For an assessment of this literature and a critique of "rational deterrence" theory as applied to proliferation, see Peter D. Feaver, "Proliferation Optimism and Theories of Nuclear Operations," *Security Studies* (Spring/Summer 1993): 159–91.

pessimists about the spread of nuclear weapons have sometimes passed one another, owing to differences in methodology and conceptual focus.[5] In the discussion that follows, I do not try to revisit all previously published arguments for and against nuclear proliferation. Instead, I review three conceptual perspectives or frames of reference through which the nuclear past can be related explicitly and systematically to prognosis about nuclear futures.

Nuclear "Realism"

Nuclear positivism based on political realism (or nuclear realism) is of value to the extent that it acknowledges the importance of the nuclear revolution.[6] The nuclear revolution separated the accomplishment of military denial from the infliction of military punishment. The meaning of this for strategists was that military victory, defined prior to the nuclear age as the ability to prevail over opposed forces in battle, was now permissible only well below the level of total war. And less-than-total wars were risky as never before. Nuclear realists admit that these profound changes have taken place in the relationship between force and policy. They argue, however, that the new relationship between force and policy strengthens rather than weakens some perennial principles of international relations theory. Power is still king, but now the king is latent power in the form of risk manipulation and threat of war, instead of power actually displayed on the battlefield.

5. For recent assessments, see Robert D. Blackwill and Albert Carnesale, eds., *New Nuclear Nations: Consequences for U.S. Policy* (New York: Council on Foreign Relations, 1993), and Jacqueline R. Smith, "Nuclear Non-Proliferation Policy in a New Strategic Environment," ch. 4 in Lewis A. Dunn and Sharon A. Squassoni, eds., *Arms Control: What Next?* (Boulder, Colo.: Westview Press, 1993), 58–78.

6. "Realists" contend that power is based on tangible resources such as population, economic capacity, and territory; the most influential among them also believe that power is both a means and an end in international politics. See Hans J. Morgenthau, *Politics among Nations: The Struggle for Power and Peace* (New York: Alfred A. Knopf, 1948). "Neorealists" hold, as do realists, that the structure of the international system, especially system polarity, is the most important determinant of the context for state decisionmaking. In contrast to realists, neorealists are more likely to acknowledge sources of power other than tangible ones and to treat power as a means but not an end in itself. For a summary and critique of neorealist views, see Robert O. Keohane, "Theory of World Politics: Structural Realism and Beyond," in Ada W. Finifter, ed., *Political Science: The State of the Discipline* (Washington, D.C.: American Political Science Association, 1983), repr. in Paul R. Viotti and Mark V. Kauppi, *International Relations Theory: Realism, Pluralism, Globalism* (New York: Macmillan, 1993), 186–227. See also Kalevi J. Holsti, *Peace and War: Armed Conflicts and International Order 1648–1989* (Cambridge: Cambridge University Press, 1991), 328–30.

Other schools can concur with the realists on some of these major points, but implicit in the realist model of deterrence stability are some theoretical (i.e., explanatory or predictive) limitations. Each of these limitations or sets of problems qualifies the inferences that can be drawn from a realist or neorealist perspective, especially from the perspective of *structural* realism. The three problem areas are (1) whether the realist view is based on exceptional cases, (2) whether the economic theories on which some neorealist arguments about deterrence stability are based can be transferred from economics to international politics, and (3) whether structural realism can account for both general and immediate deterrence situations.[7]

Exceptional Cases

First of all, realist arguments for the possibility of a stable nuclear multipolar world are based on the Cold War experiences of the United States and the Soviet Union. The supposition is that, just as the U.S. and the Soviet political-military leaderships over time worked out rules of the road for crisis management and for the avoidance of inadvertent war or escalation, so too would aspiring nuclear powers among the current nonnuclear states. However, there are reasons to doubt whether the U.S.-Soviet experience can be repeated after the Cold War. For one thing, the U.S.-Soviet nuclear relationship between 1945 and 1990 was also supported by bipolarity and by an approximate equality, albeit an asymmetrical one, in overall U.S. and Soviet military power. Neither bipolarity nor, obviously, U.S.-Russian global military equity is available to support stable relations in the post–Cold War world. In fact, both factors are irrelevant so long as Russia evolves in a democratic, capitalist direction and prefers cooperative U.S.-Russian foreign relations.

Another reason why the U.S. and Soviet Cold War experience is unlikely to be repeated by future proliferators is that the relationship between political legitimacy and military control was solid in Moscow and in Washington, but uncertain for many nuclear powers outside Europe. The issue here is not whether democracies are less warlike than dictatorships. The question is whether a given regime can impose either assertive or delegative military control over its armed forces and, if it does, what the consequences will be for its crisis management and normal nuclear operations. Assertive control implies a great deal of civilian intervention in military operations and management; delegative control, more willingness to let the military have their own way on operational and organiza-

---

7. For the distinction between general and immediate deterrence, see Patrick M. Morgan, *Deterrence: A Conceptual Approach,* 2d ed. (Beverly Hills, Calif.: Sage Publications, 1983).

tional issues. Assertive control overcompensates for "never" types of fail-ure in a nuclear command-and-control system, at the expense of "always" failures (responding promptly to authorized commands). Delegative con-trol has the reverse emphasis.[8] The timely nature of the question of stable civil–military relations, and of political accountability of militaries to civil authority in new proliferants, can be appreciated from a list of suspected current and probable future nuclear-armed states (see Table 20).

Yet another reason why the U.S.-Soviet experience may not be norma-tive for newer nuclear powers is that there were no pieces of disputed foreign territory or other vital interests for which one of the sides was committed to go to war rather than suffer defeat or stalemate. The two sides were generally satisfied by *bloc consolidation* and by *internal power balancing* instead of external adventurism and zero-sum competition for territory or resources. The preceding observation does not imply that Cold War crises, such as those which occurred over Berlin and Cuba, were not dangerous. They were dangerous; but the danger was mitigated by an awareness that neither state had to sacrifice a vital piece of its own territory or its own national values (allies were another matter) in order to avoid war. What was at stake in the most dangerous U.S.-Soviet Cold War confrontations was "extended deterrence," or the credibility of nuclear protection extended to allies, not defense of the homeland per se.

In sum, the first major problem with nuclear realism, based on the U.S.-Soviet Cold War experience, is the sampling of exceptional cases. It is as if one were to sample the opinions of the American electorate by taking polls only in Vermont and New Hampshire. The behavior of the United States and the Soviet Union with regard to nuclear weapons was unusual because their vital interests could be defended without nuclear war, be-cause their systems of civil–military relations were proof against military usurpation or command disability in crises, and because other supports for stability, especially a widely acknowledged global military bipolarity, reinforced the effects of nuclear weapons.

Microeconomic Analogies

The second major set of theoretical problems with nuclear realism has to do with the adaptation of arguments from microeconomic theory to theo-ries of interstate relations. Kenneth N. Waltz explicitly compares the be-havior of states in an international system to the behavior of firms in a

8. See Peter Douglas Feaver, *Guarding the Guardians: Civilian Control of Nuclear Weap-ons in the United States* (Ithaca, N.Y.: Cornell University Press, 1992), 3–28 et pass.

Table 20. Suspected Current and Probable New Nuclear Forces,
Late 1990s–2000+

	Nuclear Material	Warhead Design	No. of Warheads	Means of Delivery
Israel	Pu HEU (?) Adequate stocks	Advanced fission Thermonuclear (?)	>100	Missile (SRBM, IRBM) Aircraft
India	Pu Large stocks	Fission Thermonuclear (?)	>100	Missile (SRBM, IRBM) Aircraft
Pakistan	HEU Pu (?) Limited stocks	Fission	>10	Aircraft Missile (SRBM) Unconventional
Algeria	Pu (?)	Fission	1 (?)	Aircraft Unconventional
Egypt	Pu (?)	Fission	1–3	Missile Aircraft
Iran	HEU (?) Pu (?)	Fission	1–3	Aircraft Missile (SRBM) Unconventional
Iraq	HEU Very limited stocks	Fission	1–3	Aircraft Unconventional
Libya	HEU (diverted) Pu (diverted)	Fission	1–3 (?)	Missile Unconventional
North Korea	Pu Very limited stocks	Fission	<10	Aircraft Missile (SRBM) Unconventional
Syria	Pu (?)	Fission	1 (?)	Missile Unconventional

SOURCE: Adapted from Lewis A. Dunn, "New Nuclear Threats to U.S. Security," ch. 2 in Robert D. Blackwill and Albert Carnesale, eds., *New Nuclear Nations: Consequences for U.S. Policy* (New York: Council on Foreign Relations, 1993), 36–37.

NOTE: HEU = highly enriched uranium; SRBM = short-range ballistic missile; IRBM = intermediate-range ballistic missile.

market.[9] As the market forces firms into a common mode of rational decisionmaking in order to survive, so too does the international system, according to Waltz, dictate similar constraints upon the behavior of states. The analogy, however, is wrong. The international system does not domi-

9. Kenneth N. Waltz, *Theory of International Politics* (Reading, Mass.: Addison-Wesley, 1979).

nate its leading state actors: leading states define the parameters of the system.

International politics is a game of oligopoly: the few rule the many. Because this is so, there cannot be any "system" to which the leading oligopolists, unlike the remainder of the states, are subject. The system is determined by the preferred ends and means of its leading members. Structural realists assume that some "system" of interactions exists independently of the states which make it up. This is a useful heuristic for theorists, but a very mistaken view of the way in which policy is actually made in international affairs. Because structural realists insist upon reification of the system independently of the principal actors within the system, they miss the subsystemic dominance built into the international order.

An important test of whether meaningful theory can proceed on the basis of the realist, or realpolitik, premise of "system" separateness, or whether domestic political forces must also be taken into account by theorists, is to test realist and domestic/constrained hypotheses against historical evidence. According to Bruce Bueno de Mesquita and David Lalman, the realist perspective as formalized in their models is not supported by the past two centuries' experience of interstate behavior.[10] The authors deduce an "acquiescence impossibility" theorem which shows that, in a logically developed game structure based on realist assumptions, it is impossible for one state to acquiesce in the demands of another "regardless of the beliefs held by the rivals, regardless of the initial demand made by one of the states, and regardless of initial endowments of capabilities, coalitional support, propensities to take risks, or anything else."[11] None of the deductions derived from the realist or neorealist versions of their international interactions game, according to Bueno de Mesquita and Lalman, was supported in their empirical data set (which included 707 dyadic interactions).[12]

One might argue, in defense of structural realists on this point, that the assumption of system determinism is a useful fiction. It allows for parsimony in expression and in focus on the essential attributes of the interna-

10. Bruce Bueno de Mesquita and David Lalman, *War and Reason: Domestic and International Imperatives* (New Haven, Conn.: Yale University Press, 1992).

11. Ibid., 267.

12. Ibid., 267–68. The findings of Bueno de Mesquita pertinent to the limitations of realism are important in the context of debates about proliferation, since his work is cited by proliferation pessimists as representative of nuclear realist positivism. See, for example, Scott D. Sagan, "The Perils of Proliferation: Organization Theory, Deterrence Theory, and the Spread of Nuclear Weapons," *International Security* (Spring 1994): 66–108, esp. 66. Sagan cites Bueno de Mesquita and William H. Riker, "An Assessment of the Merits of Selective Nuclear Proliferation," *Journal of Conflict Resolution* (June 1982): 283.

tional system. But, again, the assumption of "apartness" of the system and its essential state or nonstate actors is useful, and methodologically defensible, only if it leads to insights which are both accurate and not otherwise attainable. Neither exceptional accuracy nor exceptional attainability of insight has been demonstrated by structural realists for the assumption of system and actor "apartness." This is probably one reason why traditional realists, as opposed to neorealists and modern structural realists, do not exclude what Waltz, in another study, refers to as first- and second-image variables.[13] Realism fails to explain the high degree of international cooperation that takes place, despite a legally anarchic international order, because of the biased manner in which realism deals with imperfect information. According to Bueno de Mesquita and Lalman:

> In the realist world, imperfect information can only encourage violence. Incorrect beliefs about the intentions of rivals can only steer disputes away from negotiation (or the status quo) and toward the blackmail inherent in a capitulation or the tragedy inherent in a war. Incorrect beliefs, secrecy, misperception, misjudgment, and miscalculation are routine features of human intercourse. In that sense, a realist world could be a dangerous world indeed.[14]

In fact, the explanations and predictions made possible by structural realism are successfully carried out only within a closed and very constrained universe. Even within that universe, structural realism works better with conventional weapons than it does with a multitude of nuclear forces. Conventional wars can be fought to rectify an imbalance of power, to challenge the hegemonic rule of imperial states, or to bring about other changes in the international political environment within which

13. Kenneth N. Waltz, *Man, the State and War* (New York: Columbia University Press, 1959). The "first image" includes human nature and individual psychological attributes pertinent to decisionmaking. The "second image" refers to state-level decisions and behaviors. An interesting anomaly is that Waltz's 1959 book offers a much more subtle appreciation of the complexity of international political interaction than does his 1979 book (see n. 9 above); yet, the latter has proved to be far more influential in spawning bandwagoning and balancing responses in the literature. The 1959 Waltz is actually far more convincing than the 1979 Waltz, although the latter book is written in a style perhaps appealing to the new wave of scholastically inclined theorists.

14. Bueno de Mesquita and Lalman, *War and Reason,* 269. The authors acknowledge that, under conditions of imperfect information, states might mistakenly stumble into war as a result of misjudgments based on inaccurate information. But in a domestically constrained as opposed to a realist model of strategic rationality, leaders may also "mistakenly" avoid war and "stumble into negotiation or other peaceful solutions to their differences" (ibid.). Waltz argues that the complexity of a multipolar nuclear world will induce risk-averse, instead of risk-acceptant, behavior on the part of leaders (*The Spread of Nuclear Weapons,* p. 30).

states must act. Conventional war and system change can go together.[15] Nuclear weapons—in particular, the spread of nuclear weapons—makes the relationship between war and system change much more pathological. War as an instrument for the attainment of policy objectives becomes more irrational with nuclear (compared with conventional) weapons. Realists actually count on this fear, on a pathological relationship between war and change, to preserve peace. Nuclear weapons will freeze the situation in favor of the defenders of the status quo and against those potential aggressors who would disturb the peace.

Structural Realism and Immediate Deterrence

This brings us to the third general set of problems with realist theories and nuclear weapons spread. The structure of the international system is not related to general deterrence in the same way as it is related to immediate deterrence. According to Patrick M. Morgan, the need for general deterrence is inherent in the normal day-to-day relations of states, based on the distribution of power and states' assumptions about each other's intentions. *General deterrence* is the latent possibility that any state may opt for war within an anarchic or nonhierarchical international order.[16] *Immediate deterrence* obtains in a situation in which one side has actually made specific threats against another, the second side perceives itself threatened, and a significant likelihood of war exists in the minds of leaders in at least one of the two states.[17] The onset of a crisis, for example, often signifies a failure of general deterrence but not of immediate deterrence, for the involved states have not yet abandoned diplomacy and crisis management.

It makes sense to assume that there might be a strong correlation between success or failure in general deterrence and such system attributes as distributions of actor capabilities and objectives. However, the relationship between international systems and failures of immediate deterrence is much more indirect. State and substate variables, including the attributes of individuals, groups, and bureaucratic organizations, are among the filters through which any "system" forces must pass before those forces are manifest in state decisions and policies. The distinction

15. On the historical relationship between war and system change, see Robert Gilpin, *War and Change in World Politics* (Cambridge: Cambridge University Press, 1981).

16. Or, as Thomas Hobbes explained it, it is a precept or general rule of reason that "every man, ought to endeavour Peace, as farre as he has hope of obtaining it; and when he cannot obtain it, that he may seek, and use, all helps, and advantages of Warre" (Hobbes, *Leviathan* [New York: Washington Square Press, 1964], 88). See Morgan, *Deterrence;* also see Hedley Bull, *The Anarchical Society: A Study of Order in World Politics* (New York: Columbia University Press, 1977).

17. For a more complete definition of immediate deterrence, see Morgan, *Deterrence.*

between general and immediate deterrence helps to explain why perfectly logical deductions from deterrence theory based on rationality postulates often fly in the face of states' actual behavior.[18]

The significance of the distinction between general and immediate deterrence is illustrated by the Cuban missile crisis. The decision by Khrushchev to put Soviet medium- and intermediate-range ballistic missiles into Cuba was intended, among other objectives, to diminish the gap (publicly acknowledged by U.S. government officials) between U.S. and Soviet strategic nuclear capabilities. Khrushchev's decision, made in the spring of 1962 after consulting very few key advisers, represented a failure of general deterrence. The Soviet leadership had decided to risk the emplacement of its nuclear weapons outside Soviet territory and within the Western Hemisphere for the first time. However, it was not yet a failure of immediate deterrence. Immediate deterrence was not involved in Khrushchev's clandestine deployment program, because the deployments were deliberately kept secret. Had Khrushchev carried through his original plans, he would have completed the missile deployments and then announced their existence.

In that eventuality, the mere existence of Khrushchev's missiles on Cuban soil, however threatening it seemed to U.S. policymakers, would not have created a situation of immediate deterrence. Only the completion of deployments followed by a coercive threat would move the situation from a failure of general deterrence (Soviets make a dangerous move in the arms race) to one of immediate deterrence (e.g., Soviets now demand that United States and allies leave West Berlin immediately). The preceding supposition is of the "what if" or counterfactual kind: we may never know the full story of Khrushchev's motives for the missile deployments.[19] The actual shift from a general to an immediate deterrence situation took place on October 22, 1962, when President Kennedy ordered the Soviet

18. As Robert Jervis explains, rationality assumptions are not necessarily falsified by cases in which leaders have chosen poorly. But in many other instances "the beliefs and policies are so removed from what a careful and disinterested analysis of the situation reveals that the failure is hard to fit into the framework generated by rationality" (intro. in Robert Jervis, Richard Ned Lebow, and Janice Gross Stein, *Psychology and Deterrence* [Baltimore: Johns Hopkins University Press, 1985], 6). In addition, leaders' beliefs about deterrence and credibility are interactive with the probability that particular strategies will succeed or fail. As Jervis acknowledges, "there is no objective answer to the question of which nuclear postures and doctrines are destabilizing, apart from the highly subjective beliefs that decision makers hold about this question. . . . Not only do each side's beliefs constitute an important part of the reality with which the other has to contend, but also states can collude or contend on the constructions of reality that frame these judgments" (Jervis, *The Meaning of the Nuclear Revolution: Statecraft and the Prospect of Armageddon* [Ithaca, N.Y.: Cornell University Press, 1989], 183).

19. See Raymond L. Garthoff, *Reflections on the Cuban Missile Crisis,* rev. ed. (Washington, D.C.: Brookings Institution, 1989), 6–42.

missiles removed from Cuba, announced that the United States was imposing a quarantine on Soviet shipments to Cuba, and stated that a nuclear
missile launched from Cuba against any target in the Western Hemisphere
would call forth a full U.S. retaliatory response against the Soviet Union.

Realist perspectives help to explain the background to general deterrence failure in this instance, but they do little to clarify why the U.S. and
Soviet political leaderships chose as they did. If the international power
positions of states yield unambiguous deductions about their crisis management strategies, Khrushchev should never have dared to put missiles
into Cuba. And the United States once the missiles had been discovered,
need not have hesitated to invade Cuba or to launch an air strike to
destroy the missile sites, collocated air-defense sites, and other nuclear-
capable weapon platforms deployed in Cuba by Moscow.[20] Realists would
argue, against the preceding statement, that nuclear weapons made the
Soviets and the Americans cautious during the Cuban missile crisis. The
danger created by nuclear weapons helped to end the crisis without war,
following the logic and against my earlier argument.

However, realist arguments will not work in this context. Nuclear weapons did not make the crisis easier to manage, but harder. They added to
the risk of escalation, to be sure, and leaders were well aware of those
risks. The United States deliberately and, some would say, successfully
manipulated the risk of escalation and war in order to force Khrushchev's
withdrawal of the missiles. But this argument (for nuclear coercion as the
path to Cuban crisis settlement) will not work, because nuclear weapons
and the Soviet sense of inferiority in the nuclear arms race were major
causes for the crisis.[21] If it is argued that nuclear weapons helped resolve

20. U.S. officials at the time of the Cuban missile crisis underestimated significantly the
size of the Soviet conventional force deployed on that island (actually some 40,000 troops).
Nor did they realize that, in addition to warheads for medium- and intermediate-range missiles deployed in Cuba, the Soviets had also deployed nuclear warheads for tactical weapon
launchers. At the time of the crisis, U.S. leaders were uncertain whether *any* Soviet warheads had actually arrived in Cuba. See Raymond L. Garthoff, "The Havana Conference on
the Cuban Missile Crisis," *Cold War International History Project Bulletin* (Washington, D.C.:
Woodrow Wilson Center) (Spring 1992): 1–4. According to Bruce Blair, orders to the senior
Soviet commander in Cuba specifically precluded the use of any nuclear weapons without
prior approval from Moscow: *The Logic of Accidental Nuclear War* (Washington, D.C.: Brookings Institution 1993), 109.

21. U.S. leaders were not well informed about the actual Soviet nuclear force deployments
in Cuba in October 1962. With regard to nuclear force loadings, Soviet *tactical* nuclear weapons (i.e., in addition to those intended for SS-4 and SS-5 launchers) numbered between 98
and 104: 80 for two regiments of front cruise missiles; 12 for Luna surface-to-surface, short-
range missiles; 6 for gravity bombs for IL-28 bombers; and possible additional charges for
nuclear-armed naval mines. The approximate maximum range for the cruise missiles, fired

the crisis, that is true only as a historical tautology: by having caused or helped to cause it and by making it more dangerous, they played a part in ending it.

The Cuban crisis example shows the limitations of realism in explaining even the most frequently proffered set piece, one-against-one confrontation between two relatively mature command-and-control systems during the Cold War. Structural realism leaves the mold in place and removes the gelatin. The essence of Cuban crisis bargaining was about Khrushchev's overestimation of his own risk-taking propensity. His military reach had exceeded his political grasp, and when discovery of the missiles blew his cover, he retreated—not only in the face of U.S. power and determination, but also because he and Kennedy recognized that they had maneuvered themselves very close to an outbreak of inadvertent war, and possible escalation to nuclear war.

The tendency of realism to reification of "systems" may have its methodological uses when systems are posited to do harmless or politically benign things. When systems are charged with the responsibility for maintaining peace and security, then one cannot exclude from the assessment of system stability the decisionmaking proclivities of states, nor the fears and perceptions of their leaders. Realist assumptions can help to explain or predict failures of general deterrence, as in the case of arms races that get out of control. But what states will choose to *do* about these systemic processes (actually a series of state decisions, but granting structural realists the benefit of the doubt) remains an open door, a "window of opportunity."

The matter raised here is not simply a level-of-analysis problem, but one of philosophy of analysis. One cannot choose preferred levels of analysis without making some assumption about which level or levels best provide explanations and predictions for those outcomes and processes which matter most. Nuclear positivists who depend upon realism can make interesting statements about the *central tendencies* of state behav-

---

from Cuban shore points nearest to U.S. territory, was ninety miles; the warheads for these cruise missiles were in the 5–12 kiloton range. The 60 warheads deployed for SS-4 and SS-5 launchers in Cuba (the latter never reached Cuba, having been turned back by the U.S. quarantine) were in addition to these tactical weapons; all but the SS-5 warheads apparently reached Cuba in a single shipment on October 4. The existence of a Soviet tactical nuclear force of this size, unknown to U.S. invasion planners, indicates that for Moscow the psychological investment in Cuban defense was much higher than Americans, both then and subsequently during the Cold War, believed. The potential for inadvertent escalation was obviously much greater than crisis participants could have known. I am very grateful to Raymond Garthoff, Brookings Institution, for updated information on Cuba, based on his extensive discussions with Russian defense experts and many years of study devoted to this issue.

iors within a particular international order. But meaningful theory must also include statements about *ranges* or variation among values taken on by causal and dependent variables. It is both true and misleading to say, for example, that because we had no nuclear wars during the Cold War era, we may conclude that states in general are risk-averse once they have acquired nuclear weapons. The point about states in general remains not proved, and it says nothing at all about what a particular state might do in a specific crisis. Unlike the world of business firms, in the world of nuclear weapons and nuclear wars, we *do* want to know the deviant cases and know them intimately: they may drive the entire system into new directions.

Nuclear Irrelevancy

A second school of thought argues that nuclear weapons were really unnecessary for Cold War stability. One can formulate this argument in harder or softer terms. The "harder" version is that nuclear weapons were irrelevant subjectively as well as objectively: not only did they have no real impact on the likelihood of major war, but, in addition, leaders paid little regard to the role of nuclear weapons in preserving stable deterrence. The "softer" form of the argument contends that leaders did pay attention to nuclear weapons and spent a great deal of time with nuclear planning, but that it was all "ceremonial," not really necessary for a basically nonmilitary relationship between the United States and NATO, on one side, and the Soviet Union and the Warsaw Pact, on the other.

Representative of the softer form of the argument is John Mueller's *Retreat from Doomsday: The Obsolescence of Major War.*[22] Mueller's book really asserts two very different theses. The first is that large-scale, interstate wars had already become obsolete by the turn of the twentieth century. Leaders, having failed to recognize this, plunged foolishly into World War I and paid an unexpectedly drastic price. After World War I, most European political and military leaders, intellectuals, and publics recognized the dysfunctional character of major war. The world was on a linear path toward the rejection of great coalition wars, which lined up numbers of major powers on each side. This path toward peaceful progress was interrupted in the 1930s, however, by the unexpected dedication of regimes in Germany and Japan to a program of achieving their objectives by conquest. After World War II, in a very new international system, the major powers resumed their linear progression toward disavowing war.

22. New York: Basic Books, 1989.

Like dueling and slavery, the argument goes, war was simply becoming an idea whose time had run out.

This idea that the states of the developed world were on a course toward eventual debellicism was not original with Mueller, of course, and the pre–World War I literature foreseeing the obsolescence of war is discussed (and critiqued extensively) by Geoffrey Blainey in his historical study *The Causes of War*.[23] Many of Mueller's references are to literary and other sources which support the idea that the cultural literati have been gradually turning away from war as an expression of anything purposive or beneficial. But the case that statesmen, generals, and publics— even in democratic societies—are now more opposed to war than they were formerly requires more evidence than Mueller offers.

The growing obsolescence of major interstate war is only one of Mueller's arguments. It is related to, but distinct from, another: that nuclear weapons had little to do with Cold War stability. One must dispose of the first argument, concerning the perceived obsolescence of major war, before addressing the second, concerning the irrelevance of nuclear weapons during the Cold War. If the first argument by Mueller is largely true, then the second argument can rest in part on a substructure provided by the first: obsolescence of war supports nuclear irrelevancy. The United States, the Soviet Union, and their major allies had had enough of fighting as a result of World War II. The possibility of a World War III fought even without nuclear weapons would have been sufficiently discouraging. Mueller contends that U.S. industrial and economic superiority would have guaranteed victory in a global war waged without nuclear weapons: America could have mobilized for victory and overwhelmed any adversary with military production after World War II, as it did between 1941 and 1945. U.S. mobilization potential and economic capacity were the great deterrent against Soviet adventurism, according to Mueller, not nuclear weapons.

Mueller's case for nuclear irrelevancy during the Cold War is supported by Robert S. McNamara, former U.S. secretary of defense. McNamara is something of a paradox. As secretary of defense he played an essential part in developing a U.S. nuclear strategy and force structure which remained influential to the very end of the Cold War.[24] In February 1963, McNamara testified before a congressional committee that Khrushchev was forced to back down: Khrushchev "knew without any question whatsoever that he faced the full military power of the United States, including its nuclear weapons," and U.S. officials had faced "the possibility of

23. Third ed. (New York: Free Press, 1988), esp. 35–56.
24. Alain C. Enthoven and K. Wayne Smith, *How Much Is Enough? Shaping the Defense Program, 1961–1969* (New York: Harper & Row, 1971), 165–96.

launching nuclear weapons and Khrushchev knew it, and that is the reason, and the only reason, why he withdrew those weapons."[25] McNamara's
reflections out of office, on the other hand, run decidedly against the
political or military significance of nuclear weapons. Writing in the 1980s,
McNamara argued that nuclear weapons "serve no military purpose whatsoever. They are totally useless—except only to deter one's opponent
from using them."[26] In 1987, reconsidering the U.S. experience in the Cuban missile crisis, McNamara reaffirmed that "all those fancy nuclear
weapons are militarily useless. You can't *use* them."[27] Note that this position is different from the position taken by some nuclear positivists and
agnostics—that nuclear *superiority* is militarily or politically useless.
McNamara would doubtless agree about the futility of nuclear superiority,
but his (most recent) position goes beyond that.

Mueller is correct to argue that the Soviet Union and its allies would
have been disadvantaged in any global conventional war vis-à-vis the
United States and its allies. U.S. economic and industrial strength, especially in the first two decades following the end of the Second World War,
must have seemed very imposing to Soviet leaders. In addition, to the
extent that they took their Marxism seriously, Soviet leaders would have
believed that military superiority flows from economic potential. Therefore, any war against the capitalist West would make long odds for Moscow.[28] In addition, U.S. maritime superiority throughout the Cold War
years would have added to American and allied advantages in any global
war of attrition against the Soviet Union and its allies. Moscow's only
hope, should war break out against NATO and remain nonnuclear, was to
attain its political and military objectives through a blitz campaign. Careful net assessment revealed that the chances of the Soviet Union succeeding, in a short-warning attack against NATO during the 1980s, ranged
from slight to nonexistent.

Just because the requirements for deterring the Soviet Union from de-

25. McNamara testimony, U.S. Congress, House of Representatives, Committee on Appropriations, "Department of Defense Appropriations for 1964," February 6, 1963, p. 31, cited in
Marc Trachtenberg, "The Influence of Nuclear Weapons in the Cuban Missile Crisis," *International Security* (Summer 1985), repr. in Sean M. Lynn-Jones, Steven E. Miller, and Stephen
Van Evera, eds., *Nuclear Diplomacy and Crisis Management* (Princeton, N.J.: Princeton University Press, 1990), 260.

26. Robert S. McNamara, "The Military Role of Nuclear Weapons: Perceptions and Misperceptions," *Foreign Affairs* (Fall 1983): 79, cited in Trachtenberg, "The Influence of Nuclear
Weapons in the Cuban Missile Crisis," 258.

27. James G. Blight and David A. Welch, *On the Brink: Americans and Soviets Reexamine
the Cuban Missile Crisis* (New York: Hill & Wang, 1989), 188.

28. On this point see P. H. Vigor, *Soviet Blitzkrieg Theory* (New York: St. Martin's Press,
1983), ch. 1.

liberate attack on NATO could have been met without nuclear weapons, however, does not mean that the necessary and sufficient conditions for prevention of war in Europe were obtained. More was involved in maintaining Cold War European stability than deterrence of the Soviet Union from any deliberate aggression which it might have contemplated. The Soviet Union also had to be persuaded that NATO was "deterred." The very statement that NATO required deterring struck Western military experts as oxymoronic during the Cold War years: it was self-evident to them that the United States and NATO would never launch an unprovoked attack on the Soviet Union. But it was not self-evident to Moscow. What seemed like an unprovoked or unjustified attack to the Soviet leadership might differ from what was defined as an unprovoked attack in Washington, Bonn, or Brussels.

Given the large arsenals of nuclear and conventional weapons and the great numbers of troops deployed in Europe by opposing military blocs poised for war, the chief risk was not deliberate but inadvertent war.[29] Incidents growing out of border clashes or other apparently minor skirmishes between NATO and Warsaw Pact forces might have escalated into major confrontations between the Cold War superpowers. Recall that nuclear deterrence theorists touted their logic of manipulation of an unknown, but significant, risk of war as a principal component of deterrence. Testimony to this theory being put into practice by NATO was NATO's forward deployment of U.S. and other short-range, or tactical, nuclear forces throughout the European theater of operations. Either these weapons would be overrun by enemy forces very early, or commanders would demand early release from NATO authority, raising the likelihood of nuclear first use to a near certainty.

Tactical nuclear weapons were capable of igniting a series of action–reaction sequences over which the combatants would rapidly lose centralized political and military control. Many wars, not one, would be going on at once: a NATO military command-and-control system cut into pieces of uneven size and complexity would be reacting to a Soviet system similarly disaggregated and confused. Stopping this kind of war would not necessarily be impossible, but it would be about as difficult an undertak-

29. Mueller addresses the problem of rationality in crisis and wartime decisionmaking and the importance of uncertainty (*Retreat from Doomsday*, 227–31), arguing that major war, though highly improbable, could still occur "if decision makers become confused or demented and act irrationally or if they undergo a change in values and perspectives so that war once again becomes a seemingly sensible procedure" (227). However, these are two very different kinds of issues, and neither says a great deal about the problem of accidental/inadvertent war. Interestingly, Mueller does allow for an important role played by fear of escalation, though not necessarily nuclear escalation (see below).

ing as theorists of war termination had ever imagined. There was very little likelihood that, had war broken out in Europe at any time between the later 1950s and the mid-1980s, NATO could have used most of its short-range nuclear forces in a controlled and purposive way.[30]

The preceding paragraph strengthens Mueller's argument to the extent that it supports the political absurdity of nuclear warfighting doctrines. However, it reminds us that deliberate war was probably not the major risk to stability in post–World War II Europe. The war machines created by the two alliances had become military museums overstuffed with useless furniture, including superfluous arms and vulnerable command-and-control systems. These war machines were designed for threatening one another, but in the event of actual war they could not have kept the level of violence proportionate to any meaningful political objective. Even throwing away nuclear weapons would have left NATO and the Warsaw Pact with military pterodactyls: forces larger than necessary for any politically acceptable mission, but forces with sufficient size and putative capability to create serious fears on both sides that the other side might launch a surprise attack.

Bernard Brodie's claim about nuclear weapons in 1946—that from the time of their invention strategy would mainly be dedicated to the avoidance of major war—was prescient. It also had an ironic destination in the Cold War armed forces and military doctrines of the United States and the Soviet Union. The skillful nonuse of military forces turned deterrence into an all-encompassing substitute for military preparedness, for usable warfighting skills and, especially in the U.S. case, for foreign policy in general. Deterrence became the tapeworm that swallowed the host. Forces and doctrines justified in the name of deterring Moscow were often perceived by the Soviets as strategic compellents. Instead of viewing U.S. forces and doctrines as defensively motivated policies of the status quo, Soviet leaders from the 1960s through the 1980s interpreted U.S. force modernizations and policy pronouncements as American efforts to force Moscow into military and political retreat.[31]

Nuclear Agnosticism

Nuclear agnosticism is the position toward which scholars and analysts who reject both the argument of nuclear positivism and that of nuclear

30. See Paul Bracken, *The Command and Control of Nuclear Forces* (New Haven, Conn.: Yale University Press, 1983), 129–78.

31. On this point see Raymond L. Garthoff, *Deterrence and the Revolution in Soviet Military Doctrine* (Washington, D.C.: Brookings Institution, 1990), 6–15.

irrelevance are driven. Nuclear agnosticism includes a variety of persons and ideas whose views are not easily summarized. The category includes, to use the language given currency by a Harvard nuclear arms control study group, "hawks, doves and owls."[32] Agnosticism shares with nuclear positivism the argument that the nuclear revolution was an important component of Cold War international stability, especially stabilizing for the relationship between the United States and the Soviet Union. At the same time, nuclear agnostics recognize that the problems of inadvertent war and escalation made stability far from a sure thing between 1945 and 1990. For agnostics, it was fortunate that Cold War stability was over-determined by factors other than fear of nuclear war, among them bipolarity. Agnostics doubt that technology fixes or new models of political decisionmaking can change the history of human folly a great deal. Thus, agnostics tend to feel that the problem of accidental or inadvertent nuclear war or escalation calls into question the assumptions made by nuclear positivists, who think that arms control can work indefinitely, and by advocates for nuclear irrelevancy, who argue that the march of history bypasses nuclear weapons.

The historian John Lewis Gaddis and the political scientist Robert Jervis are examples of prominent nuclear agnostics, although they work from very different points of departure. Gaddis has written a great deal about the development of U.S. national security policy during the Cold War.[33] He shares with other historians a sense of frustration over the approach of many social scientists with respect to explaining political causes and effects: "Theorists . . . expend so much of their energy debating methodology—what with neo-realists clashing with neo-Marxists, empiricists with deductivists, quantifiers with non-quantifiers, and behaviorists with particularists—that one wonders at times if they will ever get around to substance at all."[34] Gaddis suggests that interpreters of the Cold War, and of the role of nuclear weapons in international relations during that period, should take a "consumerist" approach toward theory. Arguing for paradigm pluralism in explaining the duration of Cold War stability, he contends that arguments drawn from theories of bipolarity, hegemonic stability, "triumphant liberalism," and long-cycle theory can be

32. Graham T. Allison, Albert Carnesale, and Joseph S. Nye, Jr., eds., *Hawks, Doves and Owls: An Agenda for Avoiding Nuclear War* (New York: W. W. Norton, 1985), esp. 206–22.
33. See, for example, John Lewis Gaddis, *Strategies of Containment: A Critical Appraisal of Postwar American National Security Policy* (New York: Oxford University Press, 1982).
34. Gaddis, "Great Illusions, the Long Peace and the Future of the International System," ch. 10 in Gaddis, *The United States and the End of the Cold War: Implications, Reconsiderations, Provocations* (New York: Oxford University Press, 1992), 169.

used, in addition to the argument for nuclear peace, to explain Cold War stability.[35]

Although arguing for paradigm pluralism, Gaddis leans more toward the perspective of nuclear positivists than he does toward those who would contend that nuclear weapons were irrelevant during the Cold War. According to Gaddis, nuclear weapons have influenced post–World War II international relations in at least four ways. First, nuclear weapons helped to support an already existing reluctance of the great powers to wage war against one another. Second, states that possessed nuclear weapons became more risk-averse. Third, nuclear weapons did not create bipolarity after World War II, but they did prolong its life and thus helped also to prolong stability. Fourth, nuclear weapons helped to perpetuate the Cold War by saving the United States, the Soviet Union, and their allies military expenditures on conventional forces—expenditures which, had they been necessary—might have forced rethinking of Cold War assumptions sooner.[36]

All four of these arguments go against the grain of nuclear irrelevancy, but only the first three are necessarily supportive of the case for nuclear stability. The fourth acknowledges that *political* relations between the United States and the Soviet Union remained adversarial longer than necessary, owing in part to ingrained habits of *military* hangover. Nuclear weapons helped to freeze a political glacis that became its own worst enemy until a new Soviet leader in 1985 began to take dramatic steps to melt the ice. To the nuclear positivists' contention that nuclear weapons made war less likely because war became more dangerous, Gaddis's fourth argument for nuclear relevancy points to the downside of that contention. The very weapons of mass destruction which some would contend were instruments of deterrence or peace were also causes of U.S. and Soviet leaders' fears of devastating surprise attack. The capabilities of those weapons were so unprecedented that the very fact of their being targeted at one's state made a relationship hostile in military-operational terms even when it had passed into a stage of nonhostility in policy.

Among political scientists writing about nuclear strategy and deterrence theory, Robert Jervis has taken the most influential agnostic position. Jervis argues assertively for the uniqueness of the nuclear revolution, and against the conventionalization of nuclear forces into warfighting strategies analogous to prenuclear thinking.[37] Thus he maintained that the Cold War U.S.-Soviet nuclear relationship was a world of

35. Ibid., 171–90.
36. Gaddis, "The Essential Relevance of Nuclear Weapons," ch. 6 in Gaddis, *The United States and the End of the Cold War,* 105–32.
37. Jervis, *The Meaning of the Nuclear Revolution,* esp. 1–45.

mutual assured destruction in fact, regardless of clever theories that might be proposed against that view.[38] On the other hand, it could not be taken for granted that a "MAD" world was an inherently stable world. Jervis's contributions to the study of decisionmaking showed how the psychological attributes of individuals and the behavior of small groups influenced the outcomes of decisions. Of particular significance were his works on the importance of perceptions, images, and other aspects of leaders' cognitive or motivational mind-sets pertinent to their normal or crisis behavior.[39]

Jervis qualifies as an agnostic because he accepts mutual deterrence through assured retaliation as a basic frame of reference for nuclear stability, but recognizes that deterrence is neither automatic nor risk-avoidant. In that recognition he is not alone among those nuclear strategists who favor assured retaliation to counterforce-damage limitation strategies.[40] But one of Jervis's special contributions, his insight into the two-sided character of escalation, stems from his agnostic appreciation of the role of nuclear weapons. Escalation is neither *impossible* nor *certain*.[41] If escalation were impossible, then war could be waged safely below the nuclear threshold. If escalation were certain, then no one would start a conventional war involving one or more nuclear powers. The indeterminacy of escalation is what makes it work; the same indeterminacy makes it dangerous. It "works" because leaders who engage in a process of competitive risk taking knowingly enter a sequence of events over

38. Ibid., 74–106. See also Jervis, "Why Nuclear Superiority Doesn't Matter," *Political Science Quarterly* (Winter 1979–80): 617–33, and id., *The Illogic of American Nuclear Strategy* (Ithaca, N.Y.: Cornell University Press, 1984).

39. Jervis, *The Logic of Images in International Relations* (Princeton, N.J.: Princeton University Press, 1970), and id., *Perception and Misperception in International Politics* (Princeton, N.J.: Princeton University Press, 1976). See also Irving Janis and Leon Mann, *Decision Making* (New York: Free Press, 1977); Patrick M. Morgan, "Saving Face for the Sake of Deterrence," ch. 6 in Jervis et al., eds., *Psychology and Deterrence,* 125–52; and Jervis, "Perceiving and Coping with Threat," ch. 2 in Jervis et al., eds., *Psychology and Deterrence,* 13–33.

40. See, for example, Lawrence Freedman, *The Evolution of Nuclear Strategy* (New York: St. Martin's Press, 1981), esp. the concluding chapter. For a classification of schools of U.S. deterrence theory into damage limitation, punitive retaliation, and military-denial schools, see Charles Glaser, "Why Do Strategists Disagree about the Requirements of Strategic Nuclear Deterrence?" ch. 2 in Lynn Eden and Steven E. Miller, eds., *Nuclear Arguments* (Ithaca, N.Y.: Cornell University Press, 1989), 109–71. I have no particular objection to this framework, although it serves a purpose different from my own: schools of thought are defined primarily on the basis of their targeting strategy. Moreover, the views of leading deterrence theorists are not necessarily static. Jervis, for example, most recently argued in favor of "MAD-4," or a version of MAD with flexible targeting: see Jervis, *The Meaning of the Nuclear Revolution,* ch. 3, esp. 79–81.

41. Jervis, *The Meaning of the Nuclear Revolution,* 80.

which they may ultimately lose control.[42] Like nuclear agnostics, some proponents of nuclear irrelevancy count on an important role for fear of escalation in dampening crises and in avoiding wars—but not necessarily, and not preferably, nuclear escalation.[43]

Jervis's insight—that deterrence worked by making escalation neither impossible nor certain—helps to arbitrate between the claims of nuclear optimists who favor post–Cold War proliferation and nuclear pessimists who warn against the potential dangers of nuclear weapons spread. In a world of nuclear certainty in which deterrence could be derived directly from nuclear balances, the spread of nuclear weapons would create more situations of military stalemate in which aggressors were inhibited and defenders were made more secure. But if nuclear deterrence works primarily by manipulation of risk or by uncertainty, then the widespread dispersal of nuclear weapons increases the insecurity of defenders and motivates them to adopt hair-trigger deterrents.

Other contributions from nuclear agnostics provide grounds for skepticism about a positive association between nuclear weapons spread and international stability, based on case studies of nuclear-crisis management and force operations or on the operations of nuclear command-and-control systems generally. Studies of nuclear-crisis management by Richard K. Betts, Alexander L. George, Richard Ned Lebow, and Scott D. Sagan, among others, have called into question many of the assumptions about decisionmaking on which "rational deterrence" theory is based.[44]

---

42. Ibid., 85. See also Thomas C. Schelling, *Arms and Influence* (New Haven, Conn.: Yale University Press, 1966), 89–99.

43. Mueller, for example, contends that the horror of repeating World War II was sufficient to prevent U.S. and Soviet leaders from direct military conflict during the Cold War (*Retreat from Doomsday,* 116 et pass.). Of course, the fear of global war which, according to Mueller, deterred any shooting war between Americans and Soviets from 1945 to 1990, is irrelevant for most potential proliferators after the Cold War. A credible threat to wage global conventional war must now be replaced by a credible threat to wage regional conventional war at an acceptable cost (e.g., Desert Storm).

44. Alexander L. George, ed., *Avoiding War: Problems of Crisis Management* (Boulder, Colo.: Westview Press, 1991), includes an insightful selection of theoretical articles and empirical case studies on crisis management. See also Richard Ned Lebow, *Nuclear Crisis Management: A Dangerous Illusion* (Ithaca, N.Y.: Cornell University Press, 1987); George's chapter on the Cuban missile crisis in George et al., *The Limits of Coercive Diplomacy: Laos, Cuba, Vietnam* (Boston: Little, Brown, 1971), 86–143; Scott D. Sagan, *Moving Targets: Nuclear Strategy and National Security* (Princeton, N.J.: Princeton University Press, 1989), ch. 4; Scott D. Sagan, "Nuclear Alerts and Crisis Management," *International Security* (Spring 1985), repr. in Lynn-Jones et al., eds., *Nuclear Diplomacy and Crisis Management,* 160–99; and Richard K. Betts, *Nuclear Blackmail and Nuclear Balance* (Washington, D.C.: Brookings Institution, 1987). See also Ole R. Holsti, "Crisis Decision Making," ch. 1 in Philip E. Tetlock et al., eds., *Behavior, Society and Nuclear War* (New York: Oxford University Press, 1989), 1:8–84,

These studies were supported by extensive analyses of the U.S. and Soviet nuclear command-and-control systems, including detailed information about operational biases and military-doctrinal proclivities, offered by Bruce Blair, Desmond Ball, Paul Bracken, and others.[45] These "crisis management/force operations" and "command and control" literatures jointly call into question the assumption made by proliferation optimists: that new nuclear states will automatically learn the stabilizing crisis-management behaviors and develop command/control systems that minimize the risks of accidental or inadvertent war.

Contributors to nuclear-crisis management and command-and-control studies have shown that (1) there is often significant tension between the requirements for crisis management and those for protecting forces against vulnerability; (2) political leaders are frequently ill-informed about the capabilities and operations of their own military forces, including nuclear forces; (3) leaders' crisis behavior is marked by very constrained perceptions, expectations, and frames of reference which filter incoming stimuli from the external environment, including deterrent threats from other states; and (4) military organizations enter a crisis with an already established repertoire of standard operating procedures and an institutional ethos which cannot be suddenly disposed of without harming organizational performance.

Peter D. Feaver has explained that nuclear command-and-control organizations must optimize between the "always" requirement (for responsiveness to authorized commands in order to avoid vulnerability) and the "never" requirement (to prevent accidental or unauthorized nuclear use).[46] He notes that one cannot infer the behavior of nuclear command systems

---

and Blight and Welch, *On the Brink*. See also Scott D. Sagan, *The Limits of Safety: Organizations, Accidents and Nuclear Weapons* (Princeton, N.J.: Princeton University Press, 1993), and id., "The Perils of Proliferation," 66–107.

45. Bruce G. Blair, *Strategic Command and Control: Redefining the Nuclear Threat* (Washington, D.C.: Brookings Institution, 1985); Blair, *The Logic of Accidental Nuclear War;* Desmond Ball, *Can Nuclear War Be Controlled?* Adelphi Paper no. 169 (London: International Institute for Strategic Studies, 1981); Desmond Ball, *Soviet Strategic Planning and the Control of Nuclear War,* Reference Paper no. 109 (Canberra: Research School of Pacific Studies, Australian National University, November 1983); Bracken, *The Command and Control of Nuclear Forces*. On nuclear operations, see the chapters in Ashton B. Carter, John D. Steinbruner, and Charles A. Zraket, eds., *Managing Nuclear Operations* (Washington, D.C.: Brookings Institution, 1987). John Steinbruner's work on command and control was also seminal: see his "Choices and Trade-offs," ch. 16 in Carter, Steinbruner, and Zraket, eds., *Managing Nuclear Operations,* 535–54, and Steinbruner, "Nuclear Decapitation," *Foreign Policy* (Winter 1981–82): 16–28.

46. Feaver, *Guarding the Guardians,* 12–25, and id., "Proliferation Optimism and Theories of Nuclear Operations," 166.

without taking into account those environments or domains which might influence nuclear-use decisions. Those environments are the following: the strategic weapon systems and force structures; the strategic environments in which a state's policy is located; and, most significant in the present context, the strategic culture of a state, including its pattern of civil–military relations and whether that pattern emphasizes "delegative" or "assertive" control by civilians over military operations.[47]

The work of Blair, Sagan, Feaver, and others who are attempting to develop testable hypotheses about nuclear organizational behavior is important for another reason. Testable propositions about leaders' decision-making and command system performances will help to settle some past disputes about how *behaviorally* correct deterrence theory really is.[48] Deterrence has always been promoted as a species of rational-decision theory: it depends upon arguments about cost–benefit ratios and calculations of expected gains and losses.[49] For many critics, however, U.S. versions of nuclear deterrence theory have suffered from vacuous arguments and insufficient validation in comparative case studies.[50] Much of the deterrence literature, like a great deal of the Marxist literature, has served as a scholastic rallying point for polemicist argument instead of a source of disinterested scientific research or policy studies.

Whether deterrence, as related to proliferation or as discussed per se, was really a behavioral science was not only a philosophical or methodological issue. The U.S. government approach to Cold War decision-

---

47. On the significance of strategic culture for U.S. and Soviet Cold War forces, see Colin S. Gray, *Nuclear Strategy and National Style* (Lanham, Md.: Hamilton Press, 1986), 33–96.

48. As an illustration of what might be done, John Gaddis notes that World War I is generally thought to have broken out after six crises, and World War II (in Europe) after five crises. He then tabulates some thirty-seven major crises between 1945 and 1991, none of which led to a world war. His point is that this may say something about the significance of nuclear weapons for stability. See Gaddis, *The United States and the End of the Cold War*, 246, n. 18, for the list of cases.

49. For a sense of the recent debates concerning deterrence, see the special issue of *World Politics* (January 1989) and the articles therein by Christopher Aachen and Duncan Snidal, Robert Jervis, Alexander L. George and Richard Smoke, Richard Ned Lebow and Janice Gross Stein, and George W. Downs. See also Lebow and Stein, *When Does Deterrence Succeed and How Do We Know?* Ottawa: Canadian Institute for International Peace and Security, 1990); Charles L. Glaser, *Analysing Strategic Nuclear Policy* (Princeton: Princeton University Press, 1990); Morgan, *Deterrence;* Alexander L. George and Richard Smoke, *Deterrence in American Foreign Policy: Theory and Practice* (New York: Columbia University Press, 1974); and the collection of articles in Steven E. Miller, ed., *Strategy and Nuclear Deterrence* (Princeton, N.J.: Princeton University Press, 1984).

50. An exception is George and Smoke, *Deterrence in American Foreign Policy,* which draws important theoretical observations from detailed case studies. See also Michael Mandelbaum, *The Fate of Nations: The Search for National Security in the Nineteenth and Twentieth Centuries* (Cambridge: Cambridge University Press, 1988).

making, including its uses of coercive diplomacy and threat, was influenced by deterrence theory. Deterrence theory, if some nuclear positivists can be believed, provided for U.S. policymakers an applied behavioral science which supported containment policy and made relations with the Soviet Union on arms control and other topics more predictable. From the standpoint of the nuclear irrelevants and agnostics, on the other hand, deterrence appeared to the Soviet military and to Soviet defense intellectuals as a confrontational, coercive strategy designed to manipulate the arms race against Moscow's interests.[51] Seen as the essence of behavioral realism by its proponents, deterrence was a conceptual void and a policy anachronism to its detractors.

Nor are agnostics of one mind concerning whether the stability of the Cold War was *overdetermined* or *multidetermined.* One does not necessarily imply the other. An overdetermined period of peace implies that, even with nuclear weapons out of the picture altogether, a great-power peace would have obtained after 1945. A multidetermined peace is one caused by nuclear deterrence among other factors, including bipolarity, an absence of issues sufficiently grave to propel the great powers into war, and so forth.[52] Gaddis, for example, argues for multidetermination: nuclear weapons had at least a supportive role to play in Cold War stability, and without nuclear weapons the U.S.-Soviet rivalry might have been more likely to erupt into war.[53] On the other hand, advocates of nuclear irrelevancy like Mueller contend that nuclear weapons were unnecessary, and therefore gratuitously dangerous, to stable Cold War international politics.[54]

Some advocates of nuclear positivism would contend that the nuclear irrelevants and nuclear agnostics have benign intentions about moderating the arms race. In the view of these positivists, though, the irrelevants and agnostics confuse the desirable with the necessary. The "balance of

51. Garthoff, *Deterrence and the Revolution in Soviet Military Doctrine,* ch. 1. See also Garthoff, "Mutual Deterrence and Strategic Arms Limitation in Soviet Policy," ch. 5 in Derek Leebaert, ed., *Soviet Military Thinking* (London: Allen & Unwin, 1981); David Holloway, *The Soviet Union and the Arms Race* (New Haven, Conn.: Yale University Press, 1983), esp. chs. 2 and 3; and Garthoff, "Soviet Perceptions of Western Strategic Thought and Doctrine," ch. 4 in Gregory Flynn, ed., *Soviet Military Doctrine and Western Policy* (London: Routledge, 1989), 197–328.

52. Feaver, "Proliferation Optimism and Theories of Nuclear Operations," 162.

53. See Gaddis's comments on the views of Waltz and Mearsheimer: *The United States and the End of the Cold War,* 171–72.

54. Although Mueller can be read to argue that nuclear weapons were irrelevant in both a positive and a negative sense: they neither supported nor undermined stability to a significant degree. However, I think a fairer reading is that they were unnecessary and gratuitously dangerous (otherwise, why devote an entire book to show that they were unnecessary, if not also dangerous?).

terror" is simply a modernized and more dangerous version of the balance of power. Failure to acknowledge this point results in weaker deterrence and an enhanced, not reduced, risk of war. States have frequently sought to escape the "perpetual quadrille of the Balance of Power," as A.J.P. Taylor has noted, but they have rarely succeeded in doing so.[55] One does not have to endorse the realist paradigm for explanation and prediction of a majority of international phenomena in order to acknowledge that a realist perspective quickly enters into the council chambers and war rooms of crisis-bound leaders. Few nuclear positivists would try to argue that the outcomes of nuclear war are acceptable or desirable. But, in contrast to nuclear agnostics and to advocates of nuclear irrelevancy, positivists do assert with greater confidence that deterrence is an acceptable and even a desirable modernized form of the balance of power. In fact, some positivists draw heavily upon the argument that nuclear deterrence is a more reliable guarantor of peace than conventional deterrence, on the evidence of an admittedly one-sided historical record.[56]

Conclusions

The views of those who argue for Cold War nuclear positivism, irrelevancy, or agnosticism are not only the stuff of theoretical debate. They are paradigms or conceptual lenses that we can use to connect arguments about nuclear weapons in the old, and newer, world orders. Scott Sagan, for example, outlines three requirements within a "rational deterrence" framework for nuclear stability and then tests whether nuclear-armed states would be likely to meet those requirements: (1) absence of preventive war motives; (2) availability of second-strike forces on both sides for potential opponents; and (3) no nuclear arsenals prone to accidental or unauthorized use.[57] Sagan's studies make a strong case for bringing the organizational level of analysis into the study of nuclear proliferation.

However, neorealists who argue that nuclear weapons spread is consistent with international stability are not entirely refuted by showing that

---

55. A.J.P. Taylor, *The Struggle for Mastery in Europe, 1848–1918* (Oxford: Clarenden Press, 1954), xix.

56. John Mearsheimer, "Disorder Restored," in Graham Allison and Gregory F. Treverton, eds., *Rethinking Security: Beyond Cold War to New World Order* (New York: W. W. Norton, 1992), 229, contends that a totally denuclearized Europe would be the most dangerous option, compared with a Europe having the current number, or an increased number, of nuclear powers. For conventional deterrence failures, see Mearsheimer, *Conventional Deterrence* (Ithaca, N.Y.: Cornell University Press, 1983), intro.

57. Sagan, "The Perils of Proliferation," 71.

accidental, inadvertent, or preventive wars could happen in a new world order. Proliferation optimists can play back the organizational card: U.S., Soviet, and other Cold War organizations learned how to reduce the risks of accidental/inadvertent war to acceptable levels and how to eliminate for all practical purposes the risks of politically usurped deterrents. Forced to the wall, proliferation positivists can and will leap the fence of rational-deterrence theory and forage into other levels of analysis.

A fundamental weakness of the realist argument for proliferation is theoretical or conceptual, not to mention empirical problems with the theory. Realism works by *simplifying* the reality of political decisionmakers. And although nuclear weapons *seem* to simplify the choices of political and military leaders, it is more probable that pandemic nuclearization would introduce unacceptable levels of international systemic complexity. The interaction dynamics of multilateral nuclear-crisis management would be many times as complicated as those of the bilateral U.S.-Soviet Cold War experience. Imagine a future world with "second-strike capable" Ukrainian, Pakistani, Iranian, and North Korean nuclear forces, and you have arrived at the "realism" to which proliferation positivism leads us.

Continuing Controversy

What Should We Do about Recalcitrant Proliferators?

The United States and other nuclear powers will not react with equal concern about the spread of nuclear weapons to all states. As the history of the Cold War demonstrated, a state views nuclear weapons in the hands of another state as threatening or reassuring on the basis of political expectations and alliances. For example, the United States did not feel threatened by Britain's or France's nuclear arsenals during the Cold War. U.S. leaders knew that none of London's or Paris's weapons was aimed at U.S. forces or territory, and that no conceivable political issue could lead to a nuclear exchange between their countries. On the other hand, American and Soviet leaders worried a great deal about one another's weapons. Symbolic of the end of the Cold War was the decision by the Yeltsin and Clinton governments to retarget strategic nuclear weapons away from one another's territory, purportedly at broad ocean areas away from either country.

There are those states regarded by most status quo powers, especially by the United States and its NATO allies, as dangerous potential proliferators. They are dangerous because they have goals and objectives threatening to U.S. security, to American allies, or to peace and stability in regions deemed vital to U.S. interests (the Persian Gulf, for example). North Korea and Iraq are two textbook cases used in discussions among U.S. policymakers. Iraq's nuclear capability was cut short and put under international monitoring after its defeat in 1991. North Korea, after a great deal of haggling with the International Atomic Energy Agency and after receiving warnings from the United States and other interested governments, agreed in 1994 to freeze its nuclear program in place in return for U.S. guarantees of aid in developing nuclear power for peaceful purposes.

Should a future North Korea, Iraq, or other state hostile to U.S. interests acquire a nuclear weapons capability and refuse to submit to international inspection, military moves would obviously be among the options reviewed by U.S. leaders. In order to determine whether the danger from nuclear weapons justified military action, American leaders would have to make judgments about at least six key issues:

1. Could the proliferators (country A) be *deterred* from using its nuclear weapons against the United States or its allies?
2. Can country A be prevented from transferring its nuclear weapons capability to other, potentially hostile, states?
3. Will development or deployment of nuclear weapons by country A increase the danger of conventional war, with the attendant risk of nuclear escalation?
4. If the answer to *any* of the questions (1–3, above) is "yes," how confident are U.S. leaders that dangers can be contained by diplomatic means, including possible economic sanctions?
5. If U.S. leaders assume that country A is preparing to use weapons of mass destruction for aggression, is offensive military preemption by the United States justified, in terms of its risks, costs, and legal justification?
6. Can U.S. and/or allied military action eliminate the danger without risk of retaliation that poses an even greater threat to U.S. interests?[58]

If the United States makes a decision to use military disarmament against a nuclear-armed state, that decision would not necessarily require the use of U.S. nuclear weapons and, preferably, would rely on conventional weapons only. As the U.S. military campaign against Iraq in Desert Storm showed, American conventional air forces can destroy large numbers of targets, including target sets vital to enemy political and military viability, in the space of a few days or weeks. U.S. planning studies

58. This list is drawn from Philip Zelikow, "Offensive Military Actions," ch. 7 in Blackwill and Carnesale, eds., *New Nuclear Nations,* 162–63.

for the Gulf War emphasized the prompt destruction of Iraq's command and control (including leadership), air defenses, offensive air power, and possible sites for the storage or manufacture of weapons of mass destruction. How different U.S. target planning might have been had Iraq already possessed a small nuclear arsenal is not known. Some experts speculate that Iraqi possession of nuclear weapons in 1990–91 might have broken apart the political coalition that eventually agreed to wage war against Saddam Hussein, especially after the first actual nuclear use by Iraq subsequent to war's outbreak.[59]

One example of the kinds of operational planning required for offensive military action against a major regional proliferator can be hypothesized for a fictional country resembling Iraq in 1990 or North Korea in 1992. Table 21 provides a notional list of targets and target complexes that would have to be attacked and the numbers of aimpoints that U.S. targeteers would have to take into account during operational planning.

Attacks of such magnitude against a state that has not yet used nuclear weapons against the United States or its allies, and that may not have explicitly threatened nuclear use, are certain to be controversial among the attentive American public and in the U.S. Congress. A difficult period of decision will develop during the opening phases of a conventional war between an aspiring regional hegemon armed with a small nuclear capability and a U.S.-allied or friendly country without nuclear weapons. One issue will be who is judged as the "aggressor" by the U.S. government and by other states. In the war against Iraq in 1991, the United States bene-

Table 21. Target List for a Disarming Attack against a Fictional Country Resembling Iraq in 1990 or North Korea in 1992

Target	No. of Targets	No. of Aimpoints
Weapons with mass destruction potential	25	200
Air superiority (not requiring attacks on individual aircraft)	100	400
Strategic (command, control, telecommunications)	75	150
Strategic (energy, transport)	70	200
Strategic (selected military production)	20	100
Military forces (missiles only)	50	100
TOTAL	340	1,150

SOURCE: Adapted from Philip Zelikow, "Offensive Military Options," ch. 7 in Robert D. Blackwill and Albert Carnesale, eds., *New Nuclear Nations: Consequences for U.S. Policy* (New York: Council on Foreign Relations, 1993), 179.

59. For this scenario, see Robert D. Blackwill and Albert Carnesale, "Introduction: Understanding the Problem," ch. 1 in Blackwill and Carnesale, eds., *New Nuclear Nations*, 3–19.

fited from the coalition partnership of major Arab governments, including Saudi Arabia and Egypt. These Arab states were willing to coalesce against Saddam Hussein because Iraq's aggression against Kuwait was unambiguous. In a more ambiguous case of aggression, the United States might not find others willing to follow its lead.

Even more difficult than preemptive attack against another state, even against a regional power with a substantial military infrastructure, would be the formulation of a response to nuclear attack or threat from a terrorist organization. Terrorists have the motive, means, and opportunity to acquire modest nuclear capabilities and to deliver nuclear charges across state borders by clandestine means. Terrorists, unlike states, have no obvious "address" to which retaliation or threat of retaliation, in order to forestall hostile attack, can be directed. The most that can be done is to announce that state governments hosting or supporting terrorists will be held accountable for actions taken by those groups, including nuclear terrorism. However, political controversy would surround a U.S. decision, for example, to retaliate against Iran for nuclear detonations in the Middle East by Hezbollah.

Interest in defenses against threats posed by proliferators has already received a boost from the performance of Patriot defense missiles in the Gulf War of 1991. Upgraded Patriots will be available for U.S. forces deployed overseas and for some American allies. Meanwhile, improved generations of theater missile defenses, or ATBMs (anti-theater ballistic missiles), are in the research-and-development stage. The Bush administration plan for Global Protection against Limited Strikes (GPALS) envisioned both ground- and spaced-based interceptors, in addition to other system components, but the Clinton administration scaled this plan back and reorganized the Strategic Defense Initiative Organization as the Ballistic Missile Defense Organization (BMDO). The highest priority of BMDO was stated as the development and deployment of theater missile defenses to meet present and increasing threats to forward-deployed U.S. forces and allies. The second Clinton priority was national missile defense: namely developing the option to deploy a missile-defense system "capable of providing a highly effective defense of the United States against limited attacks of ballistic missiles."[60]

The Clinton administration's Nuclear Posture Review, following in the spirit of Bush's Nuclear Weapons Employment Policy, anticipated Third World nuclear proliferation and the requirement to deter attacks by proliferators against U.S. allies, forces, or territory. Nuclear target planners

---

60. Secretary of Defense Les Aspin, *Annual Report to the President and the Congress* (Washington, D.C.: GPO, January 1994), 55.

at Strategic Command (STRATCOM, formerly Strategic Air Command) have begun to evaluate and compile possible target lists that include potential regional adversaries capable of developing or deploying weapons of mass destruction. The U.S. Joint Chiefs of Staff have indicated a need for the "selective capability of being able to use lower-yield weapons" in regional contingency operations.[61] Scientists in U.S. weapons laboratories have also expressed interest in low-yield nukes, including 10-ton "micronukes," 100-ton "mininukes," and 1,000-ton "tinynukes" for diverse battlefield applications.[62] Congress, out of fear that such weapons if adopted might conflict with U.S. declared policy on nonproliferation, at least temporarily put the brakes on research and development for nuclear weapons below 5 kilotons.

One can sympathize with the concern expressed by defense critics and by some military professionals: more nuclear weapons are not the answer to nuclear proliferation. Nonetheless, not all states have a U.S.-style arsenal of high-technology conventional weapons that might be used to deter an opposed state from nuclear first use or destroy its nuclear capability, either preemptively or in retaliation. A roster of those states in 1994 which had declared their nuclear weapons status, those undeclared but thought to have achieved nuclear weapons capability, and those judged by experts to be working toward nuclearization of their armed forces appears in Table 22.

The Clinton administration was the first to face explicitly the potential conflict between the objective of limiting the spread of nuclear weapons in the post–Cold War world (nonproliferation) and the goal of credible deterrence to protect U.S. allies and forces against nuclear blackmail (counterproliferation). (This topic is discussed at greater length in the "Continuing Controversy" section in Chapter 5 above.) Low-yield nuclear weapons create a marginal trade-off between these objectives. These weapons of smaller yield minimize collateral damage to surrounding territory: they are designed to approximate the precision aiming of the high-technology conventional weapons used in Desert Storm. On the other hand, by making nuclear weapons seem more useful, they may also make nuclear weapons seem more "usable." During the Cold War, it was an article of faith among nuclear powers that nuclear weapons were useful but not usable. They were useful for deterrence, but only if they were not actually used. If used, their destructive side effects were disproportionate to their military or political benefits.[63]

61. William M. Arkin, "Agnosticism When Real Values Are Needed: Nuclear Policy in the Clinton Administration," *FAS Bulletin* (September/October 1994) 8.

62. Ibid., 9.

63. Jervis, *The Meaning of the Nuclear Revolution.*

Table 22. Declared, Undeclared, and Aspiring Nuclear States, 1994

	Maximum Range of Ballistic Missiles (in miles)[a]	Chemical or Biological Weapons Available
Declared		
Britain*	>2,900	
France*	>3,100	Probably
U.S.A.*	>9,200	Yes
Russia*	>9,200	Yes
People's Republic of China*	>9,200	Probably
Belarus[†]	>6,500	Yes
Kazakhstan[†]	>6,800	Yes
Ukraine[†]	>6,200	Yes
Undeclared		
India[b]	>1,550	Probably
Israel*	>930	Probably
Pakistan	>190	Probably
Working on nuclear capability		
Algeria	<40	
Iran	>300	Probably
Iraq	>190	Yes
Libya[c]	>190	Probably
North Korea[d]	>300	Probably
Syria	>300	Probably

SOURCE: Adapted from Lt. Col. Joseph F. H. Peterson and Col. Andy McIntyre, *Ballistic Missile Proliferation: A National Security Focus for the 21st Century*, Strategic Research Project, unclassified (Carlisle Barracks, Pa.: U.S. Army War College, April 18, 1994), encl. 2, adapted from Bruce W. Nelan, "Fighting Off Dooms," *Time*, June 21, 1993.

*Capable of delivering nuclear weapons.

[†]States committed to becoming nonnuclear under the Nuclear Nonproliferation Treaty but having nuclear weapons, under Russian control, located on their territory.

[a]I have revised some of the maximum ranges and other cell entries that appeared in source.

[b]Source does not list India as having a delivery capability, but weapons could be delivered against targets in Pakistan by aircraft; the same holds for Pakistan with regard to targets in India.

[c]Almost certainly possesses chemical weapons.

[d]Thought by the CIA to possess nuclear weapons, although other members of the intelligence community disagree.

The United States would certainly feel absurd unleashing strategic nuclear weapons of high yield against the mininuclear forces of Third World dictators. Yet the conventionalization of nuclear weapons by reducing their yields and incorporating them into regional attack plans has dangers, too. The first use of nuclear weapons since Hiroshima will cross a politically useful, psychological threshold. The precedent of nuclear nonuse is one that should be maintained by present nuclear powers. The

United States, in particular, has an unrivaled superiority in high-technology conventional weapons that should preclude the need to retaliate in kind with nuclear weapons against Third World first use. One danger is that U.S. public opinion will demand nuclear retaliation for any nuclear first use against U.S. combat forces. It would be just as well if U.S. declaratory policy on nuclear retaliation against aggressive proliferation remained deliberately ambiguous.

The entire concept of "extended" nuclear deterrence needs rethinking within the frame of reference of nonproliferation and counterproliferation. U.S. extended deterrence during the Cold War cast a protective nuclear shadow over Western Europe. NATO was the institutional embodiment of the U.S. nuclear guarantee against any Soviet invasion. Although it was conceivable that conventional warfighting might take place in Europe without a nuclear first use, NATO deterrence strategy held over the heads of Soviet planners the possibility of deliberate nuclear retaliation or of inadvertent escalation. The latter threat was probably the more credible on account of its unpredictability. Both sides might lose control over a process of escalation that neither had fully intended.

This escalation uncertainty could operate to deter new nuclear proliferators from threatening American friends or allies not party to any mutual defense pact like NATO, as in the Middle East or Northeast Asia. On the other hand, it is more likely that certainty of response, not uncertainty, will deter nuclear coercion or attack against allies not already wired into a mutual defense guarantee. For example, it may be important for the United States to make clear to regional aggressors outside Europe that retaliation, though not necessarily with nuclear weapons, will follow any nuclear threat or nuclear use against a friendly state contrary to American vital interests. U.S. superiority in high-technology conventional weapons of long range should make threats of this type highly credible for most regional aggressors, excepting those who are not operating with any cost–gain calculus at all. Nothing will deter fanatic ideologues who are determined to have war at all costs.

For those ideological fanatics for whom war is their place in history, preemption of intended attack against a U.S. ally or preventive war may be the only option. These options to destroy an existing nuclear arsenal will be controversial within the American body politic and among allies unless the regional malefactor has already issued an explicit nuclear threat. Israel's attack on Iraq's Osirak reactor in 1981 does not set a useful precedent for a major power like the United States. Israel is a small state facing imminent threat by neighbors who have maintained a state of war readiness against Tel Aviv for generations. In addition, Israel's preventive attack against Iraq's nuclear option might have backfired: Iraqi planners went to ground with more covert methods for developing a nuclear weapons capability, and one which succeeded in avoiding IAEA detection until the aftermath of Desert Storm.

Preventive war or preemption in the face of imminent attack is a better option before an arsenal is created and deployed than it is afterward. Once a country has deployed even a small number of nuclear weapons, preventive war risks the cost that even one or two surviving weapons could do unacceptable damage to U.S. or allied forces or cities. U.S. regional allies may, for this reason, be less willing to engage in preemption or preventive war than is the United States. The ballistic missiles and aircraft available to most proliferators between now and the turn of the century allow for attack distances of short to medium range. The continental United States will not be within range of attack by Iraqi, North Korean, or Iranian ballistic missiles or aircraft. But the prospective regional opponents of these states, including Saudi Arabia, Israel, and South Korea, will be within range of available delivery systems held by these aspiring regional hegemons. A summary of those countries having ballistic missiles with ranges estimated at 1,000 kilometers or better appears in Table 23.

Table 23. States Having Ballistic Missiles with Range ≥ 1,000 Km, 1994

	Missile	Maximum Range	Status
People's Republic of China	M18 (Tondar-68)	1,000	D
	CSS-N-3 (JL-1) SLBM	1,700	S
	DF-25	1,700	D
	CSS-5 (DF-21)	1,800	S
	JL-1 SLBM	2,050	S
	CSS-2 (DF-3A)	2,500	S
	CSS-3 (DF-4)	4,750	S
	DF-31	8,000	D
	JL-2 SLBM	8,000	D
	CSS-4 (DF-5)	11,000	S
	DF-41	12,000	D
Egypt	Badr 2000	1,200	T
France	S-3	3,000	S
	S-4	3,500	T
	M-4 SLBM	4,000	S
	M45 SLBM	4,000	D
	M-5 SLBM	11,000	D
India	Agni	2,500	D
	Aslv	4,000	D
Iran	Labour-1 (No-dong 1)	1,000	D
	M18 (Tondar-68)	1,000	D

Table 23. *Continued*

	Missile	Maximum Range	Status
Iraq	No-dong 1	1,000	D
	Badr 2000	1,200	T
	Al-Aabed	2,000	T
Israel	Jericho (YA-3)	1,500	S
Kazakhstan	SS-18 (RS-20)	11,000	S*
Libya	No-dong 1	1,000	D
North Korea	No-dong 1	1,000	S
	Taepo-dong 1	2,000	D
	Taepo-dong 2	3,500	D
	No-dong 2	?	D
Russia	SS-NX-24	4,000	T
	SS-N-18 SLBM	6,500	S
	SS-N-6 SLBM	7,800	S
	SS-N-20 SLBM	8,300	S
	SS-N-23 SLBM	8,300	S
	SS-13 (RS-12)	9,400	S
	SS-17 (RS-16)	10,000	S
	SS-19 (RS-18)	10,000	S
	SS-24 (RS-22)	10,000	S
	SS-25 (RS-12M)	10,500	S
	SS-11 (RS-10)	13,000	S
Saudi Arabia	DF-3A	2,800	S
South Africa	Jericho 2	1,000	S
	Arniston	1,500	D
Spain	Capricornio	1,300	D
Ukraine	SS-19 (RS-18)	10,000	S*
	SS-24 (RS-22)	10,000	S*
United Kingdom	A-3TK Polaris SLBM	4,600	S
	UGM-133 Trident D-5 SLBM	12,500	S
U.S.A.	UGM-73 Poseidon SLBM	4,630	S
	UGM-96 Trident C-4 SLBM	7,400	S
	LGM-118 Peacekeeper	9,000	T
	XMGM-134 Small ICBM	11,000	T
	LGM-30F Minuteman II	12,500	S
	UGM-133 Trident D-5 SLBM	12,500	S
	LGM-30G Minuteman III	13,000	S

Table 23. *Continued*

"Almosts"			
People's Republic of China	DF-2	900	S
Iraq	Al-Abbas	900	D
	Condor 2	900	T
Israel	Shavit	930	S
Libya	Al-Fatah	950	D
Taiwan	Ching Feng (Sky Horse)	950	D

SOURCE: Adapted from Lt. Col. Joseph F. H. Peterson and Col. Andy McIntyre, *Ballistic Missile Proliferation: A National Security Focus for the 21st Century*, Strategic Research Project, unclassified (Carlisle Barracks, Pa.: U.S. Army War College, April 18, 1994). Adjustments to cell entries are solely my responsibility.

NOTE: The designation "-N-" or "-NX-" indicates sea-based missiles. SLBM = submarine-launched ballistic missile. All other missiles are land-based. D = in development; S = in service; T = declared intent to terminate.

*Scheduled to eliminate its strategic ballistic missiles (i.e., those with intercontinental ranges) and to accede to the Nuclear Nonproliferation Treaty as a nonnuclear state.

Until long-range or intercontinental ballistic missiles are available to Third World proliferators, then, the decision for preventive war against a nuclear-armed state creates a different kind of risk for the United States, compared with its allies and friends outside Europe. Reluctance of allies to participate in preventive war or to authorize antinuclear preemption may leave no option other than retaliation after the fact. There is some thinking that special operations forces could be used to disable or to destroy a "not yet ready for prime time" nuclear capability before it became fully operational. Although this approach—preventive war—cannot be ruled out, it is extremely risky: gestating nuclear weapons capabilities will undoubtedly be closely guarded and physically protected state secrets. Getting accurate intelligence about their location and vulnerability will be among the many challenges for counterproliferation planners in the next century.

Conclusion

The twentieth century is often described as a century of total war. In an important sense it has been so. The world wars of the present century have resulted in unprecedented destruction of human life and social value. The military forces created to accomplish this destruction have threatened, by their very size and diversity, to subvert the proper subordination of war to policy. Keeping war under the control of policy is inherent in the very raison d'être for the modern territorial state. However, twentieth-century wars showed that states have lost control over some of the important politics of war.

The great Prussian military theorist Carl von Clausewitz offered more insight into the important relationship between war and state policy than any other modern writer. Clausewitz anticipated that a dysfunctional relationship between war and politics could contribute to military defeat and to loss of the state. He offered a model of correct relations among army, government, and people which is still used for reference by scholars and statesmen. However, war in the later nineteenth and twentieth century became more complex than Clausewitz could have foreseen, so his insights have to be modified accordingly. No one whose last real military campaign took place during the Napoleonic Wars and who last wrote on military subjects in 1827 (published posthumously by his wife in 1832) could anticipate the features of twentieth-century warfare and conflict: weapons technology permitting unprecedented and potentially ecocidal destruction of social value; major coalition wars extending over many years with mass armies supported by fully industrialized economies;

post–World War II disintegration of the great European empires and the emergence of a global congeries of new states, vulnerable to domestic upheaval, in Asia, Africa, and the Middle East; or, a return of military primitivism, subsequent to the end of the Cold War, in the form of eth-nonationalist, religious, and other primordial political aspirants to self-rule. And by no means is this list of items pertinent to the conduct of twentieth-century war and conflict exhaustive.[1]

Yet, Clausewitz did succeed in anticipating the crux of the problem in military preparedness or in war waging: the difference between making war subordinate to "policy" and allowing war to be submerged in "politics," in present-day terminology. In war properly conducted according to Clausewitz's theory, as we have seen, the military arm would take its marching orders from the political head. But the obligation was recipro-cal: the political head would not misuse the military arm for nonmilitary objectives, nor assign to it objectives obviously beyond its reach. Many twentieth-century wars found that this desirable relationship between force and policy never obtained. Because it did not, armies marched on behalf of politically feckless purposes, or militaries usurped political power and militarized the state and its policies. The preceding chapters show how the largest and smallest twentieth-century wars, and in some cases prominent crises, became politicized (meaning politically cor-rupted) by a distorted relationship between aims and arms.

My analysis shows that larger and smaller wars are both politicized, but in different ways. Larger wars are politicized by the diversity of aims in-herent in coalitions of states. Smaller wars are politicized, as the typology developed in my introductory chapter suggests, by a lack of national unity with respect to small wars and by the consequent turbulence within, and across, civilian and military leadership circles. A paradoxical finding, but one borne out by twentieth-century experience, is that leaders may be less willing to see smaller wars, especially civil wars, through to their conclusion than they will larger conflicts. Thus, internal conflicts may be harder to terminate than interstate wars. Overall, the perspective in this book suggests that wars of the largest and smallest kinds (either major coalition wars or civil wars) are the most subject to political and military distortion: wars of intermediate scope and stake are more likely to be fought within a proper frame of political and military reference.

For U.S. and other military planners, the finding of a stronger tendency for politico-military distortion in wars at both ends of the conflict spec-

1. Martin Van Creveld, *Technology and War: From 2000 B.C. to the Present* (New York: Free Press, 1989), esp. 153–234.

trum (major coalition wars and unconventional conflicts) has an ominous ring. Present indications are that, in the post–Cold War world, unconventional conflicts involving the very definition and viability of the territorial state will assume prominence on the policy agenda. The political scientist K. J. Holsti has traced the evolution of conflict-producing issues from the foundation of the modern state system to the present.[2] His summary of the kinds of issues that led to war in each of four different international systems from 1715 to 1989 is shown in Table 24.

Table 24 shows a much higher frequency in the twentieth century, especially since 1945, of wars resulting from issues related to nation-state integration/disintegration. In the multipolar balance-of-power systems from 1715 to the present century, states fought many wars for territory, including the spoils attendant to the possession of territory. The salience of that issue, relative to issues such as "maintain integrity of state/empire" and "government composition," diminishes as we move from more remote times to more recent times. The significance of state integration/ disintegration is reinforced by the continuing salience of "human sympathy" and other issues involving primordial values: namely, concern for one's ethnic, ideological, or religious kinfolk. Wars involving issues related to human sympathy peaked in the period 1815–1914 but remained strong to the end of the present century, as conflicts in Bosnia, Rwanda, Chechnya, and elsewhere in 1994 showed all too well. If the drivers of future interstate and intrastate conflict are state integration and human

Table 24. Frequency of Issues Causing War in Four International Systems, 1715–1989 (% of Total)

	1715–1814	1815–1914	1918–1941	1945–1989
Territory	67	42	47	24
Balance of power	1	3	3	0
National liberation/state creation	8	29	13	28
Protect ethnic kin	0	16	7	9
Ethnic/religious unification, irredenta	0	6	17	12
Government composition	14	13	17	28
Maintain integrity of state/ empire	8	55	30	28

SOURCE: Adapted from Kalevi J. Holsti, *Peace and War: Armed Conflicts and International Order, 1648–1989* (Cambridge: Cambridge University Press, 1991), 308.

NOTE: Percentages do not total 100.

2. Kalevi J. Holsti, *Peace and War: Armed Conflicts and International Order, 1648–1989* (Cambridge: Cambridge University Press, 1991).

sympathy, what does this do to the classical relationship between dutiful armed forces and the politically sovereign state?

Wars of the twentieth century have not all been of one type. Nevertheless, for wars among the Eurasian and North American great powers, there were important central tendencies. Clausewitz anticipated that war would grow toward its absolute limit of violence unless it was deliberately held in check by policy. The first half of the twentieth century saw this prophecy fulfilled all too successfully. Technology and industrialism provided to military planners and to political leaders the tools with which to wage total war, against societies as well as their armed forces, without restraint. The nuclear age provided a technology even more deadly, promising if it were ever fully unleashed to destroy modern civilization.

The two world wars of the twentieth century and the Cold War from 1945 to 1990 presented one kind of relationship among policy, strategy, and weapons technology.[3] Clausewitz had asserted a normative theory of the relationship between strategy and policy. Strategy was to be the province of the military brain trust; policy, the directive of the political leadership. Policy was the controlling faculty, and strategy the instrument.[4] If war were an unrestrained and absolute expression of force, then "the moment it is called forth by policy it would step into the place of policy," becoming something quite independent of it, according to Clausewitz.[5] Although all wars began with a political cause of some sort, they were not all political wars to the same extent.

According to Clausewitz, the likelihood that political and military aims in war would coincide was stronger if the war was fought for larger stakes and aroused greater social passions. As he develops the argument:

> The more violent the excitement which precedes the War, by so much the nearer will the War approach to its abstract form, so much the more will it be directed to the destruction of the enemy, so much the nearer will the military and political ends coincide, so much the more purely military and less political the War appears to be; but the weaker the motives and tensions, so much the less will the natural direction of the military element—that is, force—be coincident with the direction which the political element indi-

3. Colin S. Gray emphasizes the interaction of these three sets of variables throughout his work. For a recent and interesting example, see Gray, *Weapons Don't Make War: Policy, Strategy, and Military Technology* (Lawrence: University Press of Kansas, 1993).

4. Gen. Carl von Clausewitz, *On War*, trans. Col. J. J. Graham, (London: Routledge & Kegan Paul, 1966), 1:23.

5. Ibid., 1:22.

cates; so much the more must, therefore, the War become diverted from its natural direction, the political object diverge from the aim of an ideal War, and the War appear to become political.[6]

This is an extremely important argument. Clausewitz had seen how the ability of revolutionary France to put an entire nation under arms through mass conscription and mobilization had helped to inspire Napoleonic conquest, including defeats inflicted on Prussia and its allies. Clausewitz regretted that the Prussian king could not muster the same sense of nationalist opposition to Napoleonic adventurism as did, for example, the Russian tsar, whose armies Clausewitz temporarily served as adviser.[7] However, this argument—that the more militarily correct and less politically distorted wars would be the larger and more costly ones—was put to a severe test by twentieth-century war.

Twentieth-century wars combined the fury of Napoleonic revolutionary imperialism with the technology of the industrial era to produce unprecedented destruction of armies and peoples. Clausewitz could not have foreseen the changes in technology which caused his model to require adaptation. The First and Second World Wars showed that, contrary to his expectation, major coalition wars are as subject to dysfunctional politicization as smaller conflicts. That is to say, the political incompetency of the major powers of Eurasia and North America dominated the prosecution of the world wars and the succeeding Cold War, often to the detriment of sound military strategy. B. H. Liddell Hart attributes some of this distortion of political or military aim, and of the relationship between the two in the world wars, to Clausewitz's abstract style of reasoning which lent itself to misinterpretation:

> By the reiteration of such phrases [Liddell Hart cites several passages from Clausewitz here, including "Let us not hear of generals who conquer without bloodshed"] Clausewitz blurred the outlines of his philosophy, already indistinct, and made it into a mere marching refrain—a Prussian *Marseillaise* which inflamed the blood and intoxicated the mind. In transfusion it became a doc-

6. Ibid., 1:24.
7. See Peter Paret, "Napoleon and the Revolution in War," ch. 5 in Paret, ed., *Makers of Modern Strategy: From Machiavelli to the Nuclear Age* (Princeton, N.J.: Princeton University Press, 1986), 123–42, and Paret, "Clausewitz," ch. 7, pp. 186–217 in the same volume. Also useful are Paret, *Clausewitz and the State* (New York: Oxford University Press, 1976), which contains an extensive bibliography of Clausewitz literature, and Michael I. Handel, ed., *Clausewitz and Modern Strategy* (London: Frank Cass, 1986), especially Handel's discussion of the omissions in Clausewitz on account of his preindustrial experience.

trine fit to form corporals, not generals. For by making battle appear the only "real warlike activity," his gospel deprived strategy of its laurels, and reduced the art of war to the mechanics of mass slaughter.[8]

The criticism is overstated, but it touches a valid point about the confusion that Clausewitz's ideal of absolute war lent itself to in later generations. Why was this so? One reason was that mass mobilization in the twentieth century went well beyond that envisioned by a nineteenth-century philosopher. Clausewitz had assumed that a mobilized population would be more likely to support the war aims of heads of state, and at the outbreak of World War I it seemed so. After several years of war and unprecedented military and social costs to all sides, the popular will turned against war. The tsar's soldiers quit the field and joined in revolutionary agitation that ultimately brought down the Russian Empire. French forces on the western front mutinied, in some cases by entire division. The British public grew sufficiently tired of war and unhappy with the direction of war policy that Lloyd George was catapulted into the political driver's seat. Although the German public had less to say about the matter compared with the British and French, its discouragement and deprivation after four years of fighting was one contributory factor in Germany's willingness to sign the armistice on November 11, 1918.

Thus, the experience of World War I could be read as a warning that national mobilization redounds against policymakers unless victory or other acceptable war termination can be obtained in a timely fashion. Otherwise the politicization of war by excessive mass antagonism, creeping from the body politic into the armed forces, will pin policy to the wall. This disposition of mobilized public involvement against policymakers is, on the evidence of twentieth-century experience, most likely in the largest and in the smallest wars. "In between" wars of limited aim have greater potential to avoid public antagonism against policymakers and against military commitments. However, this potential for wars of limited aim to avoid undue politicization is not always realized: in the Gulf War of 1991 it was; in Korea and Vietnam, it was not.

In the Vietnam War, President Johnson chose not to mobilize the country by a declaration of war and decided to fight the war with a strategy of phased escalation. In so doing, according to some of President Johnson's critics, he prevented the U.S. armed forces from applying a correct military strategy which might have led to victory.[9] This argument is seductive

---

8. B. H. Liddell Hart, *Strategy,* 2d rev. ed. (New York: Frederick A. Praeger, 1967), 355.

9. The case is argued most assertively by Col. Harry G. Summers, Jr., *On Strategy: A Critical Analysis of the Vietnam War* (New York: Dell Publications, 1984).

for American military professionals, but essentially it is incorrect. Although the White House and other civilians did involve themselves in some aspects of military operations, this was more true of the air war than of the ground war. The U.S. Army fought its ground war in South Vietnam according to the dictates of its own military doctrine, one in which Secretary of Defense Robert McNamara and other leading civilians concurred.

In addition, the Army conducted itself well in this military phase of the Vietnam War. The problem was not that the U.S. Army was defeated in battle, but that U.S. forces were fighting on behalf of a lost political cause. The government of South Vietnam lacked the political integrity and authority, especially in the countryside, to maintain the allegiance of its population in the face of subversion and revolutionary warfare. That U.S. forces were able to defeat North Vietnamese and Viet Cong main-force units in every battle shows that the American military performance through 1968 was exceptional *despite* a hostile political climate in South Vietnam and in the United States.

The Vietnam War became more politicized as the war expanded from a peripheral conflict into one which committed half a million U.S. troops to a fight with no apparent termination. President Nixon turned the Vietnam War officially into a political war by announcing his intent eventually to withdraw U.S. forces and leave the fighting to the South Vietnamese. Then the contest was between the North Vietnamese and Viet Cong and the South Vietnamese government, assisted at arm's length by the United States. It is no coincidence that it was during this period, following the announced intention of the United States to phase out its military commitment to South Vietnam, that militarily dysfunctional behavior marked the U.S. armed forces. They now had a political mission: standing fast to symbolize U.S. commitment until all American forces had been withdrawn. Who wanted to be the last enlistee or officer to be killed in action?

Limited wars can be vulnerable to politicization if their war aims and military missions undergo impromptu changes for which military leaders and publics are not prepared. For example, U.S. involvement in the Korean War became controversial because President Truman limited U.S. objectives to restoration of the status quo ante: the liberation of South Korea. The controversiality of Truman's decision was increased by the president's own earlier decision to allow commanding general Douglas MacArthur to proceed north of the 38th parallel and to unify all of Korea under U.N. control. Chinese military intervention and the unwillingness of Truman to risk escalation into war against China or world war forced a reversion to the originally proclaimed war aim of restoring South Korea.

In the five months or so of U.S. buildup prior to the Gulf War of 1991, President Bush averred that if war broke out, it would not be "another

Vietnam." Presumably he meant that U.S. force would be applied without restraints of the kind that plagued American military strategy in Vietnam. Field commander (Commander-in-Chief Central Command, or CINCCENTCOM) General Norman Schwarzkopf was given charge of all military operations in the theater of war. Reporting to him were various U.S. ground, air, and naval component commanders as well as the commanders of allied forces. It appeared that classical strategy, lost on the battlefields of Vietnam, had been regained in the Gulf.

The appearance was deceptive. The U.S. victory over Iraq was never in doubt, but the timing and character of that victory were made possible by a collapse of Saddam's war machine hitherto unexpected by military experts. Iraq had no countermeasures for U.S. advanced technology and conventional weapons, nor for overwhelming U.S. air power. Just as decisive as technology and tactics for determining the war's outcome, however, was politics. Saddam's diplomatic ineptitude and political hamhandedness allowed Bush to mobilize a majority of Arab states against Iraq, including long-term Saudi and Kuwaiti enemies like Syria. Bush also exploited the denouement of the Cold War to get Gorbachev's Soviets to vote in favor of a U.N. use of force against Iraq. The diplomatic disconnection of Iraq from the Soviet Union paved the way for unrestrained use of force for the limited and specific purpose of expelling Iraq from Kuwait.

The Gulf War was also political in other important ways that helped to determine its outcome. U.S. diplomatic strategy kept Israel out of the war. Had Israel jumped in, Saddam Hussein could have exploited Arab–Israeli hostility to divide the coalition and, perhaps, to discontinue Saudi support for American war aims. Recall that immediately after Iraq's invasion of Kuwait on August 2, 1990, the United States was uncertain whether Saudi Arabia would welcome an American troop presence on its territory. Another political constraint on prosecution of the war had to do with coalition war aims. If it went beyond the aim of expelling Iraq from Kuwait, the United States would have lost members of the coalition and left Washington open to cries of First World imperialism.

The Gulf War as a major regional conflict both confirms and disconfirms my hypothesis about the relationship between war intensity and its politico-military character. On the one hand, within carefully bounded limits imposed by politicians, U.S. and allied force was used without restraint against military targets. Efforts were made to discriminate and to spare collateral damage to Iraq civilians, but these efforts were not entirely successful.[10] This image of antiseptic war, conveyed by carefully

---

10. U.S. Department of Defense, *Gulf War Air Power Survey* (Washington, D.C.: GPO, 1993), 2:222–23 et pass.

selected and televised video of U.S. "smart bombs" going down chimneys, was a construct as much as a reality of combat. Air target planners in the "black hole" at CENTCOM were eventually directed by Schwarzkopf to avoid bridges in downtown Baghdad for fear of causing civilian casualties and adverse publicity. Command sensitivity to bad publicity was raised after February 13 attacks against the Al-Firdos bunker were followed by CNN video of dead women and children being removed from that bunker.[11]

Operations and tactics were also, contrary to popular impression, directly affected by politics. The Iraqi mobile-Scud ballistic missiles proved much more difficult to detect and to destroy than prewar estimates had held. As they began to rain down on Israel, a major diplomatic and military crisis ensued. U.S. officials sent Patriot theater ballistic-missile defenses to Tel Aviv as they implored the government of Israel to remain nonbelligerent. Defense Secretary Richard Cheney and Chairman of the Joint Chiefs of Staff General Colin Powell increased the pressure from Washington to target and to destroy the Scuds. From a military standpoint, however, the Scuds were not a priority target unless nuclear- or chemical-armed. They were a less important target for U.S. air planners than Iraq's armored divisions, artillery, or weapons of mass destruction. From the standpoint of classical strategy as articulated by Clausewitz and seconded by his latter-day admirers, the diversion of reconnaissance and firepower resources to the Great Scud hunt was a clear distortion of military logic by political expediency.

If the Gulf War is a split decision for the argument that larger wars are less political, it weighs more in the balance against the argument than in favor of it. It was a small war in two respects: (1) numbers of U.S. and friendly casualties and (2) duration. It was a major war in its intensity of firepower and in the advanced state of technology used by U.S. and allied forces. It was a limited war in terms of political objective, although within that objective, massive destruction was inflicted on Iraqi forces. On the other hand, not all the destruction that U.S. forces could have done was authorized. Saddam Hussein emerged from the war with about a third of his armored divisions intact and with his regime still in office.

Had the U.S. trimmed its political objective to fit its military means? Some suspected that this was so, since U.S. logistics for the ground war would have lasted only another few days without significant replenishment. The start of the ground war was timed, in part, because coalition aircraft had virtually run out of useful military targets. Extended military campaigning in the Gulf would have meant a continuation of the war into seasons of more adverse weather and an extension of already overtaxed

11. Ibid, 2:220.

enlisted personnel assignments. The U.S. reserves would have been further mobilized, and U.S. public support for the war would have been placed at risk. If the United States and its allies were fighting to deter future aggression in the "new world order" and not merely for oil, the war aim seemed disproportionately small and the operations abrupt. Perhaps a classical military campaign was followed in the Gulf because it was possible, though not necessarily optimal.

Intelligence, low-intensity conflict, and special operations serve as reminders that war and armed conflict are related, but distinct, concepts. They, too, tested my hypothesis that larger wars should be fought more in accord with a strictly military or classical strategy. Intelligence and special operations can serve to support military efforts in wars of all sizes, in conventional and in unconventional wars. Low-intensity conflict or unconventional wars are usually below the threshold of major conventional war, although some wars involve a peculiar conflation of both types of conflict (Vietnam, for example). Notwithstanding these qualifications, we see little evidence that smaller engagements or operations are more politicized and larger ones less so. Many Special Operations Executive activities during World War II were intentionally paramilitary and purposely deniable. So, too, were the equally controversial (to military traditionalists) efforts of the U.S. Office of Strategic Services. The U.S. Central Intelligence Agency's OSS parentage only made more controversial its adoption of clandestine operations, including clandestine military operations, as part of its assumed mission.

If more "politicized" means more charged with political controversy, then CIA paramilitary operations certainly fitted Clausewitz's expectation about the increased politicization of small wars. On the other hand, this was only true once those operations became widely visible, after the fact, for the larger body politic. So long as they were kept hidden, CIA clandestine operations were as strictly "military" as Clausewitz might have wished any tactical operation to be. The intelligence equivalent of tactical commanders (case officers and their administrative superiors) operated more or less without oversight. The CIA overthrew governments, planned assassinations, and carried out illegal domestic surveillance at the behest of various presidents and national security councils. Although carrying out the presumed political will of their superiors, CIA clandestine warriors were until the 1970s operating in a very Clausewitzian world of autonomy over operations and tactics.

U.S. experience in crisis management during the Cold War is pertinent to the hypothesis that smaller conflicts are more politicized and less likely to take the form of classical military engagements. My expectation was borne out in this regard. In fact, a hallmark of nuclear-crisis manage-

ment during the Cold War was the intrusiveness of politicians in the details of military operations. The Cuban missile crisis, according to one
very prominent student of that episode, was precedent-setting for U.S.
policymakers with respect to their micromanagement of military strategy.[12]
Therefore, nuclear-crisis management experience would seem to provide
partial confirmation of the thesis that going lower on the scale of actual
violence makes a potential military clash more political.

On the other hand, crises, especially the U.S. and Soviet management
of nuclear crises during the Cold War, are more like substitutes for war
than they are like small wars. The purpose of nuclear-crisis management
was the avoidance of war, and not only of nuclear war. Any war between
the United States and the Soviet Union was judged by leaders of both
sides to hold unacceptable risks of escalation. Crises as substitutes for
war involved a special blending of diplomatic and military signals, or a
coercive form of diplomacy short of war.[13] It follows that crises may not
be one incremental step below small wars but, rather, an entirely different qualitative step, away from mainly military conflict into diplomatic
conflict backed up by latent or manifest threats.

One issue in regard to placing crises on the spectrum of violence, in
order to test further my argument about politicization in small wars, is
whether they involve latent or manifest threats by one or both parties.
Sometimes crises can heat up without either side making an explicit military threat. The sides can maneuver their forces, for example by raising
alert status or deploying troops, without placing these maneuvers and
alerts in the context of any open warning or remonstrance. In chess, the
equivalent move is to shove a pawn into harm's way in order to draw the
attention of bigger pieces, and to reveal the strategy by which the bigger
pieces might be operating. For example, the Berlin crisis of 1948 involved
no explicit threat by the Soviet leader Joseph Stalin to force the United
States and its allies out of their rightful sectors in that divided city. Stalin
squeezed off the overland access routes from the western part of Germany into Berlin, located in eastern Germany, and waited to see how the
allies would respond. Truman, in responding, did not threaten explicitly
to wage war unless the Soviets called off the blockade. Instead, the United
States initiated an airlift of supplies into West Berlin, forcing Stalin to
choose between a war-provoking escalation (shoot the planes down) or
the eventual abandonment of his harassment of allied rights.

Much of what crises are about is the bargaining reputation of states,

12. Graham T. Allison, *Essence of Decision: Explaining the Cuban Missile Crisis* (Boston:
Little, Brown, 1971).

13. Alexander L. George et al., *The Limits of Coercive Diplomacy: Laos, Cuba, Vietnam*
(Boston: Little, Brown, 1971); see esp. George's chapter on Cuba.

independently of the immediate issue at stake: Berlin, Cuba, and so forth.[14] This has led to some mistaken attempts to treat crises as strictly psychological encounters or competitions in military bluff. But crises are serious issues because, among other reasons, they have real potential to explode into violence and because the threat of latent violence is already present. States poised to respond to a possible attack have probably alerted their military forces, primed their command-and-control systems, and adjusted their organizational responses from normal day-to-day readiness to approximate battle conditions.

Thus, state involvement in crises is a war form involving latent military threats which make crisis management "work."[15] Crisis management is an important set of approaches to the avoidance of war because the pace of crisis events may outstrip the capacity of decisionmakers to manage those events. For example, historians and political scientists have noted numerous and important failures in U.S. intelligence and warning systems during Cold War crises. Some of these failures nearly triggered unwanted crisis escalation or inadvertent nuclear first use. According to Scott Sagan's study of U.S. nuclear weapons safety during the Cuban missile crisis, "the possibility of an accidental, unauthorized, or mistaken use of a U.S. nuclear weapon" during the U-2 stray over Siberian airspace on October 27, 1962, "was not remote."[16]

Nuclear deterrence under "normal" day-to-day conditions during the Cold War, like crisis management, can also be understood as ersatz war in place of actual military fighting. U.S., Soviet, or other states' experience in nuclear deterrence may therefore have no immediate bearing on the issue of whether smaller wars are more or less political than larger ones. But it does not stretch the point to treat deterrence, like crisis management, as something more than a psychology experiment. Deterrence, as in the case of crisis management, is supported by implicit or explicit threats of violence. To credibly threaten to harm another state or its values, one must create the appropriate means of destruction and task them for first strike or retaliation, as policymakers intend.

If deterrence and crisis management are both "not quite war," then the argument that smaller wars are more politicized receives some additional support in these cases. Indeed, many insights of U.S. deterrence theorists

14. The point is emphasized in Thomas C. Schelling, *Arms and Influence* (New Haven, Conn.: Yale University Press, 1966).

15. For an explication of crisis management, see Gordon A. Craig and Alexander L. George, *Force and Statecraft: Diplomatic Problems of Our Time* (New York: Oxford University Press, 1983), 205–19.

16. Scott D. Sagan, *The Limits of Safety: Organizations, Accidents and Nuclear Weapons* (Princeton, N.J.: Princeton University Press, 1993), 138.

are based on the assumption that nuclear deterrence and crisis management are more political than military. The "threat that leaves something to chance" can be exploited for bargaining purposes by deliberately creating some indeterminate risk of uncontrolled outcomes desirable to neither party.[17]

Drawing from and expanding upon my summary in Table 1 (see Introduction above, we might now modify that table in two ways. As presented earlier, the table depicted my expectations about the probable politicization of small and large wars. We have seen that my anticipations were partly correct, and partly incorrect. A modified table, with the dimension of crisis management added to small and large wars and with the preceding chapters taken into account, might now be constructed (see Table 25).

One aspect of my argument that smaller wars are likely to be less politicized is the assumption that mass awareness and psychological involvement in such conflicts will be diminished or nonexistent, compared with larger conflicts. Yet conditions pertinent to this "visibility" hypothesis have turned inside out since Clausewitz's day. He was concerned lest Prussia's statist wars fail to mobilize sufficient popular support. Today, global media of communication create instant mass awareness of small wars and crises as well as of larger conflicts. There is no place for wars to hide from the view of masses or elites. This restricts the elites' freedom of action. CNN videos can push distant interethnic wars, as in Bosnia, to the top of the U.S. State Department and NATO agendas.

Because even smaller wars and crises now have the visibility that only very large and costly nineteenth-century and early twentieth-century wars used to have, the task of sealing off the conduct of military operations from adverse politicization is unprecedentedly difficult. In the fu-

Table 25. Dimensions of Conflict Politicization

Attributes of Politicization	Small Wars	Large Wars	Crises
Leader interference with operations	Moderate to high	High	High
Ambiguity of aims	High	Low to high	Low
Public involvement and expected costs	Low if short; high if prolonged	High	Low if short; high if prolonged

17. Thomas C. Schelling, *The Strategy of Conflict* (Cambridge, Mass.: Harvard University Press, 1960).

ture, it may prove to be impossible. The public, news media, and Congress will be looking over the operations and tactics of U.S. warriors in "real time." Clausewitz had anticipated that small wars would be less politicized than larger wars because leaders would have relatively more decisionmaking freedom in small wars. Dynastic wars over territory or spoils, characteristic of seventeenth- and eighteenth-century monarchs, rarely pushed a decision to the point at which a major power's very existence was at stake. When the visibility and costs of war were raised higher by nationalism (as prefigured by revolutionary France) or (as in the latter half of the nineteenth century) by technology, war involved major power coalitions, erroneous prewar strategic appreciations, and uncertainty about the terms of a peace settlement. Coalitions, wrongful strategic expectations, and ambiguous peace settlements are all hallmarks of politicized wars.

If the genie of warfare cannot be put back into the bottle of policy, is that necessarily bad? Some think not. The eminent military historian John Keegan argues that the Western way of warfare has outlived its usefulness.[18] The wars of the twentieth century fought by the great powers according to state policy resulted in unprecedented societal destruction and chaos. Nuclear war between the Cold War superpowers, had it erupted, would have spelled the end of civilization. The eclipse of war as a continuation of politics, though not of warriors or politics separately, may be preferable to a continued linkage between the two:

> Politics must continue; war cannot. That is not to say that the role of the warrior is over. The world community needs, more than it has ever done, skilful and disciplined warriors who are ready to put themselves at the service of its authority. Such warriors must properly be seen as the protectors of civilisation, not its enemies. The style in which they fight for civilisation—against ethnic bigots, regional warlords, ideological intransigents, common pillagers and organised international criminals—cannot derive from the Western model of warmaking alone.[19]

18. John Keegan, *A History of Warfare* (New York: Alfred A. Knopf, 1993).
19. Ibid., 391–92.

Select Bibliography

Addington, Larry H. *The Blitzkrieg Era and the German General Staff, 1865–1941.* New Brunswick, N.J.: Rutgers University Press, 1971.

Adelman, Jonathan R. *Prelude to the Cold War: The Tsarist, Soviet and U.S. Armies in the Two World Wars.* Boulder, Colo.: Lynne Rienner, 1988.

Agee, Philip. *Inside the Company: CIA Diary.* New York: Bantam Books, 1975.

Albertini, Luigi. *The Origins of the War of 1914.* Vol. 2. Translated and edited by Isabella M. Massey. London: Oxford University Press, 1953.

Allison, Graham T. *Essence of Decision: Explaining the Cuban Missile Crisis.* Boston: Little, Brown, 1971.

Allison, Graham T., Albert Carnesale, and Joseph S. Nye, eds. *Hawks, Doves and Owls: An Agenda for Avoiding Nuclear War.* New York: W. W. Norton, 1985.

Allison, Graham T., Ashton B. Carter, Steven E. Miller, and Philip Zelikow, eds. *Cooperative Denuclearization: From Pledges to Deeds.* Cambridge, Mass.: Center for Science and International Affairs, Harvard University, 1993.

Allison, Graham, and Gregory F. Treverton, eds. *Rethinking America's Security: Beyond Cold War to New World Order.* New York: W. W. Norton, 1992.

Allison, Graham, and William L. Ury with Bruce J. Allyn, eds. *Windows of Opportunity: From Cold War to Peaceful Competition.* Cambridge, Mass: Ballinger, 1989.

Ambrose, Stephen E. *Ike's Spies: Eisenhower and the Espionage Establishment.* New York: Doubleday, 1981.

———. *Rise To Globalism: American Foreign Policy since 1938.* 6th ed. New York: Penguin Books, 1991.

Andrew, Christopher, and Oleg Gordievsky. *KGB: The Inside Story of Its Foreign Operations from Lenin to Gorbachev.* New York: Harper Collins, 1991.

Arkin, William M., "Agnosticism When Real Values Are Needed: Nuclear Policy in the Clinton Administration." *FAS Bulletin* (September/October 1994): 3–10.

———. *Arms Control Implications of the Gulf War.* Project on Rethinking Arms Control. College Park: University of Maryland, Center for International and Security Studies at Maryland, November 1993.

Arquilla, John, and Paul K. Davis. *Modeling Decisionmaking of Potential Proliferators as Part of Developing Counterproliferation Strategies.* Santa Monica, Calif.: Rand, 1994.

Aspin, Rep. Les, and Rep. William Dickinson. *Defense for a New Era: Lessons of the Persian Gulf War.* Washington, D.C.: GPO, 1992.

Atkinson, Rick. *Crusade: The Untold Story of the Persian Gulf War.* New York: Houghton Mifflin, 1993.

Axelrod, Robert. *The Evolution of Cooperation.* New York: Basic Books, 1984.

Ball, Desmond, and Jeffrey Richelson, eds. *Strategic Nuclear Targeting.* Ithaca, N.Y.: Cornell University Press, 1986.

Bamford, James. *The Puzzle Palace: A Report on America's Most Secret Agency.* Boston: Houghton Mifflin, 1982.

Barnett, Frank R., B. Hugh Tovar, and Richard H. Shultz, eds. *Special Operations in U.S. Strategy.* Washington, D.C.: National Strategy Information Center, 1984.

Barron, John. *KGB Today: The Hidden Hand.* New York: Reader's Digest Press, 1983.

Beschloss, Michael R. *The Crisis Years: Kennedy and Khrushchev, 1960–1963.* New York: Harper Collins, 1991.

Betts, Richard K., "Incentives for Nuclear Weapons: India, Pakistan, Iran." *Asian Survey* (November 1979): 1053–72.

————. *Nuclear Blackmail and Nuclear Balance.* Washington, D.C.: Brookings Institution, 1987.

————. "Nuclear Proliferation after Osirak." *Arms Control Today* (September 1981): 1–2, 7–8.

————. "Nuclear Proliferation and Regional Rivalry: Speculations on South Asia." *Orbis* (Spring 1979): 167–84.

————. "Paranoids, Pygmies, Pariahs and Nonproliferation." *Foreign Policy* (Spring 1977): 157–83.

————. *Soldiers, Statesmen, and Cold War Crises.* Cambridge, Mass.: Harvard University Press, 1977.

Bittman, Ladislav. *The Deception Game.* New York: Ballantine Books, 1981.

Blackwill, Robert D., and Albert Carnesale, eds. *New Nuclear Nations: Consequences for U.S. Policy.* New York: Council on Foreign Relations, 1993.

Blainey, Geoffrey. *The Causes of War.* New York: Free Press, 1973.

Blair, Bruce G. *The Logic of Accidental Nuclear War.* Washington, D.C.: Brookings Institution, 1993.

————. *Strategic Command and Control: Redefining the Nuclear Threat.* Washington, D.C.: Brookings Institution, 1985.

Blaufarb, Douglas. *The Counterinsurgency Era: U.S. Doctrine and Performance.* New York: Free Press, 1977.

Blight, James G., and David A. Welch. *On the Brink: Americans and Soviets Reexamine the Cuban Missile Crisis.* New York: Hill & Wang, 1989.

Bond, Brian, ed. *The First World War and British Military History.* Oxford: Clarendon Press, 1991.

Bracken, Paul. *The Command and Control of Nuclear Forces.* New Haven, Conn.: Yale University Press, 1983.

Brands, H. W. *The Devil We Knew: Americans and the Cold War.* New York: Oxford University Press, 1993.

Brinton, Crane. *The Anatomy of Revolution.* New York: Vintage Books, 1938, 1965.

Brodie, Bernard M. *Strategy in the Missile Age.* Princeton, N.J.: Princeton University Press, 1959.

————. *War and Politics.* New York: Macmillan, 1973.

Brook-Shepherd, Gordon. *The Storm Birds: The Dramatic Stories of the Top Soviet Spies Who Have Defected since World War II.* New York: Weidenfeld & Nicolson, 1989.

Brown, Michael E. *The "End" of Nuclear Arms Control.* Project on Rethinking Arms Control. College Park: University of Maryland, Center for International and Security Studies at Maryland, March 1993.

Brown, Seyom. *The Causes and Prevention of War.* New York: St. Martin's Press, 1987.

Brzezinski, Zbigniew. *Out of Control: Global Turmoil on the Eve of the Twentieth Century.* New York: Charles Scribner's Sons, 1993.

Bundy, McGeorge. *Danger and Survival: Choices about the Bomb in the First Fifty Years.* New York: Random House, 1988.

Bunn, George. *Extending the Non-Proliferation Treaty: Legal Questions Faced by the Parties in 1995.* Issue Papers on World Conferences no. 2. Washington, D.C.: American Society of International Law, October 1994.

Carter, Ashton B., John D. Steinbruner, and Charles A. Zraket, eds. *Managing Nuclear Operations.* Washington, D.C.: Brookings Institution, 1987.

Carus, W. Seth. *Cruise Missile Proliferation in the 1990s.* Westport, Conn.: Praeger Publishers, 1992.

Cave Brown, Anthony. *Bodyguard of Lies.* New York: Harper & Row, 1975.

Cline, Ray S. *The CIA under Reagan, Bush and Casey.* Washington, D.C.: Acropolis Books, 1981.

Cohen, Eliot A. *Commandos and Politicians: Elite Military Units in Modern Democracies.* Cambridge, Mass.: Center for International Affairs, Harvard University, 1978.

————, dir. *Gulf War Air Power Survey.* Vols. 1, 2, 3, 5, and Summary Report. Washington, D.C.: GPO, 1993.

Colby, William, and Peter Forbath. *Honorable Men: My Life in the CIA.* New York: Simon & Schuster, 1978.

Consortium for the Study of Intelligence. *Covert Action in the 1990s.* Washington, D.C.: Working Group on Intelligence Reform, 1992.

Constantinides, George C. *Intelligence and Espionage: An Analytical Bibliography.* Boulder, Colo.: Westview Press, 1983.

Copeland, Miles. *The Game of Nations: The Amorality of Power Politics.* New York: College Notes and Texts, 1969.

Cordesman, Anthony H. *After the Storm: The Changing Military Balance in the Middle East.* Boulder, Colo.: Westview Press, 1993.

————. *The Iran-Iraq War and Western Security, 1984–87: Strategic Implications and Policy Options.* London: Jane's Publishing Co., 1987.

Coser, Lewis A. *The Functions of Social Conflict.* New York: Free Press, 1956.

Daalder, Ivo H. *Stepping Down the Thermonuclear Ladder: How Low Can We Go?* Project on Rethinking Arms Control. College Park: University of Maryland, Center for International and Security Studies at Maryland, June 1993.

Dailey, Brian D., and Patrick J. Parker, eds. *Soviet Strategic Deception.* Lexington, Mass.: D. C. Heath, 1987.

Daniel, Donald, and Katherine Herbig, eds. *Strategic Military Deception.* New York: Pergamon Press, 1982.

Danilov, Iurii. *La Russie dans la Guerre Mondiale (1914–1917).* Paris: Payot, 1927.

Divine, Robert A., ed. *Causes and Consequences of World War II.* Chicago: Quadrangle Books, 1969.

Doughty, Robert A., et al. *Warfare in the Western World,* vols. 1 and 2. Lexington, Mass.: D. C. Heath, 1996.

Dulles, Allen. *The Craft of Intelligence.* New York: New American Library/Signet Books, 1965.

Dunn, Lewis A. *Containing Nuclear Proliferation.* Adelphi Paper no. 263. London: International Institute for Strategic Studies, 1991.

———. *Controlling the Bomb: Nuclear Proliferation in the 1980s.* New Haven, Conn.: Yale University Press, 1982.

Durch, William J., ed. *The Evolution of UN Peacekeeping: Case Studies and Comparative Analysis.* New York: St. Martin's Press, 1993.

———. *The United Nations and Collective Security in the 21st Century.* Carlisle Barracks, Pa.: Strategic Studies Institute, U.S. Army War College, February 1993.

Dyson, Freeman. *Weapons and Hope.* New York: Harper & Row, 1984.

Dziak, John J. *Chekisty: A History of the KGB.* Lexington, Mass.: D. C. Heath, 1988.

Earle, Edward Mead, ed. *Makers of Modern Strategy: Military Thought from Machiavelli to Hitler.* Princeton, N.J.: Princeton University Press, 1943.

Eisenhower, David. *Eisenhower at War, 1943–1945.* New York: Random House, 1986.

Enthoven, Alain C., and K. Wayne Smith. *How Much Is Enough? Shaping the Defense Program, 1961–1969.* New York: Harper & Row, 1971.

Erickson, John. *The Road to Berlin.* Boulder, Colo.: Westview Press, 1983.

Fall, Bernard. *Street without Joy.* Harrisburg, Pa.: Stackpole Books, 1963.

Fay, Sidney Bradshaw. *The Origins of the World War.* 2d rev. ed. Vol. 2. New York: Free Press, 1966.

Feaver, Peter Douglas. *Guarding the Guardians: Civilian Control of Nuclear Weapons in the United States.* Ithaca, N.Y.: Cornell University Press, 1992.

———. "Proliferation Optimism and Theories of Nuclear Operations." *Security Studies* (Spring/Summer 1993): 159–91.

Fischer, Fritz. *War of Illusions: German Policies from 1911 to 1914.* Translated from the German by Marian Jackson. New York: W. W. Norton, 1975.

Foot, M.R.D. *SOE: An Outline History of the Special Operations Executive, 1940–46.* London: British Broadcasting Corporation, 1984.

Freedman, Lawrence. *The Evolution of Nuclear Strategy.* New York: St. Martin's Press, 1981.

———. *U.S. Intelligence and the Soviet Strategic Threat.* London: Macmillan, 1977.

Friedman, Norman. *Desert Victory: The War for Kuwait.* Annapolis, Md.: Naval Institute Press, 1991.

Fry, Earl H., Stan A. Taylor, and Robert S. Wood. *America the Vincible: U.S. Foreign Policy for the Twenty-first Century.* Englewood Cliffs, N.J.: Prentice-Hall, 1994.

Fuller, William C., *Civil–Military Conflict in Imperial Russia, 1881–1914*. Princeton, N.J.: Princeton University Press, 1985.

———. *Strategy and Power in Russia, 1600–1914*. New York: Free Press, 1992.

Gaddis, John Lewis. *The Long Peace: Inquiries into the History of the Cold War*. New York: Oxford University Press, 1987.

———. *Strategies of Containment: A Critical Appraisal of Postwar American National Security Policy*. New York: Oxford University Press, 1982.

———. *The United States and the End of the Cold War: Implications, Reconsiderations, Provocations*. New York: Oxford University Press, 1992.

———. *The United States and the Origins of the Cold War, 1941–1947*. New York: Columbia University Press, 1972.

Gallie, W. B. *Philosophers of Peace and War: Kant, Clausewitz, Marx, Engels and Tolstoy*. Cambridge: Cambridge University Press, 1978.

Garthoff, Raymond L. *Detente and Confrontation: American-Soviet Relations from Nixon to Reagan*. Washington, D.C.: Brookings Institution, 1985.

———. *Deterrence and the Revolution in Soviet Military Doctrine*. Washington, D.C.: Brookings Institution, 1990.

———. *Reflections on the Cuban Missile Crisis*. Rev.ed. Washington, D.C.: Brookings Institution, 1989.

Gelb, Leslie, with Richard Betts. *The Irony of Vietnam: The System Worked*. Washington, D.C.: Brookings Institution, 1979.

George, Alexander L., ed. *Avoiding War: Problems of Crisis Management*. Boulder, Colo.: Westview Press, 1991.

George, Alexander L., David K. Hall, and William R. Simons. *The Limits of Coercive Diplomacy: Laos, Cuba, Vietnam*. Boston: Little, Brown, 1971.

George, Alexander L., and Richard Smoke. *Deterrence in American Foreign Policy: Theory and Practice*. New York: Columbia University Press, 1974.

Gilpin, Robert. *The Political Economy of International Relations*. Princeton, N.J.: Princeton University Press, 1987.

Glantz, Col. David M., ed. *The Initial Period of War on the Eastern Front, 22 June–August 1941*. London: Frank Cass, 1993.

Godson, Roy, ed. *Comparing Foreign Intelligence: The U.S., the USSR, the U.K. and the Third World*. New York: Pergamon/Brassey's, 1988.

———, ed. *Intelligence Requirements for the 1980s: Clandestine Collection*. New Brunswick, N.J.: Transaction Books, 1982.

———, ed. *Intelligence Requirements for the 1980s: Elements of Intelligence*. New Brunswick, N.J.: Transaction Books, 1983.

———. *Intelligence Requirements for the 1980s: Intelligence and Policy*. Lexington, Mass.: D. C. Heath & Co., 1986.

———, ed. *Intelligence Requirements for the 1990s: Collection, Analysis, Counterintelligence, and Covert Action*. Lexington, Mass.: D. C. Heath, 1989.

Goldman, Emily O. *Sunken Treaties: Naval Arms Control between the Wars*. University Park: Pennsylvania State University Press, 1994.

Gompert, David C., Michael Mandelbaum, Richard L. Garwin, and John H. Barton. *Nuclear Weapons and World Politics: Alternatives for the Future.* New York: McGraw-Hill, 1977.

Gottfried, Kurt, and Bruce G. Blair. *Crisis Stability and Nuclear War.* New York: Oxford University Press, 1988.

Gray, Colin S., "Arms Control Does Not Control Arms." *SAIS Review* (Summer 1993): 333–48.

———. *House of Cards: Why Arms Control Must Fail.* Ithaca, N.Y.: Cornell University Press, 1992.

———. *Nuclear Strategy and National Style.* Lanham, Md.: Hamilton Press, 1986.

———. *Strategic Studies and Public Policy: The American Experience.* Lexington: University Press of Kentucky, 1982.

———. *Weapons Don't Make War: Policy, Strategy, and Military Technology.* Lawrence: University Press of Kansas, 1993.

Griffith, Paddy. *Forward into Battle: Fighting Tactics from Waterloo to Vietnam.* Chichester, Sussex: Antony Bird Publications, 1981.

Guderian, Gen. Heinz. *Panzer Leader.* New York: Ballantine Books, 1957.

Gurr, Ted Robert. *Why Men Rebel.* Princeton, N.J.: Princeton University Press, 1970.

Halberstam, David. *The Best and the Brightest.* New York: Random House, 1969.

Halle, Louis J. *The Cold War as History.* New York: Harper Collins, 1967, 1991.

Handel, Michael I., ed. *Clausewitz and Modern Strategy.* London: Frank Cass, 1986.

———. *Perception, Deception and Surprise: The Case of the Yom Kippur War.* Jerusalem: Leonard Davis Institute, 1976.

Hastings, Max. *Overlord: D-Day and the Battle for Normandy.* New York: Simon & Schuster, 1984.

Hersh, Seymour M. "On the Nuclear Edge." *The New Yorker* (March 29, 1993): 56–62.

———. *The Price of Power: Kissinger in the Nixon White House.* New York: Summit Books, 1983.

———. *The Samson Option: Israel's Nuclear Arsenal and American Foreign Policy.* New York: Random House, 1991.

Herzog, Chaim. *The Arab-Israeli Wars: War and Peace in the Middle East.* New York: Random House/Vintage Books, 1984.

Higgins, Trumbull. *The Perfect Failure: Kennedy, Eisenhower, and the CIA at the Bay of Pigs.* New York: W. W. Norton, 1987, 1989.

Hilsman, Roger. *To Move a Nation.* New York: Dell, 1963.

Holloway, David. *The Soviet Union and the Arms Race.* New Haven, Conn.: Yale University Press, 1983.

Holsti, Kalevi J. *Peace and War: Armed Conflicts and International Order, 1648–1989.* Cambridge: Cambridge University Press, 1991.

Hoopes, Townsend. *The Limits of Intervention.* New York: David McKay, 1969.

Huntington, Samuel P. *Political Order in Changing Societies.* New Haven, Conn.: Yale University Press, 1968.

———. *The Soldier and the State.* Cambridge, Mass.: Harvard University Press, 1957.

Iklé, Fred Charles. *Every War Must End.* New York: Columbia University Press, 1971.

Ivanov, S. P. *Nachal'nyi period voiny* [The Initial Period of War]. Moscow: Voenizdat, 1973.

Jablonsky, David. *Strategic Rationality Is Not Enough: Hitler and the Concept of Crazy States.* Carlisle Barracks, Pa.: Strategic Studies Institute, U.S. Army War College, August 1991.

———. *Why Is Strategy Difficult?* Carlisle Barracks, Pa.: Strategic Studies Institute, U.S. Army War College, June 1992.

Janis, Irving. *Victims of Groupthink.* Boston: Houghton Mifflin, 1972.

Janowitz, Morris. *The Professional Soldier.* New York: Free Press, 1960.

Jensen, Kenneth M., ed. *Origins of the Cold War: The Novikov, Kennan and Roberts "Long Telegrams" of 1946.* Washington, D.C.: U.S. Institute of Peace, 1991.

Jervis, Robert. *The Illogic of American Nuclear Strategy.* Ithaca, N.Y.: Cornell University Press, 1984.

———. *The Meaning of the Nuclear Revolution: Statecraft and the Prospect of Armageddon.* Ithaca, N.Y.: Cornell University Press, 1989.

Johnson, Loch K. *A Season of Inquiry.* Chicago: Dorsey Press, 1988.

Kagan, Donald. *On the Origins of War and the Preservation of Peace.* New York: Doubleday, 1995.

Kahn, David. *The Codebreakers.* London: Sphere Books, 1973.

Kahn, Herman. *On Thermonuclear War.* 2d ed. New York: Free Press, 1969.

Kaplan, Fred. *The Wizards of Armageddon.* New York: Simon & Schuster, 1983.

Keegan, John. *The Second World War.* New York: Viking Press, 1989.

Kellner, Douglas. *The Persian Gulf TV War.* Boulder, Colo.: Westview Press, 1992.

Kennedy, Paul M. *The Rise and Fall of the Great Powers: Economic Change and Military Conflict from 1500 to 2000.* New York: Random House, 1987.

———, ed. *The War Plans of the Great Powers, 1880–1914..* London: Allen & Unwin, 1979.

Keohane, Robert O., and Joseph S. Nye. *Power and Interdependence.* 2d ed. Glenview, Ill.: Scott, Foresman, 1989.

Knorr, Klaus, and Patrick M. Morgan, eds. *Strategic Military Surprise.* New Brunswick, N.J.: Transaction Books, 1982.

Koch, Scott A., ed. *Selected Estimates on the Soviet Union, 1950–1959: CIA Cold War Records.* Langley, Va.: Center for the Study of Intelligence, Central Intelligence Agency, 1993.

Laqueur, Walter. *Terrorism.* Boston: Little, Brown, 1977.

Lebow, Richard Ned. *Between Peace and War: The Nature of International Crisis.* Baltimore: Johns Hopkins University Press, 1981.

———. *Nuclear Crisis Management: A Dangerous Illusion.* Ithaca, N.Y.: Cornell University Press, 1987.

Lebow, Richard Ned, and Janice Gross Stein. "We Both Lost the Cold War." Draft manuscript.

Liddell Hart, Capt. B. H. *The Real War, 1914–1918.* Boston: Little, Brown, 1930, 1964.

———. *History of the Second World War.* New York: G. P. Putnam's Sons, 1971.

———. *Strategy.* 2d rev. ed. New York: Frederick A. Praeger, 1967.

Lieven, D.C.B. *Russia and the Origins of the First World War.* New York: St. Martin's Press, 1983.

Livingstone, Neil C., and Terrell E. Arnold, eds. *Fighting Back: Winning the War against Terrorism.* Lexington, Mass.: Lexington Books, 1986.

Lord, Carnes, and Frank R. Barnett, eds. *Political Warfare and Psychological Operations: Rethinking the U.S. Approach.* Washington, D.C.: National Strategy Information Center/National Defense University Press, 1989.

Luttwak, Edward. *Coup d'Etat: A Practical Handbook.* Greenwich, Conn.: Fawcett/ Premier Books, 1969.

Manchester, William. *Goodbye Darkness: A Memoir of the Pacific War.* Boston: Little, Brown, 1979.

Mandelbaum, Michael. *The Nuclear Revolution: International Politics before and after Hiroshima.* Cambridge: Cambridge University Press, 1981.

Mansbach, Richard W. *The Global Puzzle: Issues and Actors in World Politics.* Boston: Houghton Mifflin, 1994.

Manwaring, Max G., ed. *Uncomfortable Wars: Toward a New Paradigm of Low-Intensity Conflict.* Boulder, Colo.: Westview Press, 1991.

Marchetti, Victor, and John D. Marks. *The CIA and the Cult of Intelligence.* New York: Laurel, 1980.

Martin, David C. *Wilderness of Mirrors.* New York: Ballantine Books, 1980.

Maurer, Alfred C., Marion D. Tunstall, and James M. Keagle. eds. *Intelligence: Policy and Process.* Boulder, Colo.: Westview Press, 1985.

Mazarr, Michael J., Don M. Snider, and James A. Blackwell, Jr. *Desert Storm: The Gulf War and What We Learned.* Boulder, Colo.: Westview Press, 1993.

McInnes, Colin, and G. D. Sheffield, eds. *Warfare in the Twentieth Century: Theory and Practice.* London: Unwin, Hyman, 1988.

McNamara, Robert S. *Blundering into Disaster: Surviving the First Century of the Nuclear Age.* New York: Pantheon Books, 1986.

Meyer, Cord. *Facing Reality: From World Federalism to the CIA.* New York: Harper & Row, 1980.

Midlarsky, Manus I., John A. Vasquez, and Peter V. Gladkov, eds. *From Rivalry to Cooperation: Russian and American Perspectives on the Post–Cold War Era.* New York: Harper Collins, 1994.

Miller, Abraham H. *Terrorism and Hostage Negotiations.* Boulder, Colo.: Westview Press, 1980.

Miller, Steven E., ed. *Military Strategy and the Origins of the First World War.* Princeton, N.J.: Princeton University Press, 1985.

———, *Strategy and Nuclear Deterrence.* Princeton, N.J.: Princeton University Press, 1984.

Millett, Alan R., and Williamson Murray, eds. *Military Effectiveness.* 3 vols. Boston: Unwin Hyman, 1988.

Mitrany, David. *A Working Peace System: An Argument for the Functional Development of International Organization.* London: Oxford University Press, 1943.

Morgan, Patrick M. *Deterrence: A Conceptual Analysis.* 2d ed. Beverly Hills, Calif.: Sage Publications, 1983.

Mosley, Leonard. *A Biography of Eleanor, Allen and John Foster Dulles and Their Family Network.* New York: Dial Press, 1978.

Mueller, John. *Retreat from Doomsday: The Obsolescence of Major War.* New York: Basic Books, 1989.

Neuman, Stephanie G., and Robert E. Harkavy, eds. *The Lessons of Recent Wars in the Third World: Comparative Dimensions.* Vol. 2. Lexington, Mass.: Lexington Books, 1987.

Newton, Verne W. *The Cambridge Spies: The Untold Story of Maclean, Philby, and Burgess in America.* Lanham, Md.: Madison Books, 1991.

New York Times Company, ed. *The Pentagon Papers.* New York: New York Times Company, 1971.

Nieberg, H. L. *Political Violence: The Behavioral Process.* New York: St. Martin's Press, 1965.

Nolan, Janne E. *Trappings of Power: Ballistic Missiles in the Third World.* Washington, D.C.: Brookings Institution, 1991.

Nordlinger, Eric A. *Soldiers in Politics: Military Coups and Governments.* Englewood Cliffs, N.J.: Prentice-Hall, 1977.

Nye, Joseph S. *Bound to Lead: The Changing Nature of American Power.* New York: Basic Books, 1990.

Nye, Joseph S., Jr. *Understanding International Conflicts: An Introduction to Theory and History.* New York: Harper Collins, 1993.

Nye, Joseph S., Jr., Graham T. Allison, and Albert Carnesale, eds. *Fateful Visions: Avoiding Nuclear Catastrophe.* Cambridge, Mass.: Ballinger Publishing Co., 1988.

Oots, Kent Layne. *A Political Organization Approach to Transnational Terrorism.* Westport, Conn.: Greenwood Press, 1986.

Palmer, Gen. Bruce, Jr. *The 25–Year War: America's Military Role in Vietnam.* Lexington: University Press of Kentucky, 1984.

Paret, Peter, ed. *Makers of Modern Strategy: From Machiavelli to the Nuclear Age.* Princeton, N.J.: Princeton University Press, 1986.

Paschall, Rod. *LIC 2010: Special Operations and Unconventional Warfare in the Next Century.* Washington, D.C.: Brassey's, 1990.

Penkovskiy, Oleg. *The Penkovskiy Papers.* Translated by Peter Deriabin; introduction and commentary by Frank Gibney. Garden City, N.Y.: Doubleday, 1965.

Pike, Douglas. *War, Peace and the Viet Cong.* Cambridge, Mass.: MIT Press, 1969.

Pillar, Paul R. *Negotiating Peace: War Termination as a Bargaining Process.* Princeton, N.J.: Princeton University Press, 1983.

Posen, Barry. *The Sources of Military Doctrine: France, Britain and Germany between the World Wars.* Ithaca, N.Y.: Cornell University Press, 1986.

Powers, Thomas. *The Man Who Kept the Secrets: Richard Helms and the CIA.* New York: Washington Square Press, 1979.

Prados, John. *Keepers of the Keys: A History of the National Security Council from Truman to Bush.* New York: William Morrow & Co., 1991.

————. *Presidents' Secret Wars: CIA and Pentagon Covert Operations since World War II.* New York: William Morrow & Co., 1986.

Quester, George H. *Deterrence before Hiroshima: The Airpower Background of Modern Strategy.* 2d ed. New Brunswick, N.J.: Transaction Books, 1986.

————. *The Future of Nuclear Deterrence.* Lexington, Mass.: D. C. Heath, 1986.

————. *The Multilateral Management of International Security: The Nuclear Proliferation Model.* Project on Rethinking Arms Control. College Park: University of Maryland, Center for International and Security Studies at Maryland, March 1993.

Ra'anan, Uri, Robert L. Pfaltzgraff, Richard H. Shultz, Ernst Halperin, and Igor Lukes, eds. *Hydra of Carnage: International Linkages of Terrorism. The Witnesses Speak.* Lexington, Mass.: Lexington Books, 1986.

Ranelagh, John. *The Agency: The Rise and Decline of the CIA.* New York: Touchstone Books, 1986, 1987.

Ransom, Harry Howe. *The U.S. Intelligence Establishment.* Cambridge, Mass.: Harvard University Press, 1970.

Ritter, Gerhard. *The Schlieffen Plan: Critique of a Myth.* Translated from the German by Andrew and Eva Wilson. London: Oswald Wolff, 1958.

Ropp, Theodore. *War in the Modern World.* Durham, N.C.: Duke University Press, 1959.

Rose, Clive. *The Soviet Propaganda Network: A Directory of Organisations Serving Soviet Foreign Policy.* London: Pinter Publishers, 1988.

Rosenau, James N. *Turbulence in World Politics: A Theory of Change and Continuity.* Princeton, N.J.: Princeton University Press, 1990.

Rotberg, Robert I., and Theodore K. Rabb, eds. *The Origins and Prevention of Major Wars.* Cambridge: Cambridge University Press, 1989.

Rubenson, David, and Anna Slomovic. *The Impact of Missile Proliferation on U.S. Power Projection Capabilities.* Santa Monica, Calif.: Rand, June 1990.

Sagan, Scott D. *The Limits of Safety: Organizations, Accidents and Nuclear Weapons.* Princeton, N.J.: Princeton University Press, 1993.

————. *Moving Targets: Nuclear Strategy and National Security.* Princeton, N.J.: Princeton University Press, 1989.

Sarkesian, Sam C. *America's Forgotten Wars: The Counterrevolutionary Past and Lessons for the Future.* Westport, Conn.: Greenwood Press, 1984.

————. *U.S. National Security: Policymakers, Processes and Politics.* Boulder, Colo.: Lynne Rienner, 1989.

Sarkesian, Sam C., and John Allen Williams, eds. *The U.S. Army in a New Security Era.* Boulder, Colo.: Lynne Rienner, 1990.

Schecter, Jerrold, ed. and trans. *Khrushchev Remembers: The Glasnost Tapes.* Boston: Little, Brown, 1990.

Schelling, Thomas C. *Arms and Influence.* New Haven, Conn.: Yale University Press, 1966.

————. *The Strategy of Conflict.* Cambridge, Mass.: Harvard University Press, 1960.

Schlesinger, Arthur M., Jr. *The Imperial Presidency.* Boston: Houghton Mifflin, 1973.

Seaton, Albert. *The Russo-German War, 1941–45.* London: Arthur Barker, 1971.

Shulsky, Abram N. *Silent Warfare: Understanding the World of Intelligence.* New York: Brassey's, 1991.

Shultz, Richard H., and Roy Godson. *Dezinformatsia: Active Measures in Soviet Strategy.* New York: Pergamon/Brassey's, 1984.

Smith, Hedrick. *The Media and the Gulf War: The Press and Democracy in Wartime.* Washington, D.C.: Seven Locks Press, 1992.

Smith, Zachary A. *The Environmental Policy Paradox.* Englewood Cliffs, N.J.: Prentice-Hall, 1992.

Snow, Donald M. *Distant Thunder: Third World Conflict and the New International Order.* New York: St. Martin's Press, 1993.

———. *Peacekeeping, Peacemaking and Peace-Enforcement: The U.S. Role in the New International Order.* Carlisle Barracks, Pa.: Strategic Studies Institute, U.S. Army War College, February 1993.

———. *The Shape of the Future: The Post–Cold War World.* Armonk, N.Y.: M. E. Sharpe, 1991.

Snyder, Glenn H. *Deterrence and Defense: Toward a Theory of National Security.* Princeton, N.J.: Princeton University Press, 1961.

Snyder, Jack. *The Ideology of the Offensive: Military Decision Making and the Disasters of 1914.* Ithaca, N.Y.: Cornell University Press, 1984.

Spector, Leonard. *The Undeclared Bomb: The Spread of Nuclear Weapons, 1987–1988.* Cambridge, Mass.: Ballinger Publishing Co., 1988.

Spector, Leonard S., and Virginia Foran. *Preventing Weapons Proliferation: Should the Regimes Be Combined?* Warrenton, Va.: Stanley Foundation, October 1992.

Spector, Leonard S., with Jacqueline R. Smith. *Nuclear Ambitions: The Spread of Nuclear Weapons, 1989–1990.* Boulder, Colo.: Westview Press, 1990.

Stevenson, William. *90 Minutes at Entebbe.* New York: Bantam Books, 1976.

Stoessinger, John G. *The United Nations and the Superpowers: China, Russia and America.* New York: Random House, 1977.

Strachan, Hew. *European Armies and the Conduct of War.* London: Allen & Unwin, 1983.

Sturgill, Claude C. *Low-Intensity Conflict in American History.* Westport, Conn.: Praeger Publishers, 1993.

Summers, Harry G., Jr. *On Strategy: A Critical Analysis of the Vietnam War.* Novato, Calif.: Presidio Press, 1982.

Suvorov, Viktor (pseudonym). *Inside Soviet Military Intelligence.* New York: Macmillan Publishing Co., 1984.

Tarr, David W. *Nuclear Deterrence and International Security: Alternative Nuclear Regimes.* London: Longman, 1991.

Taylor, A.J.P. *The Struggle for Mastery in Europe, 1848–1918.* Oxford: Clarendon Press, 1954.

Treverton, Gregory F., with James Klocke. *The Fall of the Shah of Iran.* Intelligence and Policy Project, Case Book. Cambridge, Mass.: Harvard University, John F. Kennedy School of Government, May 1991.

Troy, Thomas F. *Donovan and the CIA: A History of the Establishment of the Central Intelligence Agency.* Washington, D.C.: Central Intelligence Agency, 1981.

Tsipis, Kosta. *Arsenal: Understanding Weapons in the Nuclear Age.* New York: Simon & Schuster, 1983.

Ullman, Richard. *Securing Europe.* Princeton, N.J.: Princeton University Press, 1991.

United Nations Organization. *The Blue Helmets: A Review of United Nations Peace-Keeping.* New York: United Nations, Department of Public Information, 1990.

U.S. Army War College. *Gulf War Air Power Survey: Abbreviated Summary.* Carlisle Barracks, Pa.: U.S. Army War College, n.d.

U.S. Department of the Army. *Peace Operations.* FM 100–23. Version #7 (Draft). Washington, D.C.: Headquarters, Department of the Army, April 1994.

U.S. Department of Defense. *Conduct of the Persian Gulf War.* Washington, D.C.: DOD, April 1992.

———. *United States Special Operations Forces: Posture Statement 1993.* Washington, D.C.: DOD, 1993.

U.S. Department of State. *Patterns of Global Terrorism 1992.* Publication 10054. Washington, D.C.: U.S. Department of State, April 1993.

U.S. General Accounting Office. *Weapons of Mass Destruction. Reducing the Threat from the Former Soviet Union: An Update.* GAO/NSIAD-95–165. Washington, D.C.: GAO, June 1995.

U.S. Joint Chiefs of Staff, *Joint Warfare of the U.S. Armed Forces.* Washington, D.C.: Office of the Chairman, U.S. Joint Chiefs of Staff, November 1991.

Van Creveld, Martin. *Technology and War: From 2000 B.C. to the Present.* New York: Free Press, 1989.

———. *The Transformation of War.* New York: Free Press, 1991.

Viotti, Paul R., and Mark V. Kauppi. *International Relations Theory: Realism, Pluralism, Globalism.* New York: Macmillan, 1993.

Von Hippel, Frank, Marvin Miller, Harold Feiveson, Anatoli Diakov, and Frans Berkhout. "Eliminating Nuclear Warheads." *Scientific American* (August 1993): 44–49.

Von Mellenthin, Maj. Gen. F. W. *Panzer Battles.* New York: Ballantine Books; Norman: University of Oklahoma Press, 1971.

Waller, Douglas C. *Commandos: The Inside Story of America's Secret Soldiers.* New York: Simon & Shuster, 1994.

Waltz, Kenneth N. *The Spread of Nuclear Weapons: More May Be Better.* Adelphi Paper no. 171. London: International Institute for Strategic Studies, Autumn 1981.

———. *Man, the State and War.* New York: Columbia University Press, 1959.

Weigley, Russell F. *The American Way of War: A History of United States Military Strategy and Policy.* New York: Macmillan, 1973.

Werth, Alexander. *Russia at War, 1941–1945.* London: Barrie & Rockliff, 1964.

Whaley, Barton. *Codeword Barbarossa.* Cambridge, Mass.: MIT Press, 1973.

Wildman, Alan K. *The End of the Russian Imperial Army.* Princeton, N.J.: Princeton University Press, 1980.

Wilensky, Harold. *Organizational Intelligence.* New York: Basic Books, 1967.

Wise, David. *Molehunt.* New York: Random House, 1992.

Wohlstetter, Roberta. *Pearl Harbor: Warning and Decision.* Stanford, Calif.: Stanford University Press, 1962.

Woodward, Bob. *The Commanders.* New York: Simon & Schuster, 1991.

Wright, Peter. *Spy Catcher: The Candid Autobiography of a Senior Intelligence Officer.* New York: Dell Publishing Co., 1987.

Yardley, Herbert O. *The American Black Chamber.* New York: Ballantine Books, 1981.

Index